THAT CUNNING ALPHABET

NEW SERIES   VOLUME XXXV

COSTERUS

AMSTERDAM 1982

Richard S. Moore

That Cunning Alphabet

Melville's Aesthetics of Nature

©Editions Rodopi B.V., Amsterdam 1982
Printed in the Netherlands
ISBN: 90–6203–734–8

For my parents

CONTENTS

CHAPTER I

THE VIEW FROM "THE PIAZZA"

In the winter of 1855-56 Melville prepared five previously published stories for the only collection of his shorter fiction issued in his lifetime. Letters to his publisher indicate that in February he abandoned an initial plan to entitle the collection *Benito Cereno and Other Sketches* and chose instead to add a new sketch, "The Piazza," as title piece.[1] As "Benito Cereno" is undoubtedly superior work, Melville's decision to give precedence to "The Piazza" suggests that this "sketch of mingled philosophy and word painted landscape,"[2] as it was described by an early commentator, had special relation to the other stories in the *Piazza Tales*. Simple in plot but allegorical and turgidly allusive in manner, "The Piazza" is a landscape sketch that establishes with great subtlety the frame of reference for the stories that follow it. What is more, as Melville's probing critique of the aesthetic conventions of his era, the sketch is profuse with biographical relevance. The view from "The Piazza" is at once a retrospect, illuminating the course of Melville's career prior to 1855, and a prospect of later work.

"The Piazza" opens with Melville's narrator pondering the question as to which side of his country home would afford the best location for a piazza. While all sides tempt with gentle prospects of rural beauty, the narrator defies common sense and neighborly advice in constructing his piazza on the exposed northern side that offers a sublime view of a Berkshire peak. In repose upon his piazza, he enjoys the seasonal changes in the mountainous prospect, but a glittering image of golden light, perceived through the veil of a rainbow on the highest mountain flank, evokes paradisiacal associations and incites him to investigate. He leaves the beauties of the garden surrounding the piazza, crossing through meadows and passing the picturesque ruins of a mill in the foothills. Ultimately he reaches the sublime realm of the mountain peak, where he finds not a divine garden but an inhuman wasteland alternately scorched

---

1. For correspondence pertaining to the collection see Merton M. Sealts, Jr., "The Publication of Melville's *Piazza Tales*," *MLN* 59 (January 1944): 56-59.

2. J.E.A. Smith, *The History of Pittsfield* (Springfield, Mass.: n.p., 1876), II, 7-8; cited in Egbert S. Oliver's edition of the *Piazza Tales* (New York: Hendricks House, 1948), p. 227.

by the sun and chilled by shadow and night. The enticing golden image of light is nothing more than the sun's reflection off the roof of a wretched hut. Marianna, its inhabitant, is a lonely, possibly demented girl to whom the narrator seems artificial and oddly out of place. Chastened and embittered, the narrator returns to the comforts of his piazza.

Perfunctorily treated in early Melville scholarship, "The Piazza" has been only recently accorded the aesthetic analysis it demands.[3] The imagery of the tale may be divided among three aesthetic categories, the beautiful, the picturesque, and the sublime. Melville's narrator assumes the role of spiritual quester seeking the perfection of beauty within the picturesque prospect viewed from his piazza. The meaning of the sketch emerges from the succession of more or less discrete perspectives that are generated as the narrator penetrates successive zones of the landscape. If the narrator's first act was to fix perspective by building his piazza, all of his subsequent actions alter that perspective. He turns first to natural beauty, which is in the foreground of his prospect, near at hand; it is imaged in a Chinese creeper climbing a post of the piazza and bursting into delightful "starry bloom." Focusing upon this image of beauty, the narrator suffers the first in a series of aesthetic disillusionments; "If you removed the leaves a little," he notes, exposed were

> millions of strange, cankerous worms, which, feeding upon those blossoms, so shared their blessed hue, as to make it unblessed evermore — worms whose germs had doubtless lurked in the very bulb which, so hopefully, I had planted.[4]

As the narrator mounts his horse and moves into the middle-ground of his prospect, he again alters perspective. In this middle-ground are found the conventional elements of the picturesque; it is a realm of pleasing contrast of light and roughness of texture, and it includes such stock-in-trade images of picturesque landscape as an ancient moss-covered gate and a ruined mill. The narrator encounters an apple tree, a reminder of the Edenic associations of his quest, and once again immediate experience exposes aesthetic illusion:

---

3. See Klaus Poenicke, "A View from the Piazza: Herman Melville and the Legacy of the European Sublime," *CLS* 4 (1967): 267-81 and Marvin Fisher, *Going Under: Melville's Short Fiction and the American 1850's* (Baton Rouge: Louisiana State University Press, 1977), pp. 13-28. Poenicke's study, to which I am indebted, is the most significant treatment of Melville's use of the natural sublime. In "Melville and the Sublime in *Moby-Dick*," *American Literature* 48 (May 1976): 165-182, Barbara Glenn focuses on Melville's debt to Burke in *Moby Dick*.

4. *"The Piazza,"* in *Piazza Tales*, ed. Egbert S. Oliver (New York: Hendricks House, Farrar and Straus, 1948), p. 6. All subsequent citations from "The Piazza" are drawn from this edition.

My horse hitched low his head. Red apples rolled before him; Eve's apples; seek-
no-furthers. He tasted one, I tasted another; it tasted of the ground. Fairy-land not
yet, thought I ... (p. 8).

As the narrator penetrates further into the landscape and achieves the
summit slopes of the mountain, the requisites of the beautiful and of the
picturesque give way to those of the sublime:

No fence was seen, no inclosure. Near by — ferns, ferns, ferns; further — woods,
woods, woods; beyond — mountains, mountains, mountains; then — sky, sky, sky.
Turned out in aerial commons, pasture for the mountain moon. Nature and but
nature ... (p. 9).

An appalling sameness governs all at the mountain peak, and the vast
prospect extends off into the infinity of sky. Melville's quester seeks the
supranatural in his sublime fairy-land, a garden free of decay where fruit
tastes not of the ground yet the mountain summit seems to offer such a
garden of redemption only when viewed from a delusive perspective of
great distance. Experienced directly, stripped of its vital requisite of
distance, the sublime mountain realm is found to lack even the cankered
fruit of the valley. On the summit images of death abound; the mildly
luminous colors of nature are absent; the oppression of the glaring sun is
relieved only by black shadow. Preferring a pleasing delusion, Melville's
landscape aesthete descends from the mountain, never to return:

I stick to the piazza. It is my box-royal; and this amphitheatre, my theatre of San
Carlo. Yes, the scenery is magical — the illusion so complete. (p. 15)

"The Piazza" raises many questions, not the least of which is why
Melville, at mid-career and in difficult financial straits, should write a
caustically ironic critique of landscape aesthetics as title piece for his only
collection of short fiction. That his was a gesture of dissent is immediately
clear, but the important personal, national, and — in the broadest sense
— cultural dimensions of that dissent may not be evident to a modern
reader. With Melville's career prior to 1856 in mind, one may ask why he
found the aesthetic of the natural sublime so unsettling as to grant
prominence to its analysis in "The Piazza." And, after he claimed the
sublime fictive settings of whole oceans in the sea romances and full half
the globe in *Moby-Dick*, why did Melville treast of the sublime with a
narrative mood of profound malaise? The gesture of dissent seems all the
more emphatic within its specifically American aesthetic context, for the
picturesque had become in Melville's day a vital element of the nation's
self-image. Juxtaposed with the profusion in the era of belletristic
sketches of picturesque American landscapes, Melville's analysis of the
picturesque as a delusion of perspective was nothing less than impious.
Furthermore, "The Piazza" is a document of dissent within the broader
context of international romanticism. From John Dyer, Thomson,

Young, and Akenside through Coleridge and Wordsworth, romantics had refined the technique of kinetic point of view in landscape art. As these poets moved through natural prospects they registered the subtle interaction of sense and sensibility and thus celebrated the dynamic connection between mind and matter. Formally "The Piazza" is in the mainstream of this tradition, yet paradoxically it exposes naturalistic aesthetics as a matrix of deception; beauty masks disease, the picturesque is a delusion of perspective and a form of egregious sentimentalism, and the sublime portends not God's immediacy but the hellish absence of God. Why did Melville choose a romantic mode developed to celebrate the senses and the idea of cosmic unity in order to expose the senses as deceptive and to present one man's profound estrangement from the natural world? To answer these questions we must first put into historical focus the view from Melville's piazza by reconstructing his aesthetic milieu.

The Sublime of Nature in America

When Melville wrote "The Piazza" the aesthetic of the natural sublime had already passed through two centuries of change and refinement.[5]- Rooted in a complex of seventeenth-century scientific, theological, and epistemological developments, it was formally espoused as an aesthetic in the middle decades of the eighteenth century.[6] Through the Augustan and Johnsonian periods in British arts and letters, the sublime remained a submerged but ever-present undercurrent, the obverse of the general cultural climate of the Enlightenment. Essentially "inimical to the well-

5. Standard critical treatments of the sublime are Samuel Holt Monk, *The Sublime; a Study of Critical Theories in Eighteenth-Century England* (New York: Modern Language Association, 1935; repr. Ann Arbor: University of Michigan Press, 1960); Walter John Hipple, *The Beautiful, the Sublime, and the Picturesque in Eighteenth-Century British Aesthetic Theory* (Carbondale: Southern Illinois University Press, 1957); Marjorie Hope Nicolson, *Mountain Gloom and Mountain Glory: The Development of the Aesthetics of the Infinite* (Ithaca: Cornell University Press, 1959). See also Ernest Lee Tuveson, "Space, Deity, and the 'Natural Sublime'," *Modern Language Quarterly* 12 (Spring 1951): 20-38 and "The Rationale of the "Natural Sublime'," *The Imagination as a Means of Grace: Locke and the Aesthetics of Romanticism* (Berkeley: University of California Press, 1960), pp. 56-71.

6. Many Augustan writers, including Dennis, Shaftesbury, Hutcheson, and Thomson, took up the sublime of nature well before John Baillie's *Essay on the Sublime* (1747) and, most important, Edmund Burke's *Philosophical Enquiry into the Origin of Our Ideas of the Sublime and the Beautiful* (1756). Although Addison carefully restricted use of the term "sublime" to the arts, his reflections on the "great" in nature in "The Pleasures of the Imagination" (1711-12) represent the first rigorous attempt to distinguish between the sublime of nature and its rhetorical counterpart, the Longinian sublime.

5

ordered and rational world that the neo-classical age had erected on the foundation of Cartesianism,"[7] the aesthetic achieved its apotheosis in the age of romanticism. After a period of virtual omnipresence in British and continental art, it came to a general demise in the third and fourth decades of the nineteenth century.[8] The vital currency of the aesthetic continued in American culture, however, at least through the middle decades of the last century. An adjunct to the movement toward American cultural nationalism, the natural sublime was a contentious aesthetic issue throughout the American romantic period. Indeed, the aesthetic is vestigially but potently at work in modern American literature as well as in our contemporary national self-consciousness.

The origins of the sublime of nature as aesthetic lie not in aesthetic theory but in the development of post-Renaissance science. Medieval conceptions of time and space — and the theological adjuncts which adhered to these conceptions — were overthrown by post-Copernican astronomy and mathematics. As Tuveson has written,

> The medieval universe was great, but limited in size and harmonious in form; about its center, our own planet, the heavenly bodies were arranged in beautiful concentric spheres, according to a scale of immutable values. The telescope and new developments in mathematics, however, in an unbelievably short time shattered this image which had existed for centuries; the new universe was a terrifying one with no form no center, above all, no plan perceptible to human reason.[9]

The seventeenth-century scientific revolution necessitated a philosophic revolution in which a new and ingenious cosmic image was devised. This essentially involved a redefinition and relocation of God. Henry More and other seventeenth-century thinkers removed the threat of chaos from an infinite universe by postulating that God's attributes were absolute time and absolute space. The gnostic and neo-Platonist strains of Christianity, which had directed human speculation away from a corrupt material world to things ideal, were superseded by a new theological interest in physical nature. The characteristic upward direction of medieval mysticism gave way to an outward ranging of speculation as the infinite universe, penetrated by the new empiricism, became the foundation of a theodicy of the infinite. The process was abetted, of course, by the advent of telescope and microscope, which vastly extended the range

7. Monk, *The Sublime*, p. 3.
8. While there can be no doubt that interest in the sublime crested in the romantic period, it lingered among some Victorian artists, most notably Tennyson, Hopkins, and William Turner; see Jerome Bump, "'The Wreck of the Deutschland' and the Dynamic Sublime," *ELH* 41 (Spring 1974): 106-129 as well as Curtis Dahl, "Bulwer Lytton and the School of Catastrophe," *Philological Quarterly* 32 (October 1953): 428-42 and "The American School of Catastrophe," *American Quarterly* 11 (Fall 1959): 380-90.
9. "Space, Deity, and the 'Natural Sublime'," pp. 21-22.

of visual perception. The new mode of theological reasoning is aptly summarized by Tuveson:

> The nexus between the infinite Spirit and his finite manifestations is space or indefinite extension, independent of that body. Thus spiritual omnipresence takes on a physical nature.[10]

This nexus, located in the grand and vast aspects of nature, in forests, deserts, oceans, mountains, sky, and wilderness, became the cornerstone of a new cosmic image which in turn gave rise to the aesthetic of the natural sublime.

Perhaps the most common critical dictum about the American arts is that they have taken as their paramount theme the conflict between nature and civilization. Whether couched in different but analogical antipodes, such as wilderness versus city, or among more political conceptions, the theme extends into every recess of our cultural history.[11] The reasons for the pre-eminence of this national theme — indeed, national obsession — extend from the obvious fact of the vastness of the American wilderness to the subtlest aspects of our European philosophical legacy. The value and moral significance of wilderness has been

10. "Space, Deity, and the 'Natural Sublime'," p. 23.
11. Scholarship on this matter is vast. Classic treatments from an historical perspective are Frederick Jackson Turner, *The Frontier in American History* (New York: Holt and Company, 1921) and Henry Nash Smith, *Virgin Land: The American West as Symbol and Myth* (Cambridge: Harvard University Press, 1950); see also David W. Noble, *Historians Against History: The Frontier Thesis and the National Covenant in American Historical Writing Since 1830* (Minneapolis: University of Minnesota Press, 1965). Excellent general surveys are Hans Huth, *Nature and the American: Three Centuries of Changing Attitudes* (Berkeley: University of California Press, 1957) and Roderick Nash, *Wilderness and the American Mind* (New Haven: Yale University Press, 1967). Literary dimensions are explored in Lucy Lockwood Hazard's early survey, *The Frontier in American Literature* (New York: Thomas Y. Crowell Company, 1927) and in the provocative study by Edwin Fussell, *Frontier: American Literature and the American West* (Princeton: Princeton University Press, 1965). More specialized studies of the literary dimension are Leo Marx, *The Machine in the Garden: Technology and the Pastoral Ideal in America* (New York: Oxford University Press, 1964), R.W.B. Lewis, *The American Adam; Innocence, Tragedy, and Tradition in the Nineteenth Century* (Chicago: University of Chicago Press, 1955), David W. Noble, *The Eternal Adam and the New World Garden* (New York: George Braziller, 1968), and Harold P. Simonson, *The Closed Frontier: Studies in American Literary Tragedy* (New York: Holt, Rinehart & Winston, 1970). Outstanding studies of wilderness and American culture from the viewpoint of intellectual history are Charles Sanford, *The Quest for Paradise: Europe and the American Moral Imagination* (Urbana: University of Illinois Press, 1961), Richard Slotkin, *Regeneration Through Violence: The Mythology of the American Frontier, 1600-1860* (Middletown, Conn.: Wesleyan University Press, 1973), and the essays in Perry Miller, *Nature's Nation* (Cambridge: Harvard University Press, 1967) and *Errand into the Wilderness* (Cambridge: Harvard University Press, 1956).

among the most contentious of issues since the earliest exploratory probings of the American coastline. Yet, between the establishment of the first precarious colonial settlements and the middle decades of nineteenth-century American history, wilderness came to be claimed as the nation's distinctive moral resource as well as the basis of the nation's greatness. Concurrently the sublime, salient aesthetic quality of wilderness, became an idea of special and important significance for Americans.

Behind the nineteenth-century American conception of wilderness as moral resource lie philosophical developments of which only the latest dimensions are peculiarly American. They are precisely the same developments which culminated in the eighteenth-century British aesthetic of the natural sublime. Professor Nicolson has explained that in the course of the sixteenth and seventeenth centuries the medieval aversion to wild nature as ungodly was superseded by a conception of the natural sublime as revelation of God's glorious presence, a revelation rivaled in authority only by Scripture:

> Awe, compounded of mingled terror and exultation, once reserved for God, passed over in the 17th century first to an expanded cosmos, then from the macrocosm to the greatest objects in the geocosm — mountains, ocean, desert. "Mountains, who to your Maker's view, seem less than molehills do to you" are only relatively vast, yet except for the heavens they are the grandest and most majestic objects known to man. Scientifically minded Platonists, reading their ideas of infinity into a God of Plenitude, then reading them out again, transferred from God to Space to Nature conceptions of majesty, grandeur, vastness in which both admiration and awe were combined.[12]

Aesthetic appreciation of wild nature was thus preceded by concern with the theological import of the sublime, and, since the seventeenth and eighteenth centuries, religious response to the sublime of nature has never been wholly extricable from its sensational effects upon the emotions. From its inception the sublime aesthetic was connected with mixed emotional response, a compound of dread and exultation; this fact in large measure accounts for the persistent instability of the term "sublime" as employed in literature and aesthetic discourse.

Seventeenth-century American views of the sublime of nature essentially mirrored the contemporary European conception of untamed nature as the abode of evil. The city was of God, the wilderness was of the Devil. Outside of the early settlements the American colonist confronted "A waste and howling wilderness, / Where none inhabited / But hellish fiends."[13] Abhorrence and dread of the wilderness was no doubt part of

12. Marjorie Hope Nicolson, *Mountain Gloom and Mountain Glory: The Development of the Aesthetics of the Infinite* (Ithaca, N.Y.: Cornell University Press, 1959), p. 143.

13. Michael Wigglesworth, "God's Controversy with New England," Massachusetts Historical Society, *Proceedings* 12 (1871-1873): 83-84.

the common experience of the colonists. Exceptions to the view of wilderness as loathsome existed, to be sure, but these are chiefly found in the writings of the propagandists of colonization. Such a propagandist was Captain John Smith, who wrote, in 1612, of the divine and healing efficacy of the American wilderness; Virginia, argued Smith, is

> a nurse for soldiers, a practice for mariners, a trade for merchants, a reward for the good, and that which is most of all a business (most acceptable to God) to bring such poor infidels to the true knowledge of God and his Holy Gospell.[14]

Smith's estimation of the Virginia wilds was addressed to a sceptical but by no means untutored public, as favorable conceptions of the wilderness were at work in the tradition of the noble savage as well as in the paradisiacal element which had accreted to the European conception of the wild Americas.[15]

While the English gentleman might be intrigued and delighted by the primitivist vein in the writings of Shaftesbury, Defoe, and Montaigne, the American colonist of the seventeenth and early eighteenth century could afford no such indulgence. To insure his survival he brought not fanciful pen but broad-axe and musket to bear on the wilderness. In the Connecticut mountains John Josselyn saw no healing bounty but a frightening mass of rubble offering a prospect of "the whole country round about, being daunting terrible, full of rocky hills thick as mole-hills in a meadow, and cloathed with infinite thick woods."[16] The first to report upon what has become America's most popular spectacle of sublimity, a Father Hennepin bespoke his dread when writing of his visit to Niagara Falls in 1679. Noting the "horrible Precipice" of the Niagara gorge, he observed that

> the Waters, which fall from this vast height, do foam and boyl after the most hideous manner imaginable, making an outrageous Noise, more terrible than that of Thunder.[17]

Behind the horrific response to wild nature voiced by Hennepin, Josselyn, and their contemporaries is a cosmological view the demise of which would signal the rise of eighteenth-century theodicy. For these seventeenth-century writers, topographical sublimities — infinite forests, mountain heights, fathomless gorges — comprised a world not of

4

14. *Works*, ed. Edwin Arber and A.G. Bradley (Edinburgh: J. Grant, 1910), p. 64.
15. See Nash, *Wilderness and the American Mind*, pp. 44-49. The best general treatment of early European conceptions of wild nature is George Boas, *Essays on Primitivism and Related Ideas in the Middle Ages* (Baltimore: Johns Hopkins University Press, 1948).
16. "New England Rarities Discovered," American Antiquarian Society, *Transactions and Collections* 4 (1860): 134.
17. Louis Hennepin, *A New Discovery of a Vast Country in America* (London, 1698), pp. 29-30.

divinely ordained order but of ghastly ruin. The psychological sense of exile which would inevitably attend their venture into an unknown wilderness was compounded by the conviction that the sublime American topography was mute but terrific testimony of a world fallen from grace. The American landscape, scarred with mountain barriers and pocked with gorges and canyons, was the type of the post-Adamic world; it seemed the product of some unimaginable cataclysm.[18]

While the antipathy toward wilderness continued to dominate American consciousness through the eighteenth century, elements of a dissenting opinion were imported from Europe. Deistic tracts, such as Shaftesbury's *The Moralists*, became well known among the more cultivated Americans who were anxious as the English to reconcile Christian faith with the Newtonian universe. The revised attitude toward nature which is manifest in eighteenth-century topographical poetry was gradually transmitted to colonial readers. Of course, aesthetic appreciation of nature in England began in the city and in America it appeared first in those sectors which had been rendered secure by the incursion of civilization. Hence the gentleman farmer, familiar with deistic doctrine and provided with ample security and leisure, could accommodate aesthetic naturalism more readily than the pioneer. We have such a gentlman farmer in the figure of Crevecoeur, who saw fit to defend nature's sublime phenomena in 1769:

> A great thunderstorm; an extensive flood; a desolating hurricane; a sudden and intense frost; an overwhelming snowstorm; ... each of these different scenes exhibits singular beauties even in spite of the damage they cause.[19]

Crevecoeur need not have tagged his aesthetic response with a concluding apologetic phrase, for even the modestly cultured among his readers were familiar with a broad variety of British literary and philosophical works which had embraced the sublime of nature as a source of legitimate aesthetic response. An educated American could hardly be unfamiliar, in 1769, with Addison's *Spectator* papers on the pleasures of the imagination (1711-12), Thomson's *Seasons* (1746), Young's *Night Thoughts* (1742-45), Akenside's *Pleasures of the Imagination* (1744) and, perhaps most important, Burke's *Philosophical Enquiry into the Origin of Our Ideas of the Sublime and Beautiful* (1756). In the later decades of the eighteenth century Americans began to see the American landscape anew, but their vision was framed and directed by British aestheticians. Thus Jefferson,

---

18. Nicolson has explored the advent in the late seventeenth century of a new cosmology which could admit of an aesthetic of natural sublimity; see "The Burnet Controversey" in *Mountain Gloom and Mountain Glory*, pp. 225-270.

19. Michel Guillaume St. Jean de Crevecoeur, *Letters from an American Farmer* (London: Chatto and Windus, 1908), p. 4.

whose *Notes on Virginia* (1784) contain some of the first sophisticated evocations of a sense of place in American literature, is prototypical in rendering his response to Virginia's Natural Bridge through a vision shaped by British aestheticians:

> If the view from the top be painful and intolerable, that from below is delightful in an equal extreme. It is impossible for the emotions arising from the sublime to be felt beyond what they are here; so beautiful an arch, so elevated, so light and springing as it were up to heaven; the rapture of the spectator is really indescribable.[20]

Although few eighteenth-century Europeans — or present-day Americans, for that matter — would be inclined to agree with Jefferson that the sight of such topography is worth a voyage across the Atlantic, *Notes on Virginia* no doubt convinced some foreign readers that the new nation was at least aesthetically redeemable. Jefferson and Crevecoeur were among many who faced the wilderness in the eighteenth century not as pioneers but as scientists, surveyors, artists, or vacationers. Free from the demands — and liabilities — of a mission of conquest, these gentlemen were prepared to sing enthusiastic, if often qualified, praise of wild nature's sublime features.

Perhaps the earliest to react to the wilderness with unchecked enthusiasm was William Byrd II, who was commissioned in 1728 to survey and establish the boundary between the Virginia and North Carolina colonies. Fraught with primitivistic notions, his *History of the Dividing Line* extolled the healthiness of the wilderness life over the corrupting comforts of civilization. "Mankind are the great Losers by the Luxury of Feather-Beds and warm apartments," argued Byrd. Seeking sublimity in a mountainous "wild prospect," he and his companions found themselves "climbing up to a Neighboring eminence, that we might enjoy it in more Perfection."[21] Another American who displayed an early appreciation of the sublime of nature was William Bartram, son of the famous botanist, John Bartram. The younger Bartram was prepossessed by the vast and grand aspects of nature rather than its more delicate beauty, and the concept of sublimity is pervasive in his *Travels* (1791). Reporting on the Carolina mountains, he recalled his "rapture and astonishment" in beholding a "sublimely awful scene of power and magnificence, a world of mountains piled upon mountains."[22] While Bartram's taste for the sublime of nature was shared by a rather limited group in America, his

20. *The Complete Jefferson*, ed. Saul K. Padover (New York: Duell, Sloan & Pearce, 1943), p. 581.

21. *The Writings of Colonel William Byrd of Westover in Virginia*, ed. John Spencer Bassett (New York: Doubleday, Page & Co., 1901), p. 51.

22. *The Travels of William Bartram*, ed. Francis Harper (New Haven: Yale University Press, 1958), p. 120.

Travels found a highly receptive readership abroad, most notably among the Lake Poets.[23] Chateaubriand, an early enthusiast of the American wilderness, utilized some of Bartram's descriptive passages in his romances *Atala* and *Rene*. And, as Huth has noted, Carlyle would later commend the *Travels* to Emerson as "a kind of future biblical article."[24]

Through the closing decades of the eighteenth century the conception of natural wildness as moral resource rose as the complement of deistic and primitivistic thought. In "The Philosopher of the Forest" (1781-1782) and the "Tomo-Cheeki Essays" (1792), Philip Freneau contrasted the decadent, corrupting influences of civilization with the virtuous life of the noble American savage. Dr. Benjamin Rush, like Freneau a Philadelphian, posited the view in 1800 that love of wilderness was an element of human instinct. Yet another Philadelphian, Alexander Wilson, published a journal of a pedestrian tour to Niagara Falls wherein the healing bounty of wilderness is held in contrast to "the burning streets, the growling oyster men, the stinking sewers and the polite company of Philadelphia."[25] While they bear distinctively American emphases, such views of nature as refuge are contiguous with the long-standing British literary tradition of rural retirement.

Around the turn of the century a commingling of primitivism, of sublime aesthetics, and of specifically theological notions is discernible in a number of American writers. Notable for our present purposes are the opinions of the Reverend Thaddeau Mason Harris. In 1803 Harris embarked from Philadelphia on a wilderness tour for the purpose of restoring his health. Rejoicing in the sublime aspects of wilderness, Harris wrote that

> there is something which impresses the mind with awe in the shade and silence of these vast forests. In deep solitude, alone with nature, we converse with God.[26]

Within Harris' journal is the distinction between the efficacies of two types of natural landscapes, the pastoral, which bears the mark of man's altering hand, and the sublime, which signals the awful presence of God. While Harris found pleasure in the pastures and cultivated fields which he encountered, he judged the realm of untouched wilderness to be more

23. The European reception of Bartram's *Travels* is discussed by Huth, *Nature and the American*, pp. 21-22. Further information on Bartram's significance is found in N. Bryllion Fagin, *William Bartram: Interpreter of the American Landscape* (Baltimore: Johns hopkins University Press, 1933).

24. *The Correspondence of Thomas Carlyle and Ralph Waldo Emerson, 1834-1872*, ed. C.E. Norton (Boston: J.R. osgood, 1883), II, 98; cited by Huth, p. 21.

25. *Poems and Literary Prose*, ed. Alexander B. Grosart (Boston: Paisley, 1876), pp. 111-112.

26. *The Journal of a Tour into the Territory Northwest of the Alleghany Mountains* (Boston: Manning and Loring, 1805), p. 60.

12

grand and noble: "THE SUBLIME IN NATURE captivates while it awes, and charms while it elevates and expands the soul."[37] Harris' dual aesthetic, his distinction between the beauties of the pastoral and the sublimity of the wild, is in no way remarkable, for the distinction between the sublime and the beautiful had been a critical commonplace at least since the publication of Addison's papers on the imagination in 1711-12. Most prophetic, however, are Harris' emphasis on the wildest topographical features and his preference for the sublime of nature as he compares its effects upon the emotions with those of pastoral scenes. During the first half of the nineteenth century the natural sublime became at once the dominant feature of America's landscape aesthetics and the aesthetic cornerstone of nationalist ideology.

In the early decades of the nineteenth century Americans turned to nature with an enthusiasm which was intensified by the winning of independence. They did so, to be sure, under the aegis of European romanticism, but their aesthetic vision, which had been all but wholly derivative, began to acquire peculiarly American dimensions. The Revolution and the War of 1812 compelled American artists and writers to seek in nature a basis of national distinction and self-esteem. In addition to a supremely rich cultural heritage which was everywhere evident, continental Europe and Britain also had nature. But America had wilderness, and, insofar as nature was sublime to the degree that she was wild and untouched, little in Europe could match the sublimity of the vast tracts of the American wilderness. While Harris, Bartram, Byrd, Jefferson, Crevecoeur, and other enthusiasts of the American wilderness characteristically qualified their praise of sublimity, paying due respect to the requisite of civil life, the literati and artists of the third, fourth and fifth decades of the nineteenth century found an almost limitless moral, religious, and political significance in the sublime of American nature.[28]

The following passage by James Brooks characterizes the mode in which countless Americans of this period suffused both covenant theology and fervid nationalism in the image of the sublime wilderness:

God has promised us a renowned existence, if we will but deserve it. He speaks this promise in the sublimity of Nature. It resounds all along the crags of the Alleghanies. It is uttered in the thunder of Niagara. It is heard in the roar of two oceans, from the great Pacific to the rocky ramparts of the Bay of Fundy. His finger has written it in the broad expanse of our Inland Seas, and traced it out by

27. Ibid., p. 72.
28. Valuable studies of the significance of the sublime of nature in America are Perry Miller, "The Romantic Dilemma in American Nationalism and the Concept of Nature," *Nature's Nation*, pp. 197-207; Charles L. Sanford, "National Self-Consciousness and the Concept of the Sublime," *The Quest for Paradise*, pp. 134-154; Roderick Nash, "The American Wilderness," *Wilderness and the American Mind*, pp. 67-83; Leo Marx, *The Machine in the Garden*, pp. 1-226.

the mighty Father of Waters! The august TEMPLE in which we dwell was built for lofty purposes. Oh! that we may consecrate it to LIBERTY AND CONCORD, and be found fit worshippers within its holy wall![29]

Brooks has postulated here nothing less than a new divine covenant, the promise of a new Eden bounded by the holy walls of the American wilderness. The Edenic image had been prefigured, of course, in the earliest European conceptions of America.[30] What is distinctive in Books's declamation is its purely visionary quality, its contention that the sublime American wilderness bespeaks God's promise of unique political and cultural potentialities for Americans, not the least of which is that of a future of unlimited glory unencumbered by the past. Such patriotic naturalists as Brooks developed as a kind of formulaic convention the imaging of America's *tabula rasa* of futurity in American natural sublimity. A passage from George W. Curtis, who published five of Melville's *Piazza Tales* in *Putnam's* magazine, typifies the convention:

> Space and wildness are the proper praises of American scenery. The American in Europe, with the blood of a new race and the hope of a proportioned future tingling in his veins, with a profound conviction that Niagara annihilates all other scenery in the world, and with a decided disposition to assert that Niagara is the type of the country, proclaims the extent of that country as the final argument in the discussion of scenery and bears down with inland seas and the Father of Waters, and primeval forests and prairies and Andes, to conclude his triumph.[31]

The couching of a nationalistic adulation of wild nature in religious terms would seem to gloss the disparateness of the life of the senses and matters divine. But the King James Bible, graced as it is with images of the sublime of nature, had done much to establish in the minds of Americans a connection between wilderness and divine revelation. Among Americans, even orthodox Calvinists found it possible to reconcile convenant theology with a romantic conception of nature.[32] This is not to suggest, of course, that the foundation of a national self-image upon the sublimity of wilderness was not vexed with difficulties and unresolved contradictions. Close at the heels of explorers like Lewis and Clark, or naturalists like Bartram, Wilson, and Audubon, came those who wielded the axe. The tide of westward expansion carried with it the inevitable clash of wilderness and civilization, and the writings of American celebrants of nature undoubtedly served as a literature of protest. Those cultural nationalists who hailed undefiled nature as the

29. Passage from Brooks is cited by Miller, *Nature's Nation*, p. 201.
30. See Marx, *The Machine in the Garden*, pp. 34-72.
31. *Lotus-Eating: A Summer Book* (New York: Harper & Brothers, 1852), pp. 137-138.
32. Most enlightening in regard to this point are Miller's *Errand into the Wilderness*, pp. 153-166, 184-203; *Nature's Nation*, pp. 90-120, 279-290.

spiritual image of everything of promise in America were continuously
confronted with that obtruding mainspring of the Republic, utility:

> The most utilitarian conquest known to history had somehow to be viewed not as
> inspired by a calculus of rising land values and investments but (despite the orgies
> of speculation) as an immense exertion of the spirit. Those who made articulate the
> meaning of this drama found their frames of reference not in political economy but
> in ... visions of "sublimity." The more rapidly, the more voraciously, the
> primordial forest was felled, the more desperately poets and painters — and also
> preachers — strove to identify personality of this republic with the virtues of
> pristine and untarnished, of "Romantic," Nature.[33]

Patriotic naturalists could, in their more ecstatic moments, ignore the
onslaught of civilization; in the rarified heights of Brooks's sublime
temple there is no sign of axe, plow, or railroad. But the conflict of city
and forest was ineluctable, and through the 'thirties, 'forties, and 'fifties
countless efforts were made to uphold wild nature, especially as imaged
in sublime topographical features, as symbol of national promise.

Before the aesthetic of the natural sublime could be enlisted in the
cause of cultural nationalism it had to be refashioned in such a way as to
meet certain American moral and aesthetic imperatives. In the arts of late
eighteenth- and early nineteenth-century Europe the sublime of nature
had become associated with sensationalism of an often lurid sort. It had
been employed in countless Gothic novels to evoke mystification and terror
rather than awe. The enormously popular canvases of Salvator Rosa,
which were mined by Gothic novelists in search of scenic techniques, had
suggested a savage lawlessness of spirit in portraying bandits hidden
among decaying ruins and sublime mountain scenery. American nationalists, anxious to promote the nation's lack of a rich cultural past as an
asset rather than a liability, perceived the Gothic strain of European
sublimity as testimony to the effeteness and decadence of the Old World.
If the European sublime pointed to the ravages of history, the American
sublime would be the telling symbol of a glorious future. Thus we find
Fenimore Cooper, who championed European culture to the detriment
of his domestic reputation, contrasting the American and European
landscapes:

> Europe claims superiority in its objects of art, as a matter of course; in all those
> effects which depend on time and association, in its monuments, and in this
> impress of the past which may be said to be relfected in its countenance; while we
> claim for America the freshness of a most promising youth, and a species of natural
> radiance that carries the mind with reverence to the source of all that is glorious
> around us.[34]

33. Miller, *Nature's Nation*, p. 199.
34. "American and European Scenery," *The Home Book of the Picturesque* (New
York: G.P. Putnam, 1852), p. 69.

In the writings of Cooper and his contemporaries, the European sublime was stripped of its more sensational aspects and fashioned into an American nationalist aesthetic with associations of glorious futurity and divine promise. Melville, who steeped himself in Cooper's novels at an early age and who was enmeshed in the most ardently nationalist circle of New York literati, was fully aware of the emerging American convention of sublimity. In the late eighteen-forties he wrote:

> Seventy years ago we escaped from thrall; and, besides our first birthright — embracing one continent of earth — God has given to us, for a future inheritance, the broad domains of the political pagans, that shall yet come and lie down under the shade of our ark, without bloody hands being lifted. God has predestined, mankind expects, great things from our race; and great things we feel in our souls. The rest of the nations must soon be in our rear. We are the pioneers of the world; the advance guard, sent on through the wilderness of untried things, to break a new path in the New World that is ours.[35]

The covenant theology and the image of wilderness dominate Melville's passage and body forth his notion that the American national venture constituted an utter break with history. The writer of such a passage could be confident, in the eighteen-forties, of an enthusiastic reception among readers familiar with the nationalist formula.

The emphasis upon the divine and moral import of the sublime as opposed to its sensational emotional effects was most insistent among Americans, who were inclined to hold suspect the major British poets of sublimity, particularly Byron. Mountain gloom and mountain glory might serve as correlatives of the alienation and stupendous egoism of such a decadent as Manfred, but the pristine American wilds could abide no Old World *Angst*. For Brooks, for Cooper, and for Melville in 1848, the sublimities of wilderness were emphatically *ours*, and we were new Israelites in a New World. Decadent Europeans might posture and blaspheme in the Alps, but Americans had a mission in the Alleghanies and the Rockies. Which is to say that "the sublime" had for Americans a distinctly moral and communal semantic emphasis. It would be inaccurate to suggest, however, that in formulating what would be called the "true" or "moral sublime" American artists and literati worked independently of Britain. They may have rejected the Byronic sublime and found the Gothic sublime irrelevant to their largely vacant wilderness, but in insisting on a moral or pietistic dimension as the dominant feature of the aesthetic they followed a major direction of eighteenth- and early nineteenth-century British aesthetic discourse.

A cultural climate in which natural sublimities could be accepted —

35. *White-Jacket* (Evanston and Chicago: Northwestern University Press and The Newberry Library, 1970), p. 151. All subsequent quotations from *White-Jacket* are drawn from this edition.

indeed, savored — as aesthetically pleasing may have evolved from seventeenth-century theological and cosmological developments, but the advent of Lockean epistemology was the primary factor behind the evolution of the sublime as aesthetic in eighteenth-century discourse. Locke's view that all knowledge originates in sensation did much to set in motion the eighteenth-century aesthetic revolution that culminated in romantic subjectivism.[36] Concurrent with the gradual shift of artistic attention from reason to the imagination was a shift in the focus of aesthetic from knowledge to sensation itself. Addison's papers on the "Pleasures of the Imagination" are an early manifestation of this change of focus, for, following the implications of Locke's ideas, they are a typology of sensational pleasures. Even for the pre-eminently reasonable Addison, these pleasures — imaginative and aesthetic in spite of the fact that neither word had then much currency — were suprarational and therefore not amenable to rational criteria of judgment.[37] This was especially the case in regard to Addison's category of the "great" — which is to say, the sublime — for as early as Burnet's *Sacred Theory of the Earth* (1681-89) the mixed feeling of terror and exultation evoked by the vast in nature was seen as rising not from the "Understanding" but from "phansy."[38] The sublime was an irrational "enthusiasm," and the Augustans were quick to perceive in the new aesthetic the destruction of a classical verity, the unity of aesthetic and reason, beauty and truth. But if romantic subjectivism would be, by the end of the century, the ineluctable result of the new epistemology, subjectivism in aesthetic was held in partial check by the Augustans through appeals to a community of taste and the verities of psychology. Locke may have seemed to reduce aesthetic ideals to mere sensations, sensations which, Newton had demonstrated, were themselves suspect, but he also provided in associationism the means of stabilizing aesthetic. Augustan "Nature" was, after all, human as well as external nature, and the aesthetic faculties were-

36. Definitive on this subject is Tuveson's *The Imagination as a Means of Grace: Locke and the Aesthetics of Romanticism.*

37. It should be noted, however, that Addison sought to preserve a relation between a kind of knowledge (however ill-defined) and the experience of the great in nature. He did so through appeal to final cause: "One of the Final Causes of our Delight in any thing that is *great*, may be this. The Supreme Author of our Being has so formed the Soul of Man, that nothing but himself can be its last, adequate, and proper Happiness. Because, therefore, a great Part of our Happiness must arise from the Contemplation of his Being, that he might give our Souls a just Relish of such a Contemplation, he has made them naturally delight in the Apprehension of what is Great or Unlimited" (*The Spectator*,ed. Donald Bond [Oxford: Clarendon Press, 1965], III, 545). As long as the cosmos was teleologically conceived, some relation between the sublime and intellection could be retained. Only with Burke was this relation wholly rejected; ignorance itself is connected with the sublime in the *Enquiry*.

presumably fixed and knowable aspects of human nature. Thus from Addison's "Pleasures of the Imagination" through Archibald Alison's *Essays on the Nature and Principles of Taste* (1790), aesthetic discourse took on a strongly psychological cast. Its purposes were to catalogue sensations in accordance with the aesthetic faculties to which they appealed and to expose the fixed laws of human psychology by demonstrating how sensations were transformed through mental association into such complex aesthetic ideas as "beauty" and "sublimity." Truth of aesthetic became psychological truth. A classical principle was, after a fashion, preserved.[39]

However, another traditional equation, that of aesthetic and moral truth, the beautiful and the good,[40] was to be all but wholly nullified. The manner by which this occurred is most strikingly evinced in young Edmund Burke's *Philosophical Enquiry into the Origin of Our Ideas of the Sublime and Beautiful* (1756). Written partly as a critique of Locke's associationism, Burke's treatise applies a radical sensationism to aesthetics. Finding the machinery of mental association too cumbrous and slow to obtrude between a percipient and the raw data of sensation, Burke maintains that aesthetic judgments are instantaneous, the product of physiological response rather than elaborate relation of ideas.[41] Bifurcating human nature into the instinct for propagation and the instinct for self-preservation, he defines beauty as a response to the former need and connects sublimity to the latter. Aesthetic becomes, in the *Enquiry*, the physiology of pleasure and pain.

Significantly, Burke's primary interest is in the sublime rather than the beautiful. The latter he reduces from a general, all-inclusive aesthetic quality to something like tactile smoothness or grace of line. Beauty is

38. Cited by Nicolson, *Mountain Gloom and Mountain Glory*, p. 216.

39. The usurpation of aesthetics by the eighteenth-century faculty psychologists was in some respects undeniably pernicious; as J.T. Boulton has remarked in his edition of Edmund Burke's *Philosophical Enquiry into the Origins of Our Ideas of the Sublime and Beautiful* (London: Routledge and Paul, 1958), p. xxxiv, "The habit of elevating personal predilections into general truths" became "widespread among eighteenth-century aestheticians."

40. The equation of beauty with truth and moral perfection is of course common from Plato through the aestheticians of the early eighteenth century. Shaftesbury's formulation may be typical: "What is BEAUTIFUL is *Harmonious* and *Proportionable*; what is Harmonious and Proportionable, is TRUE; and what is at once both *Beautiful* and *True*, is, of consequence, Agreeable and GOOD" (*Characteristics of Men, Manners, Opinions, Times* [London: n.p., 1714], III, 182-183).

41. Although in many respects the *Enquiry* departs radically from the mainstream of eighteenthcentury aesthetic tradition, its sensationism is consistent with the growing interest of the age in immediacy of aesthetic response; see Wallace Jackson, *Immediacy: The Development of a Critical Concept from Addison to Coleridge* (Amsterdam: Rodopi, 1973).

equated not with truth but with pleasure of an unmistakably erotic quality. Burke departs from the tradition of sublimity established by Blackmore, Thomson, and other physico-theological poets in stressing the horrific effects rather than transcendental import of the sublime. The experience of the sublime is for him one of terror that overwhelms the rational faculties. Burke's attributes of the sublime read like a catalogue of the attributes of romantic art: obscurity; power; privations, including vacuity, darkness, solitude, and silence; vastness; and infinity, which could be manifest in two "artificial" forms, succession and uniformity. Beauty, Burke explained, occasions a pleasing relaxation of the nerves and muscles. The physiology of the sublime was more complex. Through the threat of annihilation, the sublime effects an emotional state of terror which subsequently resolves itself into pleasure as the percipient becomes reassured of his security.[42] Burke restricts his analytic of the sublime to the physiology of stimulus and response; references to God or to any final cause whatever are conspicuously and tellingly few in the *Enquiry*.

The aesthetic ideas Burke articulated in his *Enquiry* influenced the direction of the arts in the late eighteenth century by legitimizing the irrational as an artistic resource. To be sure, horror, obscurity, vastness, and power had emerged as artistic material before Burke wrote, but the *Enquiry* contributed an important measure of order to this new aesthetic world and stimulated discourse about it. Burke's ideas also had the effect of extending immediacy and intensity, aesthetic criteria that had been largely restricted to tragedy and lyric verse, to other literary genres. As Robert Kiely has reflected,

> Behind the apparent morbidity of an aesthetic theory which, like "graveyard" poetry and Gothic fictioin, seems obsessed with the fearful, lies a quest for the ultimate. Burke's discussion of the sublime, like most early romantic fiction, is a parade of superlatives. He attempts to describe the *strongest* of emotions, the *most* engrossing of ideas, the *greatest* of pleasures, the *most* dreadful of pains, in an effort to ascertain what inventions of the imagination might produce them.[43]

That the aesthetic climate Burke helped to cultivate endured more than a century there can be no doubt, for we know in Moby Dick an invention of the imagination apposite to those of the *Enquiry* . To Burke's mind no beast could exceed in sublimity the biblical Leviathan.

British aestheticians of the later eighteenth century respected Burke as

---

42. Burke's unconvincing explanation evinces the underlying difficulty of his aesthetic; the second phase of the experience of the sublime restores what sensationism denies — aesthetic distance. A degree of cultural estrangement from nature is very likely a necessay condition for the rise of any formal aesthetic of nature.

43. *The Romantic Novel in England* (Cambridge: Harvard University Press, 1972), p. 13. Kiely's introduction is a cogent survey of the influence of Burke's aesthetics on romantic fiction.

an estimable forerunner, but none among them could accept his basic principles. They found his sensationism chiefly objectionable, and, rightly perceiving that Burke's epistemology could admit of no moral dimension in aesthetic, they attacked the more vulnerable portions of the *Enquiry* with the virulence of the righteous. Their criticisms were complicated but not complex and were addressed to Burke's untenable physiology of stimulus and response that, in fact, was founded on a slight and inconsistent body of empirical knowledge. Here Burke was open to such witty abuse as that of Francis Jeffrey, who, remarking Burke's notion that a languorous relaxation of the nerves was the source of the feeling of beauty, defined the perfection of the beautiful as a hot bath.[44] More kind but not less incisive were the Scottish Common Sense philosphers, Kames, Blair, Alison, Stewart, and Payne Knight. Quick to point out such difficulties in Burke's sensationist line as the apparent incapacity of the iris to feel pain or pleasure, these conservatives eschewed sensationism in favor of an associationist epistemology which, originating in Hobbes and Locke, had been developed by Hartley in his *Observations on Man* (1749).[45] In their aesthetic tracts, which were laced with critical comments on Burke, the Common Sense school worked toward ends emphatically moral. They sought to arrest the tide of subjectivism evinced in Burke's sensationist aesthetic as well as in the skeptic Hume by maintaining a type of cognition as a mediating factor between sense and sensibility. Aesthetic experience was valuation and revaluation of sense data throught the association of ideas.

While Burke's *Enquiry*, as well as the Gothic literature it helped to spawn, achieved immense popularity in America, the associationist ideas of the Common Sense school had become aesthetic orthodoxy on this side of the Atlantic by the early decades of the nineteenth century.[46]

44. Cited by Hussey, *The Picturesque*, p. 60.

45. On associationism and eighteenth-century aesthetics see Gorden McKenzie, *Critical Responsiveness: A Study of the Psychological Current in Later Eighteenth-Century Criticism*, University of California Studies in English, No. 20 (1949), especially Chapter VI, "Imagination," pp. 180-206; Walter Jackson Bate, "The Growth of Individualism," *From Classic to Romantic: Premises of Taste in Eighteenth-Century England* (New York: Harper & Row, 1961), pp. 129-259; and M.H. Abrams, *The Mirror and the Lamp: Romantic Theory and the Critical Tradition* (New York: W.W. Norton & Company, 1958), pp. 177-181 and passim.

46. At least ten American editions of the *Enquiry* appeared between 1800 and 1856; see Sanford, p. 137n. Burke's influence accounts in part for an American climate of opinion receptive to the horrific Gothicism in the fiction of Brockden Brown and Poe. The latter may be directly indebted to Burke in his denial of any relation between aesthetic and the true or the good. The most complete treatment of Common Sense philosophy and the American arts is Terence Martin, *The Instructed Vision: Scottish Common Sense Philosophy and the Origins of American Fiction* (Bloomington: Indiana University Press, 1961).

American academies were receptive to the Scottish associationists because, as Merle Curti has noted, these institutions sought a viable alternative to the "idealism of Berkeley, the negations of Hume, and the quasi-materialism of Locke."[47] As regards aesthetic, the Common Sense school offered the means of exalting the sublime of nature in a manner compatible with Christian orthodoxy, for they consistently attributed the feeling of sublimity to divine associations set in motion by grandeur in nature. We find their views at work in the writings of Washington Allston (1779-1843), American painter, friend to Coleridge, and author of "Lectures on Art," which, written in the 1830's, comprise the first American art treatise. Although Allston's relationship with Coleridge led to an unmistably idealist strain of thought, his introductory discourse to the lectures on art displays most clearly the influence of the Common Sense school. Following the line of Kames, Blair, and Alison, Alllston attacks the Burkean, horrific sublime as false:

> The horrible, the loathesome, the hideous, and the monstrous: these form the impassable boundaries to the true sublime.

From the "false sublime," argues Allston, we recoil "in revulsion of our moral nature." Perhaps echoing Wordsworth, who had achieved by the 1830's a broad and enthusiastic readership in America, Allston claims that the "true sublime" may be *initially* set in motion by the terrible or obscure in nature, but that the feeling of true sublimity can only exist in a tranquil state of contemplation.[48]

Refinement of the "true sublime" as a peculiarly American aesthetic was achieved most strikingly through the efforts of native painters, chiefly those of the Hudson River School.[49] Trained in the techniques of Slavator Rosa and Claude Lorraine, Allston, Thomas Cole, and Asher Durand were well equipped to capture on canvas the sublimity of the American wilderness. Sharing the aversion of their countryment to the decadent, sensational aspects of the European sublime, these painters and their followers sought a means of embodying a morally and nationalistic-

47. *The Growth of American Thought* (New York: Harper & Row, 1943), p. 236.
48. *"Lectures on Art" and "Poems," and "Monaldi,"* ed. Nathalia Wright (Gainesville, Florida: Scholar's Facsimiles & Reprints, 1967), pp. 66-67. Allston would surely recognize Wordsworth's theory of poetic creation in the prefaces to *Lyrical Ballads as* as a struggle to reconcile moral reflection and immediate, intense sensation. The "spots of time" of the *Prelude* are encounters with sublimity — of an often horrific tincture — which accrete through tranquil retrospection associations of decidedly moral emphasis.
49. The best overview of the Hudson River group, our first nativist school of painters, remains Frederick A. Sweet, *The Hudson River School* (Chicago: The Art Institute of Chicago, 1945); see also John K. Howat, *The Hudson River and Its Painters* (New York: Viking Press, 1972) and Wolfgang Born, *American Landscape Painting* (New Haven: Yale University Press, 1948), pp. 3-117.

ally expressive dimension in their compositional schemes. A mirror image in paint of the spectacular aspects of American topography would all too readily suggest the sensationalism Americans found repugnant, and duplication of the idealized landscapes of the European masters would do nothing for the cause of cultural nationalism. Some index of social man, some image of the unique potentialities and values of American life, had to enter the sublime landscape in order to meet the moral imperatives of the culture. If Rosa's bandits and ruined castles would not do, neither would the American railroad or factory. In the agrarian image, in pastoral, the American painter found the element of social man that could be reconciled with the sublimity of wilderness. Wild topographical sublimities in paint could be all the more "true" — which is to say, moral — if they were at once tempered and complemented by images of felicitous agrarian life. Background sublimites could image the promise of the nation's special covenant with God, while pastoral foreground could body forth fulfillment of the covenant. This compositional program came to be known as the American "picturesque."

The Politics of Vision: Picturesque America

The chronic instability of the term "picturesque" no doubt stems in part from the multifarious complex of forces which gave rise to its currency in the eighteenth century.[50] William Gilpin, champion of the aesthetic in the late eighteenth century, was correct in pointing to its etymological origins in the French "pittoresque": "Picturesque," he flatly remarked in 1768, is "a term expressive of that peculiar kind of beauty, which is agreeable in a picture."[51] In spite of the efforts of subsquent commentators — as well as Gilpin himself — to achieve more precision, this curiously tautological definition retains a certain unique cogency. Reflecting the fact that through the course of the seventeenth and eighteenth centuries painters rather than writers were the exploratory vanguard of the new aesthetic world of landscape, Gilpin's definition

50. Standard treatments of the picturesque are Christopher Hussey, *The Picturesque: Studies in a Point of View* (New York: Oxford University Press, 1925) and John W. Hipple, *The Beautiful, the Sublime, and the Picturesque in Eighteenth-Century Aesthetic Theory* (Carbondale: Southern Illinois University Press, 1957). More recent discussions suggest that the picturesque is not a dead aesthetic or a vogue exhausted by of the romantic period but rather a point of view of current and important appeal. See especially Martin Price, "The Picturesque Moment," *From Sensibility to Romanticism: Essays Presented to Frederick A. Pottle*, ed. Frederick W. Hilles and Harold Bloom (New York: Oxford University Press, 1965), pp. 259-292 and Marshall McLuhan, *The Interior Landscape: The Literary Criticism of Marshall McLuhan, 1943-1962* (New York and Toronto: McGraw-HIll Book Co., 1969), pp. 135-168.
51. *An Essay upon Prints, containing Remarks upon the Principles of Picturesque Beauty* (London: J. Robson, 1768), p. 2.

accommodates the historical sources of the aesthetic in a way that more abstract definitions cannot. The landscapes of eighteent- and nineteenth-century literature comprised a world first mapped — in fact, created — by pictorial artists.[52]

In spite of the appearance of specifically literary applications of the term "picturesque" as early as the first decade of the eighteenth century, the inception of picturesque as something approximating a literary aesthetic has been most convincingly located in the odes of Collins and of the Wartons.[53] To be sure, earlier poets such as Thomson and Dyer incorporated new and immensely important pictorial detail in their landscape, but their work, insofar as it subordinates affective qualities of landscape to graphic presentation, is less important in the development of the literary picturesque than are the mid-century odes. Taking up the iconographic tradition as it was developed in the tableaux of their Augustan predecessors, Collins and the Wartons fashioned landscapes as correlatives for spiritual states. By complementing natural features with the fanciful machinery of allegory, they could invoke Fear or Melancholy or Indolence as the spirit or genius of a locale. They stressed the affective dimension of the landscapes discovered by the physico-theological poets, and in so doing they prepared the way for the complex matrices of mind and landscape fashioned by Wordsworth and Coleridge.[54]

As Price has argued, the picturesque as aesthetic theory emerged from Edmund Burke's discussion of the sublime and the beautiful:

> By reducing the beautiful from a comprehensive aesthetic term to the name of a limited and lesser experience, Burke opened the way for others to identify new aesthetic categories.[55]

Burke maintained that the beautiful and the sublime are distinct and, what is more important, irreconcilable. "The ideas of the sublime and the beautiful," he wrote,

52. See Elizabeth W. Manwaring, *Italian Landscape in Eighteenth-Century England* (New York: Modern Language Association, 1925) and Jean H. Hagstrum, *The Sister Arts: The Tradition of Literary Pictorialism and English Poetry from Dryden to Gray* (Chicago: University of Chicago Press, 1958). Hussey remarks with some justice that "It was not until Englishmen became familiar with the landscapes of Claude Lorraine and Salvator Rosa, Ruysdael and Hobbema, that they were able to receive any visual pleasure from their surroundings" (*The Picturesque*, p. 2).

53. See Angus Fletcher, "Thematic Effects: Ambivalence, the Sublime, and the Picturesque," in *Allegory: The Theory of a Symbolic Mode* (Ithaca: Cornell University Press, 1964), pp. 220-278 and Hagstrum, especially pp. 157-162 and, on Collins in particular, pp. 268-286.

54. On the relation of Wordsworth to the mid-century poets, see Wallace Jackson, "Wordsworth and His Predecessors: Private Sensations and Public Tones," *Criticism* 17 (Winter 1975): 41-58.

55. "The Picturesque Moment," p. 262.

stand on foundations so different, that it is hard, I had almost said impossible, to think of reconciling them in the same subject, without considerably lessening the effect of the one or the other upon the passions.[56]

Such a radically bifurcated aesthetic theory was unacceptably restrictive, especially in regard to literary or pictorial landscape art. Clearly there was a wealth of aesthetically pleasing natural phenomena that conformed to neither of Burke's categories. A third category, the picturesque, was developed to accommodate these phenomena and to reconcile, so far as it was possible, the beautiful and the sublime. Adumbrating roughness, irregularity of line, and contrast — which had been subordinate sources of the sublime in Burke — William Gilpin developed a catalogue of the requisites of the picturesque in his popular guidebooks, while Uvedale Price, who followed Gilpin's lead, defined the picturesque as a discrete aesthetic category and related it to the beautiful and the sublime.[57] Unlike Gilpin, whose formulation of the picturesque was so flexible as to be easily conflated with the sublime, Price maintained that the picturesque was restricted to complexity, irregularity, and contrast of line, and that it had nothing to do with the sense of the unlimited or infinite.

Price's requisites of the picturesque are remarkably abstract, relating neither to feelings nor to precise qualities of landscape but rather to intellect; in divorcing the picturesque from the sublime, Price had divorced the aesthetic from the passions. Picturesqueness was the capacity of a landscape to stimulate mental play, which is to say the association of ideas. Thus it immediately found its epistemological complement in associationism, the school which was achieving epistemological orthodoxy in respect to aesthetic largely through the work of Archibald Alison.[58] In incorporating the picturesque into associationist epistemology, Price, Richard Payne Knight, Dugald Stewart, and other aestheticians were, of course, building on a venerable tradition, for the encoding of ideas in images drawn from nature is at least as old as

56. *A Philosophical Enquiry into the Origin of Our Ideas of the Sublime and Beautiful*, ed. J.T. Boulton (London: Routledge and Paul, 1958), p. 212; all subsequent citations refer to this edition.

57. Gilpin celebrated the picturesque in six guidebooks with aquatint illustrations; published between 1782 and 1798, all have extensive titles of the form "*Observations* [upon some part of Britain] *Relative Chiefly to Picturesque Beauty.*" The authoritative treatment remains William D. Templeman, *The Life and Work of William Gilpin* (Urbana: Southern Illinois University Press, 1939). Price published his reflections as *An Essays on the Picturesque, as Compared with the Sublime and the Beautiful* (London: J. Robson, 1794).

58. Alison's associationist *Essays on the Nature and Principles of Taste* achieved a wide following on both sides of the Atlantic almost immediately after its publication in 1790. It was regarded as authoritative after Francis Jeffrey's important assessment (*Edinburgh Review* XVIII [May 1811], 1-45).

medieval iconography and perhaps older than language itself. In the eighteenth century the tradition had become a widespread convention, as the sister arts were brought into increasing intimacy. In the prospect poetry of the period, topographical features were so presented as to evoke a train of associated ideas, and in the eighteenth-century garden the quickening and controlling of the process of association through the use of mottoes, literary inscriptions, statues of gods, and other architectural machinery had achieved the status of a sophisticated art. The association-ist aestheticians departed from their eighteenth-century predecessors, however, in the degree to which they emphasized the affective capacities of landscape rather than landscape as rationally perceived fact. Professor Wasserman has put the new development in proper perspective:

> The eighteenth-century analogist was striving to report "truth and reason ... as they are reflected in the glass of the visible forms, and the sensible qualities of outward things." The image is not specially shaped by the creative mind so that it will take on the power of an emblem. But the whole bent of eighteenth-century esthetics — associationism and the theories of the sublime and the picturesque, for instance — was to root the relationship of image and value in an emotive act instead of an outward perception.[59]

A manifestation of the rising tide of subjectivism, the new preoccupation with aesthetic effects, valuable as effects, is everywhere evinced in discourse on the picturesque. For the subtitle of his *Essay on the Picturesque*, for example, Price chose the words, "*on the Use of Studying Pictures for the Purpose of Improving Real Landscape*"; by imposing the values of painting — which is to say, artifice — upon "real landscape," enthusiasts of the picturesque evoked effects previously restricted to the plastic arts alone.

Price's *Essay* narrowed and refined Gilpin's notion of the picturesque and, more importantly, established the new aesthetic as coequal with the beautiful and the sublime. After Price, naturalistic aesthetics were tripartite, with the beautiful, the picturesque, and the sublime encom-passing all aesthetic value in nature. The particular requisites of each category remained a point of some contention, but it is generally true that the beautiful, the picturesque, and the sublime were thought to correspond, respectively, to the emotive effects of pleasure, curiosity or interest, and awe. In its mediate position, the picturesque offered the means of reconciling the beautiful and the sublime, especially in the compositional format of landscape painting and description.

In important respects the development of the picturesque aesthetic parallels that of the sublime. The initial inception of both the natural

---

59. Earl Wasserman, "Nature Moralized: The Divine Analogy in the Eighteenth Century," *ELH* 20 (March 1953); 75; Wasserman cites Sir William Jones, the British orientalist and aesthetician.

sublime and the picturesque as aesthetics is in large measure attributable to Burke and Gilpin, thinkers of an extreme sensationist bias. The ideas of both pioneers had immediate influence on popular culture as well as fine art. Burke added a measure of order to the new frontier of the irrational for his times and prepared the grounds for the discovery of the visual in the novel. Gilpin fostered and legitimized romantic interest in antiquity, inspired droves of landscapes aesthetes, and conditioned a public taste for the descriptive particularity that would enter poetry as well as prose. Yet, in regard to their fundamental tenets, the thought of neither Burke nor Gilpin was acceptable to later aesthetic theorists; almost immediately after these sensationists opened the sublime and the picturesque as new aesthetic realms, associationist aestheticians set to work restoring to aesthetic the moral dimension which had been denied or ignored.

The associationists found the sublime more amenable to a moral dimension than the picturesque because, in spite of the growing interest in Burke's horrific sublime, the physico-theological conception of the sublime remained a strong and viable tradition throughout the eighteenth century. But for a complex of reasons, the picturesque resisted convincing relation to the good. To be sure, a picturesque ruin — Gilpin as well as Price were willing to damage a building for picturesque effect — might be associated with the ephemerality of worldly things, but such an idea is only obliquely if at all moral and exponents of the picturesque were not interested in the idea of mutability *per se* but rather in its effects. A sense of how the picturesque resisted a moral component is suggested in qualities Price defines as central to the aesthetic:

> The recognition of the value of roughness and complexity as "interesting"; the adjective is cool and noncommittal, an assertion of aesthetic appeal without any attempt to characterize it.

And,

> The dissociation of visual, pictorial, or generally aesthetic elements from other values in contemplating a scene.[60]

These requisites of the picturesque expose the emphasis that the adherents of the aesthetic placed on the play of ideas rather than on ideas themselves. The primary effect of the picturesque was "interest," and, to enjoy this dispassionate state, one had only to cultivate a rich store of ideas and be passively receptive to the stimulus of a natural prospect. Thus, while Augustans could experience a natural prospect as an image of a larger, supra-natural reality, the late eighteenth-century enthusiasts of the picturesque found in landscape stimulus for a complex but limited mental state.

60. "The Picturesque Moment," pp. 260-261.

For its seeming meretriciousness the picturesque came eventually to be attacked; notable satiric treatments are Peacock's *Headlong Hall* (1816) and *Nightmare Abbey* (1818), and Combe's *Dr. Syntax in Search of the Picturesque* (1809). The dates of these titles suggest the fact that the picturesque, always unstable and ill-defined, had become hackneyed and empty of specificity by the end of the first decade of the nineteenth century. Because of the tendency of its enthusiasts to concentrate on its effects and to abstract its requisites, the picturesque had come to be related to all manner of disparate phenomena; "picturesque" might mean precisely delineated, obscure, austerely sublime, pathetic, quaint, motley, sentimental, beautiful, or, indeed, nearly any affective quality. For our purposes, two transmutations of picturesque are of special interest: the human or "moral picturesque" and the picturesque of literary style.

As the phrase suggests, the "moral picturesque" stemmed from an effort to find in the picturesque the moral component so conspicuously absent in Gilpin and Price. Although he never uses the phrase, Wordsworth is the master of the aesthetic. The dynamic of the conventional picturesque had essentially one stage: the perception of affective objects evoked — "excited" would be too emphatic — a pleasing state of interest.[61] Inclined always towards transcendence, Wordsworth and Coleridge sought to append to the picturesque dynamic a second stage wherein effect led to transcendental perception of moral truth. The technique is at work in Coleridge's conversational poems and most of Wordsworth's more important verse; their characteristic method is to move from picturesque, sensational experience to transcendence, from mere aestheticism to moral insight. The roughness and irregularity — to borrow Gilpin's requisites — of the Leech Gatherer and his rugged moor in "Resolution and Independence" are valued not for their sentimental affectivity but rather for the sense in which they may seem to image moral truth. If, as Professor Fletcher has argued, the cool aestheticism of the picturesque is an outgrowth of ennui and estrangement from nature among the educated,[62] then Wordsworth's conspicuous malaise at the opening of "Resolution and Independence" illuminates the poet's movement toward the moral picturesque and away from the superficial — which is to say, merely sensational — picturesque. While Gilpin, Price, and others commended the mechanical alteration of landscape to rectify an inherent paucity of "interesting" features, Wordsworth follows an imaginative rather than rational course of landscape modification. His landscape is transformed from a world of estrangement to one of hope

---

61. The state of mind Gilpin and Price most often related to the picturesque was dispassionate "curiosity."

62. *Allegory: The Theory of a Symbolic Mode*, p. 266n.

through the picturesque Leech Gatherer's catalytic effect upon his moral sensibility.

Wordsworth's tendency is to conflate the picturesque and the sublime, or, perhaps more accurately, to move from picturesque sensation to the sublime. The Leech Gatherer or the crumbled stone fence of "Michael" were little more than stock-in-trade images of the picturesque, and yet, lacking the picturesque requisite of detachment, they become timeless and profound. Wordsworth's objections to the conventional picturesque are articulated in his remarks on Foxley, the estate of Uvedale Price. Reacting to picturesque aestheticism, he found Foxley wanting in the "relish of humanity";

> A man by little and little becomes so delicate and fastidious with respect to forms in scenery, where he has a power to exercise a controul over them, that if they do not exactly please him in all moods, and every point of view, his power becomes his law; he banishes one, and then rids himself of another, impoverishing and *monotonizing* Landscapes, which, if not originally distinguished by the bounty of Nature, must be ill able to spare the inspiriting varieties which Art, and the occupations and wants of life in a country left more to itself never fail to produce.[63]

Further impetus for the development of the moral picturesque stems from Ruskin's discussion of the "surface" and the "noble picturesque" in *Modern Painters*. Like Wordsworth, Ruskin was repelled by the inclination of enthusiasts of the conventional picturesque to take a certain detached pleasure in images of suffering, poverty, or decay. He contrasted the "surface picturesque," which "dwells on texture at the expense of emotion," with the "noble picturesque," which, as a highly subjective aesthetic, demands the emphatic treatment of ruin, old age, and sorrow.[64] Thus Ruskin and Wordsworth sought to restore the identity of aesthetic and moral truth through the moral picturesque.

If the emphasis on abstracted effects in discourse on the picturesque set in motion a movement toward a moral picturesque, it also fostered the application of the term to literary style. In its simplest form, picturesque as a quality of style meant pictorially detailed, although it also suggested the capacity to evoke associative mental play. Payne Knight wrote that

63. *Letters of William and Dorothy Wordsworth: The Middle Years*, ed. E. de Selincourt (Cambridge: Oxford University Press, 1937), II, p. 466 (To Sir George Beaumont, 28 August 1811); cited by Price, p. 288. Price, to whose argument I am indebted, further points out that in a note to *Descriptive Sketches* Wordsworth remarked, "I had once given to these sketches the title of Picturesque, but the Alps are insulted in applying to them that term." The Alps, he added, are impossible to describe according to the "cold rules of painting" (Price, p. 289).

64. George P. Landow, *The Aesthetic and Critical Theories of John Ruskin* (Princeton: Princeton University Press, 1971), p. 238; for an overview of Ruskin and the "Two modes of the picturesque," see pp. 221-240. Most of Ruskin's important remarks on the matter are in Book IV of *Modern Painters*, although the moral implications of picturesque are an abiding concern throughout his writings.

Lately, too, the word picturesqueness has been extended to criticism, and employed to signify that clear and vivid style of narration and description, which *paints to the imagination*, and shows every event or object distinctly, as if presented in a picture.[65]

Tension, apparent to a modern reader, between clarity and distinctiveness, on the one hand, and imaginative appeal, on the other, would occasion no difficulty for an associationist like Knight. Prose was picturesque if it evoked in the mind associated pictorial images. The process could be complicated, as Knight's remark on picturesque landscape suggests:

The spectator, having his mind enriched with the embellishments of the painter and poet, applies them, by the spontaneous association of ideas, to the natural objects presented to the eye, which thus acquire ideal and imaginary beauties; that is, beauties that are *not felt by the organic sense of vision, but by the intellect and the imagination through that sense.*[66]

The same process might be — and indeed was — applied to prose. Picturesque prose set in motion mental play through pictorial detail, allusiveness, irregularity of syntax, and other features that might be described as correlatives of the picturesque in paint and landscape. The faculty it demanded was less the transcendent imagination of which the romantics would speak than fancy or invention.[67]

As has been pointed out, affectivity, the pre-eminent requisite of the sublime, was also, in limited intensity, a critical quality of the picturesque. The requisite was retained in both sublime and picturesque prose styles. Interest in the sublime of nature arose concurrently with the revival of the Longinian tradition of language as an instrument for the excitation of the passions.[68] Picturesque prose might evoke sentiments but they had to be sufficiently constrained so as to allow continuous mental play. The picturesque, in short, demanded a less tendentious rhetorical mode than the sublime. Syntax, idiom, and imagery had to be "interesting."

The British incorporation of picturesque into associationist epistem-

65. Richard Payne Knight, *Analytical Inquiry into the Principles of Taste* (London: T. Payne and J. White, 1805), p. 151.

66. Ibid., (italics are mine).

67. Note in this connection Price's comment that the picturesque "looks back to the earlier discussions of wit and forward to later conceptions of imagination" (The Picturesque Moment," p. 263).

68. In his edition of Burke's *Enquiry* (p. xlvii), Boulton notes that prior to Burke "sublime" was primarily a rhetorical term applied by literary critics. It is difficult — perhaps impossible — to ascertain whether the Longinian sublime was an important factor in the advent of the natural sublime or merely a classical precedent revived to legitimize a new and suspect aesthetic interest. The scholarly tendency has been to postulate multiple and discrete aesthetics of sublimity.

ology, the development of a moral picturesque, the perception of the picturesque as a mediate aesthetic between the beautiful and the sublime, and the extension of the picturesque to literary style were all manifest in American arts and popular culture in the first half of the nineteenth century. The picturesque in American arts, however, differed in important respects from the aesthetic as it developed in Britain. Interest in the picturesque in England crested early in the century, but, for a variety of reasons, the prominence of the aesthetic grew in America through the 'thirties and 'forties and did not abate at least until the 'sixties. A sense of the historical forces behind the delayed inception of naturalistic aesthetics in America is suggested in the anecdote of one Andrew Robertson, an English drawing teacher. In 1835, Robertson

> ... took an American gentleman possessing no uncommon power of understanding, and quickness of observation, to an eminence commanding the most beautiful, varied and extensive views, near London. The whole scene was a garden in cultivation, every field enclosed by hedgerows. As these receded in distance, less and less could be seen of the fields, but trees could be seen at the extreme distance. "And do you call this beautiful?" said my friend. "In America we would consider it one of the most desolate scenes that the mind can conceive. It resembles a country that has never been clear of wood."[69]

For this American gentleman landscape was still an antagonist. The nation's utilitarian exigencies in the early decades of the century could admit little aesthetic response to nature, let alone abide by the deliberate cultivation of picturesque disorder and wildness commended by Gilpin, Price, and English landscape architects. The full tide of landscape aestheticism in America had to await the substantial subjugation of the wilderness as well as the movement toward cultural nationalism, and when it did come it came with distinctively American emphases. These included, most importantly, the tendency to conflate the moral picturesque and the moral sublime in a politically expressive aesthetic vision.

Representative of the distinctively American picturesque is Thomas Cole's "Essay on American Scenery."[70] Like most of the painters of the Hudson River School, Cole toured Europe and returned a champion of the American landscape. Positing the supremacy of American topography, Cole argues in his essay that the traveller in our wilderness will

---

69. Cited by Shepard, *Man in the Landscape*, p. 131. Cf. the remark of Billy Kirby in *The Pioneers*: "'Now, I call no country much improved, that is pretty well covered with trees. Stumps are a different thing, for they don't shade the land; and besides, if you dig them, they will make a fence that will turn any thing bigger than a hog, being grand for breachy cattle" (*Works on J. Fenimore Cooper*, 10 vols. [New York: P.F. Collier, 1891], I, 664).

70. *American Monthly Magazine*, n.s., I (1836): 1. The essay is reprinted in John W. McCoubrey, ed., *American Art, 1700-1960: Sources and Documents* (Englewood Cliffs, N.J.: Prentice-Hall, Inc., 1965), pp. 98-109.

find that nowhere has nature "so completely married together grandeur and loveliness; there he sees the sublime melting into the beautiful, the savage tempered by the magnificent." The American picturesque landscape, combining the rural agrarian image with that of wild sublimity, offers both "a keener perception of the beauty of our existence, and a more profound reverence for the Creator of all things." Conservative, possessed of an emphatically moral conception of aesthetic, Cole adamantly insists on the moral import of the beautiful and the sublime, there being "in the human mind an almost inseparable connexion between the beautiful and the good." Not content with his image of the "sublime melting into the beautiful," he further underscores what would become the obsessive concern of a generation of American artists and writers, the symbolic reconciliation of the pastoral with the wild. The sublime in American nature suggests the awful magnificence of God, he argues,

> ... but the cultivated must not be forgotten, for it is still more important to man in his social capacity; it encompasses our homes, and though devoid of the stern sublimity of the wild, its quieter spirit steals tenderly into our bosoms, mingled with a thousand domestic affections and heart-touching association human hands have wrought and human deeds hallowed all around.

Cole next turns to the comparison of European and American landscape that had become, by the 'thirties, a bellestristic convention. While the European landscape may be rich in historic symbols, our land possesses the greater degree of sublimity: "The most distinctive, and perhaps, the most impressive, characteristic of American scenery, is its wildness." American natural sublimity, Cole argues, signals forth no burdensome past:

> He who stands on Mount Albano and looks down on ancient Rome has his mind peopled with the gigantic associations of the storied past; but he who stands on the mounds of the west, the most venerable remains of American antiquity, MAY experience the emotion of the sublime, but it is the sublimity of the shoreless ocean, unislanded by the recorded deeds of man.

That is to say, Europe may have the historical sublime, but America has the sublime of eternity.

As Cole turns his attention to America's future, the essential incompatibility of civilization and wild nature is predictably glossed:

> Where the wolf roams, the plow shall glisten; on the gray crag shall rise temple and tower; mighty deeds shall be done in the yet pathless wilderness; and poets yet unborn shall sanctify the soil.

Standing between America and its future promise is the spirit of utilitarianism. Attacking the "sordid tendencies of modern civilization," Cole calls for the preservation of the solitude and sublimity of wilderness, which "affect the mind with more deep-toned emotion than aught which the hand of man has touched." American destiny is inevitably couched in convenantal terms:

> It was on Mount Horeb that Elijah witnessed the mighty wind, the earthquake and heard the "still small voice"; that voice is YET heard among the mountains! Nature has spread for us a rich and delightful banquet — shall we turn away from it? We are still in Eden: the wall that shuts us out of the garden is our own ignorance and folly.

While a younger generation, that of Hawthorne and Melville, would devote much of their life's work to the demonstration that the Edenic wall is built of stronger, more tragic stuff than ignorance and folly, painters of Cole's generation set themselves to the task of imaging the "sublime melting into the beautiful." Countering the tendency of late eighteenth-century British aesthetics to postulate multiple and discrete landscape categories, they nevertheless accepted Price's mediate picturesque aesthetic as the means to harmonize prospects of disparate topographical values. The picturesque would mediate compositionally between pleasing beauty and awesome sublimity.

As Cole, Washington Allston, Asher Durand, Thomas Doughty, and other landscapists glossed distinctions among naturalistic aesthetic categories, they were abetted by an instinctively conservative aesthetic climate. American critics tended to concur with the view of Archibald Alison and other aestheticians of the Common Sense School, that beauty was not the subordinate category of Burke's *Enquiry* but rather an all-inclusive aesthetic and cognate, as it were, of the good.[71] We find, for example, that the categories of Burke were utterly broken down by the influential American critic James Jackson Jarves, who argued that the "true sublime," imbued with "Divine essence," represents the "highest manifestation of those qualities which constitute Beauty."[72] Paradoxically, the unified aesthetic implied in such a view is closer to transcendentalist aesthetic — and to the suspect "German" metaphysics that lay behind it — than to the less radical Scotch associationists. The view that one principle of beauty pervades all things was celebrated by New England Transcendentalists, who merged man and universe in the image of the transparent eye, and by less philosophically minded Americans, who vacationed as landscape aesthetes, framing picturesque scenes through Claude glasses. In the paintings which graced the parlors of the latter group, the picturesque was not merely an aesthetic of "effects," but the

---

71. Alison's unified aesthetic, which rejects Burke's relation of sublimity to terror, seems to have been the inevitable result of an associationist approach to aesthetic; the sublime, the picturesque, and the beautiful had, according to Alison, a common source in pleasing mental association.

72. *Art Hints; Architecture, Sculpture, and Painting* (New York: Hurd and Houghton, 1855), p. 82; cited by Sanford, *The Quest for Paradise*, p. 143.

compositional means by which the key to the nation's bright promise might be imaged.

The compositional program with which the American painters reconciled sublime wilderness and cultivated nature is clearly exemplified in Cole's *The Oxbow* (1846) [Pl. I]. The most common version of the program was to distribute the topographical correlatives of beauty, picturesqueness, and sublimity in the vertical zones of foreground, middleground, and background, but Cole's slightly deviating lateral arrangement simply underscores the intention of the program. The chief technical problem of this characteristically American picturesque was to image the middle zone in such a way as to meld rather than divorce the garden and the wilderness, and Cole's use of a body of water is a typical solution. The sinuous river mediates between the glowing zone of cultivated nature and the rough, shadowy, and minutely textured zone of sublimity to the left. The ancient, blasted tree in the left foreground, a signature-motif of the Hudson River School, indicates the American movement, concurrent with that of Wordsworth and Ruskin, toward a conflation of picturesque and sublime with a distinctly moral emphasis; an essentially new, unhistoried nation could find no better image of the heroic endurance of ravaging time than the blasted tree. Apposite to the British picturesque in only limited respects, Cole's painting displays tellingly American emphases. While all landscape painting symbolizes and assesses a relationship between man and nature, British landscapists were inclined to subordinate statement to picturesque effects. Cole's statement about man's — or more accurately, America's — relationship to the land looms so prominently in the canvas as to render it allegorical. The focal point of interest is not in the glowing cultivated zone, which, suggestively, resembles the English lake district, but rather in the tangled sublimities of the foreground. There we find the painter at work demonstrating, to recall Cole's "Essay," that Americans are yet in Eden and that no wall divides the garden and the wilderness. The position of the painter on the wild side of the mediating river carries with it the implication of personal and — as Cole would have it — national alliance with the sublime of nature.

Water could not, of course, consistently function as the mediator between the beautiful and the sublime, for the locus of landscape values of wildness and cultivation had to be inhabitable. What Marx has described as the all-important American "middle landscape" was to be located in a "middle ground somewhere 'between,' yet in a transcendent relation to, the opposing forces of civilization and nature."[73] Anxious to differentiate between the American version of this essentially pastoral

73. *The Machine in the Garden*, p. 23.

Plate I.   Thomas Cole, *The Oxbow* (1846). The Metropolitan Museum of Art, New
York. Gift of Mrs. Russell Sage.

Plate II.   Jasper Cropsey, *Bareford Mountains, New Jersey* (1850). The Brooklyn
Museum. Dick S. Ramsey Fund.

Plate III. Asher B. Durand, *Landscape* (1853). The Metropolitan Museum of Art, New York. Bequest of Sarah Ann Ludlum.

Plate IV. Asher B. Durand, *Woodland Interior* (ca. 1855). Museum of Fine Arts, Boston. Bequest of Mary Fuller Wilson.

ideal and the aristocratic form it had taken in eighteenth-century British prospect and rural retirement poetry, nationalistic American artists stressed the intimate contiguity of the wild and the cultivated. Their image of cultivated nature was at once felicitous and rude. The substantial farmhouses of Jasper Cropsey's *Bareford Mountains, New Jersey* (1850) [Pl. II] are estimable, to be sure, but the golden hayfield that functions as the "middle landscape" is barely set off from the wilderness by a tellingly fragile, dilapidated, and casually aligned fence. Nearby the inevitable signature of sublimity, a crumbling boulder, the wilderness blends through the fence into the hayfield. Cropsey's American pastoral is embraced by the wild.

To reconcile the beautiful and the sublime was of necessity to idealize the American wilderness and to conceal the ineluctable tensions between it and civilization. Ideal landscapes in the first half of the nineteenth century could take distorted and even bizarre form. In its milder manifestations the distortion has become so commonplace that we now often fail to recognize it as such. There is, for example, the "cow theme," a motif exemplified by Asher Durand's *Landscape* (1843) [Pl. III]; as Professor Shepard has remarked, only as a sign of America's new Edenic promise is this "odd juxtaposition of sleek cows in the wilderness comprehensible."[74] That the American middle landscape was primarily an idea rather than a specific kind of locale is evinced through dozens of canvases which postulate the harmony of civilization and wildness simply by depicting human figures who are evidently at their ease in the most savage terrain. A case in point is Asher Durand's famous painting, *Kindred Spirits* (1849), which depicts the painter Cole and William Cullen Bryant, both tastefully attired, calmly conversing at the edge of a precipitous gorge.[75] While this juxtaposition may seem, like sleek cows in the wilderness, to be simply odd, other landscapes reconciling man and wildness went beyond the idea to the bizarre. Reflecting the excesses of the Greek Revival in America, a spate of paintings appeared in which all manner of classical constructions were placed in the wildest, most unlikely places; they stand as mute testimony to the compositional necessity of the mediating middle landscape.[76]

74. *Man in the Landscape*, p. 111.
75. The painting is often cited as evidence of the reciprocal influence of American painters and writers; the aesthetic failure of the piece is too seldom noted.
76. A passage in John Muir's "A Near View of the High Sierra" offers evidence that as late as the 1890's the middle landscape was regarded as the essential compositional component of the picturesque; Muir reports an encounter with a group of artists who found the walled Yosemite Valley unpaintable; "'All this is huge and sublime,'" they complained, "'but we see nothing as yet at all available for effective pictures. Art is long, and art is limited, you know; and here are foregrounds, middle-grounds, backgrounds, all alike'" (Cited by Conron, *The American Landscape: A Critical Anthology of Prose and Poetry* (New York: Oxford University Press, 1974), p. 255.

The American Renaissance became an age marked by confluence among the arts as painters and writers came to share the conviction that the nation's destiny was in a special sense immanent in its landscape. Cole, Durand, Allston, Quidor, and other landscapists began as illustrators of books, and they were all inclined to literary subject matter. Iriving, Cooper, and Bryant were, in turn, influenced in important ways by contemporaneous painters.[77] The profusion of pictorial detail in Cooper's novels stands as the literary correlative of the burgeoning of landscape art in America, and his pictorial mode is apposite in important respects to the distinctively American picturesque of the Hudson River School. The inclination among the painters of the day to move from picturesquely detailed landscape to ideal landscape and on to allegory — that latent but ever-present dimension of the picturesque — corresponds to Cooper's tendency to arrest his narrative progression in allegorical tableaux. Cooper characteristically moves from landscape effects to landscape symbolism. Perhaps even more important is the manner in which the middle landscape of American painting surfaces as an obsessive concern in Cooper. The struggle of the Hudson River School to realize in paint this semi-primitive ideal is related to the restless shuttling of Cooper's characters between village and wilderness. Aware — perhaps not consciously — of the potency of the middle landscape as symbol, Cooper drew upon its topographical, political, and moral dimensions in *The Spy: A Tale of the Neutral Ground* (1821). His setting, the environs of Westchester, New York, during the Revolution, is a neutral ground that mediates physically between the urban settlement of New York and wilderness sublimity, politically between Royalist and Republican, and morally between Old and New World values.

Like Cooper, Irving found it convenient to place his neutral ground in the past, although his American past is more imagined and less historically founded than Cooper's. In the "Author's Account of Himself" in the *Sketch Book* (1819), he announces himself as lover of the picturesque in a manner that underscores forces that would have a profound effect on the American arts of his epoch:

> I visited various parts of my own country, and had I been merely a lover of fine scenery I should have felt little desire to seek elsewhere its gratifications, for on no country have the charms of nature been more prodigally lavished.

To this remark Irving appends a catalogue of American natural sublimities, after which he concludes that "never need an American look beyond

77. See Donald A. Ringe, *The Pictorial Mode; Space and Time in the Art of Bryant, Irving, and Cooper* (Lexington: University of Kentucky Press, 1971); James T. Callow, *Kindred Spirits: Knickerbocker Writers and Artists, 1807-1855* (Chapel Hill: University of North Carolina Press, 1967); and Blake Nevius, *Cooper's Landscapes: An Essay on the Picturesque Vision* (Berkeley: University of California Press, 1976).

his own country for the sublime and beautiful of natural scenery." The all-important qualification, however, immediately follows:

> But Europe held forth *the charms of storied and poetical association.* There were to be seen the masterpieces of art, the refinements of highly cultivated society, the quaint peculiarities of ancient and local custom. *My native country was full of youthful promise: Europe was rich in the accumulated treasures of age.* Her very ruins told the history of times gone by, and every moldering stone was a chronicle. I longed to wander over the scenes of renowned achievement — to tread, as it were, in the footsteps of antiquity, to loiter about the ruined castle, to meditate on the falling tower, *to escape, in short, from the commonplace realities of the present and lose myself among the shadowy grandeurs of the past.*[78]

Speaking here is a man of sensibility who seeks the affective landscape of the picturesque, a landscape he finds conspicuously absent in America. The passage outlines the dilemma of the American artist in Irving's age: How might imagination flourish in a nation all but wholly defined by the "commonplace realities of the present"? The creative strategies with which artists of the American Renaissance resolved or attempted to resolve this dilemma determined the generic as well as thematic shape of the arts in the period. Irivng quite simply turned to Europe. When he dealt with native materials, he avoided the broad daylight of the American present by reverting, as in "Rip Van Winkle" and the "Legend of Sleepy Hollow," to a shadowy and fanciful past. Cooper and Simms followed Scott's lead, so far as it was possible in America, by finding romance in frontier history; they skirted the commonplace as well as America's paucity of "storied and poetical association" by bringing the romance closer to the values of epic than to those of the historical novel. Poe turned his back entirely on the American scene and fashioned landscapes of fancy and invention. Hawthorne, perhaps the subtlest strategist, postulated a neutral imaginative territory in the Puritan past, and avoided the obtrusion of commonplace reality by exploiting the inherent imaginative latitude of the romance. He found the allegory a means of supplying the richness of meaning and association that the native scene seemed to lack.

After the romance, perhaps the most popular genre in antebellum America was the sketch.[79] Rising concurrently with the picturesque, it is the ideal expressive vehicle for the aesthetic. The enthusiasm with which Americans took up the genre after Irving's success is in large measure attributable to the importance the nation came to invest in landscape as

78, *The Sketch Book*, ed. M.E. Litchfield (Boston: Athenaeum Press, 1904), p. 12-13, italics added.

79. For a general assessment of the significance of the sketch with commentary on its relation to the picturesque, see Thomas H. Pauly, "The Literary Sketch in Nineteenth-Century America," *Texas Studies in Literature and Language* 17 (Summer 1975): 489-503.

cultural symbol. Sketches of picturesque scenery, often illustrated with engravings, became extraordinarily profuse between 1820 and 1860. Newspapers and especially magazines abounded with them, and the popularity of the genre gave rise to new publishing specialties, the gift book and the summer book. Three types of picturesque sketches have been distinguished: the "rough sketch," which stressed the delineation of significant forms in landscape; the "adorned sketch," which carefully manipulated effects of lighting and composition, and which admitted considerable latitude in treatment of actual scenes; the sketch of fancy, which "begins not as an observed landscape but as a dream-like mood projected into an imagined landscape."[81] The rough sketch was more often than not a type of travel literature; the sketches of Timothy Dwight's *Travels in New England and New York* (1821-1822), Bayard Taylor's foreign travel books, and Nathaniel P. Willis' *American Scenery* (1840) are better than common performances in the mode. Hawthorne and Thoreau were the masters of the adorned sketch, and in their hands the picturesque was put to new and subtle use.[82] Poe, who eschewed the "mere Flemish devotion to matter of fact," was the champion of the fanciful sketch as a vehicle of "general ideas only."[83]

The bellestristic sketch, which might be rough or adorned, was issued in monthly magazines or gift books. Gracefully illustrated monthlies which gave emphasis to the sketch were *Putnam's*, *Sartain's*, and *Holden's Dollar Magazine*. Notable gift books were the *Token* (1827-1842), to which Hawthorne was a frequent contributor, *Godey's Lady's Book* (1830-1898), in which Poe's sketches appeared, the lavishly illustrated *Picturesque America* (1872), which was edited by Bryant, and the *Home Book of the Picturesque* (1852). The last of these may be regarded as archetypical of the American picturesque; comprised by essays and sketches by Irving, Cooper, Bryant, and others, the collection celebrates,

80. The typology and terms are from Conron, *The American Landscape*, p. 165.
81. On Thoreau and the picturesque see William D. Templeman, Thoreau, Moralist of the Picturesque," *PMLA* 47 (September 1932): 864-889 and Gordon V. Boudreau's corrective paper, "H.D. Thoreau, William Gilpin, and the Metaphysical Ground of the Picturesque," *American Literature* 45 (November 1973): 357-369. On the aesthetic in Hawthorne see Leo B. Levy, "The Landscape Modes of *The Scarlet Letter*," *Nineteenth-Century Fiction* 23 (March 1969): 377-392 and "Picturesque Style in *The House of the Seven Gables*," *New England Quarterly* 39 (June 1966), and Buford Jones, "'The Man of Adamant' and the Moral Picturesque," *American Transcendental Quarterly* 14 (Spring 1972): 33-41.
82. See Boudreau, especially pp. 361-369, and Levy, "The Landscape Modes of *The Scarlet Letter*," 377-385.
83. Cited by Conron, *The American Landscape*, p. 165.

with chauvinistic emphasis, the sublimity of the American landscape.[84]
The bulk of the numberless sketches in the picturesque manner was
unredeemable hack work, but Hawthorne, Poe, Thoreau, and Melville
devoted no small measure of their first-rate talent to the genre. By
catering to the belletristic — and largely feminine — tastes of gift book
and periodical readers, they availed themselves of the means to produce
more lasting work. But factors more subtle than economic necessity lie
behind the predilection for the sketch among writers of genius.

The artistic dilemma which has been discussed in connection with
Irving was exacerbated by contradictions in the American critical milieu.
As numerous scholars have maintained and as is abundantly manifest in
the literature, the newness of the nation was ineluctably confronted by
American artists as a paucity of creatively malleable material. A characteristic mode of resolving or perhaps evading the problem is typified by
Emerson's essays, wherein history is emphatically regarded as burdensome and newness is celebrated as a cultural asset. The image of the busk
or ritually purgative bonfire, recurrent in Hawthorne and Thoreau,
suggests that others shared Emerson's point of view. Yet the denigration
of history could by no means solve the problem of subject matter for
American art and, by extension, genre in the new nation. A literature of
social life and the novel of manners would not do, for, as the British were
endlessly fond of pointing out, America had no manners and no social
hierarchy of class. Feasible alternatives to the novel, which was in fact
morally suspect in America as late as the eighteen-thirties, were the
hybrid romance-epics of Cooper and Simms and the romance of Hawthorne. By placing *The Scarlet Letter* and part of *The House of the Seven
Gables* in the shadowy past, Hawthorne could exploit the imaginative
latitude of the romance. When he turned to the present in *The Marble
Faun*, he chose Italy as a setting that could afford a "sort of poetic or fairy
precinct, where actualities would not be so terribly insisted upon as they
are, and must needs be, in America."[85] Generically, the same all-
important imaginative latitude of the romance was available in the tale,
as opposed to the short story, and in the sketch. America was a young
nation, but patriotic Americans insisted that it was an adult nation that
could abide no childish deviation from "actualities."[86] Manifest intellectually in the Common Sense realism of the critical community, native
hostility to the imagination placed strictures upon creastive possibilities

84. The *The Home Book* was ussed by Putnam in New York in 1852, four years
before the same house published Melville's *Piazza Tales*. A curious manifestation of
the subordination of the beautiful as aesthetic — a development which Burke's
Enquiry had begun — might be *The Home Book of Beauty*, a companion gift book
issued by Putnam in the same year; it consists entirely of engravings of women.

85. Preface to *The Marble Faun*, Centenary Edition (Columbus: Ohio State
University Press, 1968), p. 3; subsequent citations refer to this edition.

86. See Martin, *The Instructed Vision*, especially "The Case Against Fiction," pp.
60-76.

that might be partly evaded through the sketch and tale. These genres
carried with them the implicit understanding that the writer was indulg-
ing in play of mind, in sensibility, and in fancy. The sketch especially was
a genre of gesture, allusion, and picturesque "effects."

Taking up the modulation of light and shadow of the picturesque,
Irving employed the device as a means of playing actualities and fancy,
the American present and an imagined past, against each other. He
fashioned in "Rip Van Winkle" and "The Legend of Sleepy Hollow"
richly fanciful tales that escaped critical condemnation through their
apparent ridicule of the supernatural. The former tale is rendered feasible
in terms of the American critical climate only through Rip's patently
absurd sleep. A vestage of a fictive, legendary past, Rip is ridiculous in
the broad daylight of the new republic, and Ichabod Crane, a man of
fancy who believes in the supernatural, suffers defeat by the virile and
eminently practical Brom Bones. Yet, read with Irving's lamentation of
the unhistoried American landscape in mind, the stories are an oblique
protest of the predicament of the artist in America.

The problem of the neutral ground is focal, perhaps obsessive, in
Hawthorne's prefaces.[87] While Irving inverted his allegiances, ultimately
permitting the light of common day and common sense to dispel the
fanciful world of shadow, Hawthorne fashioned in his prefaces a subtler
form of duplicity. Overtly apologic for his departures from the actualities
of the American present, the prefaces function as covert protests against
the tyranny of the present that, he confessed, had "always pressed very
heavily"[88] upon him. "No author, without a trial," he wrote in the
preface to The Marble Faun,

> can conceive of the difficulty of writing a romance about a country where there is no
> shadow, no antiquity, no mystery, no picturesque and gloomy wrong, nor anything
> but a commonplace prosperity, in broad and simple daylight, as is happily the case
> with my dear native land.[89]

The European artist has a richly historical landscape in which to build his
fictions, but the American artist can less easily avail himself of the "Faery
Land" of romance: "This atmosphere," Hawthorne notes in the preface
to The Blithedale Romance,

87. See Terence Martin, "The Neutral Ground of Fiction," in Nathaniel Hawthorne
(New York: Twayne Publishers, Inc., 1965), pp. 38-48; Jesse Bier, "Hawthorne on the
Romance: His Prefaces Related and Examined," Modern Philology 53 (August 1955):
17-24; and Buford Jones, "The Faery Land of Hawthorne's Romances," Emerson
Society Quarterly (Third Quarter 1967): 106-124. Millicent Bell presents a general
assessment of Hawthorne's view of the artist's relation to society in Hawthorne's View
of the Artist (New York: State University of New York, 1962).
88. Preface to The Blithedale Romance, Centenary Edition (Columbus: Ohio State
University Press, 1971), p. 2.
89. The Marble Faun, p. 3.

is what the American romancer needs. In its absence, the beings of imagination are compelled to show themselves in the same category as actually living mortals; a necessity that generally renders the paint and pasteboard of their composition but too painfully discernible.[90]

Hawthorne's position was rendered all the more difficult by the fact that his career spans decades during which American artists were expected to contribute to the cause of cultural nationalism. He was compelled to concede — and perhaps was convinced — that the source of his creative difficulties was also his nation's most valuable asset, a pristine landscape largely free of cultural or historical associations.

Nowhere is Hawthorne's use of the neutral ground more revealing than in "The Old Manse," the sketch that functions, like Melville's "The Piazza," as a thematic frame for the collection of tales that it precedes. The subtitle of the piece — "The Author Makes the Reader Acquainted with His Abode" — is appropriately unassuming insofar as it prepares the reader for a sketch as opposed to an essay, for the collocation of effects rather than exposition on a particular subject. Taking actuality as its point of departure, the sketch is itself a neutral or mediating genre between the real and the imagined. Professor Price's remarks on the picturesque relate the aesthetic to the sketch in a fashion most relevant to "The Old Manse"; the favorite scens of the picturesque

are those in which form emerges only with study or is at the point of dissolution. It turns to the sketch, which precedes formal perfection, and the ruin, which succeeds it. Where it concentrates upon a particular object, the aesthetic interest lies in the emergence of formal interest from an unlikely source ... or in the internal conflict between the centrifugal forces of dissolution and the centripetal pull of form... .

Hawthorne's sketch is by turns shadowy and pictorially focused, endlessly digressive yet ordered by a delicately rendered sense of place and painterly manipulation of light, shadow, and detail. The Old Manse with its overgrown and untended orchard, the unlikely source of formal interest, seems like the sketch itself to be poised between order and dissolution. Price speaks of the emergence of interest rather than subject, for the picturesque has no subject in the conventional sense. "The center of attention" in picturesque art

is displaced from the work of art as we traditionally conceive it to the larger sphere in which it plays its role, and the drama is readily cast into the form of the energies of art wrestling with resistant materials or the alternative form of the genius of nature or time overcoming the upstart achievements of a fragile but self-assertive art[91]

The relevance of this picturesque displacement of attention to Hawthorne's sketches and tales should be immediately apparent to those

90. *The Blithedale Romance*, p. 2.
91. "The Picturesque Moment," p. 277.

40

familiar with the critical heritage of the writer's work. It illuminates responses ranging from Henry James's contention that most of Hawthorne's *Twice-Told Tales* are "so tenderly trivial, that simply to mention them is to put them in a false position" to Professor Breinig's remark that

> The reader of Hawthorne's sketches often feels that there is a story hidden behind the description, and many of the author's shorter pieces might appropriately be called not "twice-told" but "untold" tales.[92]

The tendency of Hawthorne's tales — and picturesque art in general — to displace attention to a larger sphere of reference stems in part from the sense in which the picturesque is defined by abstracted effects; after associationist aestheticians had shifted the locus of naturalistic aesthetics from qualities inhering in objects to the perceiving mind, the *subject* of art — particularly picturesque art — was radically subordinated to *effects*. The logical extension of this development is the elimination of subject altogether, which is the defining characteristic of modern abstract art.[93] Of course, the public — and especially the American public — were by no means prepared in the middle decades of the nineteenth century for the abandonment of the actual in art. Yet American landscape painting of the period evinces the movement away from the primacy of subject. Asher B. Durand's *Woodland Interior* (1843?) [Pl. IV] departs from the conventional American picturesque as a device for the mediation of topographical zones and presents the aesthetic discretely; atmosphere displaces subject in the painting, and instead of fostering statement the artist concentrates on evoking a mood through interesting contrasts of texture and light. Such performances are relatively rare in the period, however, as most American landscapists turned, as did Hawthorne, to a

92. James's remark is drawn form *Hawthorne* (New York: Harper & Row, 1956), p. 94; Breinig's view is in "The Destruction of Fairyland," p. 266. Cf. Poe's ascerbic suggestion ("Tale-Writing: Nathaniel Hawthorne," *Godey's Lady's Book* 35 [November 1847]: 259) that Hawthorne should avail himself of a "bottle of visible ink," and, perhaps most important, Hawthorne's own self-effacing remarks in "The Old Manse": "These fitful sketches, with so little of external life about them, yet claiming no profundity of purpose, — so reserved, even while they sometimes seem so frank, — often but half in earnest, and never, even when most so, expressing satisfactorily the thoughts which they profess to image — such trifles, I truly feel, afford no solid basis for a literary reputation" (*Mosses from an Old Manse*, Centenary Edition [Columbus: Ohio State University Press, 1974], p. 34; subsequent citations refer to this edition).
93. The continuity of picturesque and abstract art is evinced in Francis Jeffrey's review of Alison's *Essay on Taste*; discussing Payne Knight's contention that any object, including a dunghill, might possess picturesque beauty if properly presented, Jeffrey speculates that "if tints and shades were the exclusive sources of our gratification, ... pleasure and beauty would be much enhanced if there was *no imitation of any thing*" in a painting (*Edinburgh Review* 18 [May 1811]: 38). For further remarks on picturesque and abstract art, see Fletcher, p. 257 ff.

mixture of the picturesque with the allegorical so as to complement statement with atmospheric effects.

If "The Old Manse" may be said to have asubject at all, it is the atmosphere and point of view that gave rise to the tales that the sketch introduces. Spatially, the Old Manse mediates between the actual and the imagined:

> The glimmering shadows that lay half asleep between the door of the house and the public highway were a kind of spiritual medium, seen through which the edifice had not quite the aspect of belonging to the material world. (p. 3)

As Irving had done before him Hawthorne employs picturesque contrasts of shadow and light, a "veil woven of intermingled gloom and brightness" (p. 4), to carry the interplay of the imagined and the actual. The Old Manse, like the aesthetic position which it images, stands at slight but critical remove from the brightly illuminated "public highway" of actuality. A correlative of aesthetic distance, this remove is also imaged in the reflective surface of the Concord River, which reveals and intensifies beauty latent in the environs of the Old Manse:

> In the light of a calm and golden sunset it becomes lovely beyond expression; the more lovely for the quietude that so well accords with the hour, when even the wind, after blustering all day long, usually hushes itself to rest. Each tree and rock, and every blade of grass, is distinctly imaged, and, however unsightly in reality, assumes ideal beauty in the reflection.

Through the tawny hue and the muddiness" of the Concord — low, surprising, and therefore typically picturesque sources of interest — Hawthorne turns to a Wordsworthian or moral picturesque; let the dusky river, with its reflective, transforming surface, be a symbol that

> the earthliest human soul has an infinite spiritual capacity and may contain the better world within its depths. But, indeed, the same lesson might be drawn out of any mud puddle in the streets of a city; and, being taught us everywhere, it must be true. (p. 7)

Again following Irving's precedent, Hawthorne employs the picturesque as a device for the mediation of shadowy past with present actuality. On the northern side of the Manse a window offers a prospect of Concord bridge, scene of the famous Revolutionary battle that marked the inception of the new republic. Between this spot — already steeped in legend — and the Old Manse lies an Orchard that offers to every wayfarer "apples that are bitter sweet with the moral of Time's vicissitude" (p. 12). These "bear the closest resemblance to those that grew in Eden" (p. 13), yet, Hawthorne suggests, they are the fruit of a New World and perhaps of a better Eden; in bad weather, he jests, "Eve's bower in Paradise must have been but a cheerless and anguish kind of shelter, nowise comparable to the old parsonage" (p. 16). Past and present may intermingle in the

Old Manse, but Hawthorne is clearly allied with the past as source of fictive materials. Of the Indian artifacts which abound in the neighborhood of the Manse he remarks that "their great charm consists in ... rudeness and in the individuality of each article, so different from the productions of civilized machinery, which shapes everything on one pattern." His sympathies are evinced as he remarks that "It can hardly be told whether it is a joy or a pain," after a momentary vision of the Indian past, "to gaze around in the broad daylight of reality and see stone fences, white houses, potato fields, and men doggedly hoeing in their shirt-sleeves and homespun pantaloons" (p. 11). Perhaps alluding to Irving, Hawthorne recommends that the world "recline its vast head on the first convenient pillow and take an age-long nap" so as to elude a present that is "distracted through a morbid activity" (p. 29).

Hawthorne claims for the Old Manse and its grounds something more than pleasingly soporific effects and the means of escaping a reality from which he is estranged. The neutral imaginative ground for which the Manse stands has ontological validity, for it is the locus of sensation and meaning. The Concord environs are as profuse with meaning as landscape in Spenser, and they are the fit setting for such an allegorical quest as Bunyan's; "Our precincts," notes Hawthorne, "were like the Enchanted Ground through which the pilgrim travelled on his way to the Celestial City" (p. 28). This "fairyland" has a certain timeless validity underscored by Hawthorne's allusion to Plato's allegory: "We have been standing on the greensward, but just within the cavern's mouth, where the common sunshine is free to penetrate" (p. 32). The validity of fiction, Hawthorne suggests, lies in the artist's creative stance between common sunshine and imaginative shadow. The epistemological difficulty of this stance is so obtrusive that Hawthorne can only face it in the form of a question; of the "dream picture" reflected in that correlative of the imagination, the Concord River, he asks, "Which, after all, was the most real — the picture, or the original? — the objects palpable to our grosser sense, or their apotheosis in the stream beneath?" (p. 22). Melville, who wrote the prefatory sketch for the *Piazza Tales* with the important precedent of Hawthorne's "Old Manse" before him, faced Hawthorne's question in a radically different way. An incisive anatomy of a "dream picture," "The Piazza" fosters aesthetic, epistemological, and moral doubts that are, in a profound sense, antecedent to Hawthorne's question of the relative ontological merits of the imagined or of the sensational world. While Hawthorne's sketch defends the neutral ground as a realm wherein sensation and meaning, the actual and the ideal, and the American present and past exist contiguously, Melville's sketch exposes the deceptiveness of sensation as well as an impassable gulf between the actual and the ideal.

43

Greylock Ascended: Anatomy of an Aesthetic

The prospect of the narrator of "The Piazza" is literally and meta-phorically that of Melville in the early eighteen-fifties. "The Piazza," like "The Old Manse," is an account of the author's abode, for it describes the Berkshire environs of "Arrowhead," the Pittsfield estate at which Melville lived and worked from 1850 to 1863.[93] The locale figures vitally in the most important phase of the writer's career; there he befriended Hawthorne and wrote *Moby-Dick, Pierre, Israel Potter, The Confidence-Man*, and all of his great shorter fiction excepting *Billy-Budd*. That "Arrowhead" and the landscape surrounding it had significant impact on the writer's sensibility there can be no doubt, for they figure directly in "The Piazza," *Pierre*, "The Apple-Tree Table," "The Lightning-Rod Man," "I and My Chimney," "Cock-A-Doodle-Doo!" and "The Tartarus of Maids." On its northern side, where Melville constructed a piazza in 1851, "Arrowhead" offered a fine prospect of Mount Greylock, the highest peak in Massachusetts; the south offered views of Mount Washington, renamed by Melville October Mountain, and Monument Mountain.

Graced by mountain peaks, wooded foothills, and rolling meadows, the Pittsfield area became by mid-century a mecca for enthusiasts of the picturesque. The pleasing compound of cultivated and wild nature celebrated by the Hudson River painters could be immediately experienced in the mountain prospect of the area. Mountain excursions in search of the picturesque were very much in vogue, and, beyond Melville's solitary ramblings reported by his friend Evert Duyckinck,[94] two such excursions bear tellingly on the relation between "The Piazza" and its milieu. On August 5, 1850, Melville met Hawthorne for the first time at Stockbridge. On the same day the two joined a party composed of Duyckinck, Cornelius Mathews, Oliver Wendell Holmes, James T. Fields, Henry Dwight Sedgwick, Jr., and Joel Tyler Headley for an

93. The most valuable sources of information on Melville's life in Pittsfield are the essays in *Melville & Hawthorne in the Berkshires,* ed. Howard P. Vincent (Kent, Ohio: Kent State University Press, 1968). See also Luther S. Mansfield, "Glimpses of Herman Melville's Life in Pittsfield, 1850-1851," *American Literature* (March 1937): 26-48. In the 1830's young Melville enjoyed extended visits to Broadhall, the Pittsfield home of his uncle Thomas Melville; see Jeanne C. Howes, "Melville's Sensitive Years," *Melville & Hawthorne in the Berkshires,* pp. 22-41 and William H. Gilman *Melville's Early Life and "Redburn"* (New York: New York University Press, 1951), pp. 83-122.
94. "Melville knows every stone & tree & will probably make a book of its [the Pittsfield locale's] features," wrote Duyckinck in a letter to his wife on August 4, 1850 (Mansfield, "Glimpses of Herman Melville's Life," p. 28).

ascent of Monument Mountain.[94] The several accounts of this momen-
tous and delightful occasion suggest that a mountain excursion was a
natural form of recreation for the literati of the day; the pleasures were
aesthetic, the talk literary.[95] Perhaps the best account is Duyckinck's
letter to his wife written on August 6: "We took to our feet" on the
mountain's slopes, he wrote,

> and strode upward Hawthorne and myself in advance, talking of the Scarlet Letter
> ... The rain did not do its worst and we scattered over the cliffs, Herman Melville to
> seat himself, the boldest of all, astride a projecting low stick of rock while Dr.
> Holmes peeped about the cliffs ... Hawthorne looked wildly about for the great
> carbuncle. Mathews read Bryant's poem. The exercise was glorious.[96]

Duyckinck alludes to Hawthorne's "The Great Carbuncle," an allegorical tale which explores the moral dimension of sublimity in a mountain
setting, and the poem read aloud by Mathews is Bryant's "Monument
Mountain," a typical manifestation of the current American vogue
for the sublime of nature. The most prominent literary issue of the
day was cultural nationalism, and, as the ardently nationalistic Duyckinck
circle saw in the American landscape the nation's cultural promise, the issue
was inevitably broached on the summit of Greylock. Duyckinck reports
that

> Dr. Holmes said some of his best things and drew the whole company out by laying
> down various propositions of the superiority of the Englishmen. Melville attacked
> him vigorously.[97]

Duyckinck's letters of August, 1851, indicate that Melville's nationalistic
fervor had not diminished during the composition of Moby-Dick; he
reports that Melville entertained him and a group of mountain picnickers
by reading unidentified verse that glorified "the United States in particular with a polite slanging of all other nations in general."[98] Duyckinck's
second visit included an ascent of Greylock led by Melville. An account

---

94. Mathews (1817-1889) was a frequent contributor to the *Literary World* and
author of *Behemoth* (1839), *The Career of Puffer Hopkins*, and several plays; James T.
Fields was the publisher of *The Scarlet Letter*; Sedgwick was a new York attorney;
Headley was the author of the picturesque *Adirondack; or Life in the Woods* (1849).
95. See Duyckinck's letters of August 3 through 9, 1850, in Mansfield, "Glimpses of
Herman Melville's Life," pp. 27-35 and Cornelius Mathews, "Several Days in
Berkshire," *Literary World* VII (August 24, 1850): 145; (August 31, 1850): 166;
(September 7, 1850): 185-186; as well as James T. Fields, *Yesterdays with Authors*
(Boston: J.R. Osgood, 1872), pp. 52-53; Henry Dwight Sedgwick, "Reminiscences of
Literary Berkshire," *Century Magazine* L (August 1895): 562; Godfrey Greylock
[pseud. J.E.A. Smith] *Taghconic: The Romance and Beauty of the Hills* (Boston: Lee
and Shepard, 1879, p. 318.
96. Manfield, "Glimpses of Herman Melville's Life," p. 30.
97. Ibid.
98. Mansfield, "Glimpses of Herman Melville's Life," pp. 39-40.

of the second ascent that he published in the *Literary World* underscores
the ideas Americans were investing in landscape aesthetics and reveals the
difficulties they faced in reconciling those ideas with direct experience of
the sublime. Duyckinck remarks the refreshing brooks and wild berries
that grace the picturesque slopes of the mountain, but he has difficulty
bringing the summit sublimities into human relation. Noting the "Bel-
ows" and the "Hopper," local names for a pass and glen through which
the narrator of "The Piazza" passes on his way from "Arrowhead" to the
peak of Greylock, Duyckinck remarks rather lamely that "It is a curious
effect that sublimity is enhanced by the suggestion of a small, familiar
household object."[99] On the summit he makes a reluctant observation:

> The near view is of desolation, a wilderness of barren mountains. The New
> Englander's contest with the soil and elements is understood. He is not sublimated
> or refined by this scenery: it works no spiritual miracle in his case, but dooms him
> to a keener struggle with everyday actualities.[100]

In his ascent Duyckinck has discovered that for any but aesthetes like
himself the sublime is not a source of elevation but rather of anguish and
alienation. For Duyckinck this fact emerges only as an unpleasant
admission; bolstered with champagne brought to the mountain summit,
he turns quickly to literary, "Ossianic" associations evoked by the
mountain mists. For Melville the gulf between aesthetic convention and
acutality could not be so easily forgotten. The narrator who ascends
Greylock in "The Piazza" is haunted by the image of a mountain girl not
sublimated or refined by scenery but doomed, maddened, by a keen
struggle with actuality.

Melville was unmatched among writers for his assimilative powers, his
capacity to appropriate and to parody literary resources, and in the brief
piazza sketch he achieved referential intensity and allusiveness perhaps
unparalleled in the period. In the six thousand words of "The Piazza" he
parodies, quotes, refers directly or alludes to Bunyan, Spenser, Cervantes, Milton, Tennyson, Wordsworth, Hawthorne, Irving, Emerson, Thoreau; he refers to or quotes no fewer than four of Shakespeare's plays and
four books of the Bible, and possibly alludes to Pope's *Dunciad* and
Addison's *Spectator* papers on the imagination.[101] Such rich literary

99. "An Ascent of Mount Saddleback," *Literary World* IX (August 30, 1851): 163.
Greylock was known variously as Saddleback or Saddleball.
100. Ibid. Duyckinck's letters to his wife indicate that Melville was very nearly
arrested after the excursion for refusing to pay the extortionary fees of a local
townsman who had driven the party to the mountain's base; see Mansfield "Glimpses
of Herman Melville's Life," p. 46.
101. Nearly all critical treatments of "The Piazza" have been addressed in some
measure to the allusive currents of the sketch; Breinig ("The Destruction of
Fairyland") and Poenicke ("A View from the Piazza") offer the most complete
explications of the literary allusions.

allusiveness is, as has been noted, a standard feature of the landscape sketch as genre; by gracing the texture of their prose with references to literary tradition, sketch writers achieved effects analogous to those evoked by the iconographic or allegorical machinery of eighteenth-century garden architecture and landscape verse. Even Duyckinck's report of the Greylock ascent, a piece which claims no literary merit, makes reference to Scott, Aeschylus, Puritan chronicles, Greek and Scandinavian myth, the Bible, and Thoreau. In respect to allusiveness, "The Piazza" is, as one critic insists, "dangerously overwrought,"[102] but it is overwrought for an important purpose. The sketch is an allegory of the loss of personal faith; Melville vastly extends the referential range of faith and its loss by lacing his simple plot with references to the literature of quest (Bunyan, Spenser, Cervantes), of Christian mythology (the Bible, Milton), of romance (Shakespeare, Tennyson), of romantic transcendence (Wordsworth, Emerson, Thoreau), and of the American imaginative "fairyland" (Irving, Hawthorne). The landscape of "The Piazza" is properly saturated with literary associations because for Melville the legitimacy of cultural tradition — especially romantic tradition — rests on the success or failure of his narrator's quest. The sketch traces the narrator's progression from a state of delusion to a state of embittered realism as he discovers facts inimical to (1) faith in art, (2) faith in sensational experience, (3) faith in aesthetic convention, (4) faith in the immanence of a benign God in nature.

A pattern of disillusionment is first set in motion in Melville's sketch by the epigraph from *Cymbeline* IV, ii, 218-219: "With fairest flowers, / Whist summer lasts, and I live here, Fidele —." The lines are drawn from Arviragus' exquisitely phrased vow of fidelity over the body of the supposedly dead Imogen. As Professor Stein has pointed out,[103] Guiderius' response deprecates Arviragus' romantic effusion:

> Prithee have done,
> And do not play in wench-like words with that
> Which is so serious. Let us bury him,
> And not protract with admiration what
> Is now due debt. To th' grave.

Often woven into sustained iambics, the "richly ornate, self-consciously agreeable, sentimentally fanciful"[104] language of Melville's narrator is the analogue of Arviragus' "wench-like words," and, rising from a facile sensibility, it collapses into irrelevance when the narrator confronts so serious a matter as the plight of the mountain girl, Marianna. That a type of aestheticism is among things "now due debt" is suggested in the

102. Fogle, *Melville's Shorter Tales*, p. 85.
103. "Melville's Comedy of Faith," p. 316.
104. Fogle, p. 85.

complacency of the narrator, who, after the deceptively lovely epigraph, commends the piazza

> as somehow combining the coziness of in-doors with the freedom of out-doors, and it is so pleasant to inspect your thermometer there. (p. 1)

As the language in which the entire sketch is presented is laced with literary artifacts, so the prospect afforded by the piazza is an artifact; the view is

> such a picture, that in berry time no boy climbs hill or crosses vale without coming upon easels planted in every nook, and sunburnt painters painting there. A very paradise of painters.

Immediately the meretriciousness of art — and of picturesque art in particular — is insinuated; from the piazza one seems to see nature unified,

> The circle of the stars cut by the circle of the mountains. At least, so looks it from the house; though, once upon the mountains, no circle of them can you see. had the site been chosen five rods off, this charmed ring would not have been. (p. 1)

If nature pictured is one vast Emersonian circle only through a trick of perspective, so nature dramatized is also deception. During the narrator's dialogue with Marianna, Melville appropriately shifts from a pictorial to a theatrical trope. The piazza becomes a "box-royal" in a landscape amphitheatre, distancing the narrator from the painful actuality of mad Marianna. "But, every night, when the curtain falls," he confesses, "truth comes in with darkness."[105] As the illusion of landscape as theater dissolves he is "haunted by Marianna's face" (p. 15).

The gulf between art and actuality is also insinuated in the complex of allusions to fairytale, folklore, and literary tradition. A measure of archaic diction, anachronistic imagery and symbol, folklore and mythology conduce in the literary picturesque something like the poignant effects of architectural ruin. But in Melville's sketch these elements suggest a disparate body of traditions now bereft of meaning. His narrator invokes Bunyan and Spenser as antecedents, yet describes a third quester, Don Quixote, as "that sagest sage that ever lived" (p. 7). In his quest for the "far cot in fairyland" that lies at a rainbow's end, the narrator is at once a Red-cross Knight, a holy pilgrim, a quixotic fool, and, in Marianna's eyes, "King Charming" (p. 7). The mountain girl, orphaned and exiled with her wood-cutter brother, is taken from fairytale as well as from *Measure for Measure*.[106] Her vision is no less distorted than

105. Inversion of traditional use of light imagery is characteristic of Melville's art. Poenicke (p. 270) suggests that the conclusion of "The Piazza" was inspired by the *Dunciad* (IV, ii, 629-633 and 652-656) an edition of which Melville purchased in 1856; the values of Pope's light imagery are, however, not inverted but conventional.
106. Melville may have also had in mind Tennyson's lyric "Mariana," which was itself inspired by *Measure for Measure* III.i.277.

48

the narrator's, for, as her collapsing cottage seemed to him a "cot of fairyland," she regards his farmhouse in the azure distance as King Charming's Castle. To relieve her tormenting loneliness, her knight-errant can only recommend woodland walks, sleep, and prayer.

So as to underscore the disparity between the actualities of the mountain landscape and traditional — which is to say, European — aesthetic values, Melville develops a courtly language and idiom. Grey-lock, monarch among Pittsfield mountains, is renamed "Charlemagne":[107]

> During the first year of my residence, the more leisurely to witness the coronation of Charlemagne (weather permitting, they crown him every sunrise and sunset), I chose me, on the hill-side bank near by, a royal lounge of turf — a green velvet lounge, with long, moss-padded back; while at the head, strangely enough, they grew (but, I suppose, for heraldry) three tufts of blue violets in a field-argent of wild strawberries; and a trellis, with honeysuckle, I set for canopy. Very majestical lounge, indeed. (p. 2)

Disillusionment obtrudes into this ornate landscape-as-court conceit through Shakespearian allusion; so "majestical" is the narrator's lounge that

> here, as with the reclining majesty of Denmark in his orchard, a sly ear-ache invaded me. But, if damps abound at times in Westminster Abbey, because it is so old, why not within this monastery of mountains, which is older? (p. 2)

Melville's knight-errant is perhaps parodic of the crusader in Irving's "Westminster Abbey" sketch. Remarking the "damps" and picturesque gloom of the Abbey, Irving had been fascinated by the tomb of a crusader,

> one of those military enthusiasts who so strangely mingled religion and romance and whose exploits form the connecting link between fact and fiction, between history and the fairy tale.[108]

The abortive exploit of Melville's rather different knight divorces fact and fiction as he founders somewhere between history and fairytale, reality and literature.

Faith in sensational experience is no less suspect in "The Piazza" than faith in art. Those familiar with Professor Nicolson's studies[109] in the aesthetic of the natural sublime will find most telling Melville's recurrent reference to optical phenomena, particularly optical illusion. As is now widely known, the theory of light refraction published by Newton in his

107. Note Melville's sly irony at the expense of his narrator's courtly gesture: "It was not long after 1848; and, somehow, about that time, all round the world, these kings, they had the casting vote, and voted for themselves" (p. 3).

108. *The Sketch Book*, ed. M.E. Litchfield (Boston: Athenaeum Press, 1904), p. 203.

109. Marjorie Hope Nicolson, *Newton Demands the Muse: Newton's "Opticks" and the Eighteenth-Century Poets* (Princeton: Princeton University Press, 1946); other relevant commentary is in Nicolson's *Mountain Gloom and mountain Glory: The Development of the Aesthetics of the Infinite* (Ithaca: Cornell University Press, 1959).

Opticks had far-reaching effects upon poetry and aesthetics in the eighteenth century. Newton's explanation of the rainbow's colors as refractions of the sun's rays underlies Locke's distinction between primary qualities and secondary attributes of matter, a distinction that figures importantly in eighteenth-century discourse on aesthetics of nature. From Addison onward, aestheticians and psychological theorists argued that the sublime was distinguished from the beautiful insofar as it inhered in or was evoked by primary qualities and not secondary or apparent attributes of matter. Light and dark as well as the abstract quality of vast extension became the signal attributes of the sublime, while beauty was relegated to such apparent qualities as color, distinction, and proportion. Doubtless Melville had this aesthetic dualism and its epistemological origins in mind when writing "The Piazza."[110]

The pleasantly luminous colors of the lower valley in the sketch distinguish that zone from the sublime realm of the mountain summit, which is dominated by the colorless chiaroscuro of light and shadow. On the mountain slopes the narrator's attention is focused on the intricate contrasts of texture in the picturesque terrain, while on the summit he remarks the "oceanic" vastness and lonesomeness, "the silence and the sameness" (p. 4) of sublimity. Each of the many references to color phenomena in the sketch insinuates their ephemerality and deceptiveness. The narrator's delight in the white "starry bloom" of his Chinese creeper is destroyed when he discovers the plant is infested by "millions of strange, cankerous worms, which, feeding upon those blossoms, so shared their blessed hue, as to make it unblessed evermore" (p. 6). He is stirred from the "ingrate peevishness of [his] weary convalescence" (p. 6) by the grail-like golden light on the mountaintop. Yet even gold, supreme among colors, is but delusive refraction of light from the roof of Marianna's hut; "Sir, the sun gilds not this roof," she laments, "it first scorches, and then rots" (p. 12). The narrator is drawn to the golden light by a rainbow, which is itself composed by the refraction of colorless light. Not color alone but optical phenomena generally are suspect in "The Piazza." The golden light on Greylock, first sighted on a "wizard

---

110. Melville personally owned a complete edition of the *Speçtator* and American editions of Burke's *Enquiry*, which he annotated, and Akenside's *Pleasures of the Imagination*, which explores Addison's aesthetics in verse; see Merton M. Sealts, Jr., *Melville's Reading: A Check-List of Books Owned and Borrowed* (Madison: University of Wisconsin Press, 1966), pp. 35, 36, 44. The theory of color perception at work in early conceptions of the sublime would be available to Melville in Pierre Bayle's *Dictionary*, an edition of which he purchased and read in 1849 (Sealts, p. 39); on his use of Bayle, see Millicent Bell, "Pierre Bayle and *Moby-Dick*," *PMLA* 65 (September 1951): 626-648.

afternoon," "a mad poet's afternoon," is "only visible, and then but vaguely, under certain witching conditions of light and shadow" among mountains which "somehow ... play at hide-and-seek, and all before one's eyes" (p. 4).[111]

If the eye deceives, Melville's sketch suggests, then picturesque aesthetic conventions founded on visual experience must surely deceive. The picturesque unification of the beautiful and the sublime in Melville's prospect depends, as has been noted, on carefuly manipulated perspective; had the site for the piazza been "chosen five rods off, this charmed ring would not have been." In remarking the well chosen site, Melville employs three curiously disparate allusions:

> Whoever built the house, he builded better than he knew; or else Orion in the zenith flashed down his Damocles' sword to him some starry night, and said, "Build there." For how, otherwise, could it have entered the builder's mind, that, upon the clearing being made, such a purple prospect would be his? (p. 1)

The second phrase of the first line is borrowed, without quotation marks, from Emerson's "The Problem," a poem on the relations of religion and art:[112]

> The hand that rounded Peter's dome
> And groined the aisles of Christian Rome
> Wrought in a sad sincerity;
> Himself from God he could not free
> He builded better than he knew; —
> The conscious stone to beauty grew.

The borrowed line and its source suggest that art — here, specifically landscape art — draws its inspiration and form from the divinity in nature. Yet the implied transcendental piety is immediately qualified by the enjambed references to Orion and Damocles. Orion carries the suggestion of a cyclical regeneration of nature that the narrator contemplates from his piazza. To arm Orion with Damocles' sword engenders a paradox; after extolling the happiness of Dionysius, the flatterer Damocles was seated with a sword hung over his head by a single hair to remind him of the perilousness of happiness. The narrator's home was situated in the landscape by a man who builded better than he knew, for, while it

---

111. The deceptive color imagery of "The Piazza" seems to be a subtle rendering of Ishmael's idea that "all deified Nature absolutely paints like the harlot" (*Moby-Dick*, ed. Luther S. Mansfiedl and Howard P. Vincent [New York: Hendricks House, 1962], p. 193. Cf. Pierre Bayle, *Historical and Critical Dictionary*, 5 vols. (London: J.J. and P. Knapton, 1734-1738), IV, 654, who asked, rhetorically, if God deceives men in respect to colors, "what hinders but he may deceive them with respect to extension?"

112. The source of Melville's phrase was first discovered by Marvin Fisher ("Prospect and Perspective in Melville's 'Piazza,'" p. 208) to whose explication I am indebted.

offers a view of nature as one "charmed circle," it exposes the darker truth that all prospects, literally and metaphorically speaking, are ultimately delusive. This is of course as true of the view from Greylock's summit as it is of the view from the piazza. For Marianna, the narrator's house seems a King Charming's palace only through a "mirage haze." To the narrator Marianna appears as a "fairy queen, sitting at her fairy window," a conceit deflated by the embittered girl's assessment:

> In the morning, the sun comes in at this old window, to be sure — boarded up, when first we came; a window I can't keep clean, do what I may — and half burns, and nearly blinds me at my sewing, besides setting the flies and wasps astir — such flies as only mountain houses know. (p. 11)

Disturbed by the girl's mad musings — she speaks of the shadow of her lost dog Tray, named, possibly, for blind Lear's dog — the narrator opens a brief dialogue that underscores epistemological dilemma:

> "Yours are strange fancies, Marianna."
> "They but reflect the things."
> "Then I should have said, 'These are strange things.'" (p. 12)

As aesthetic anatomy, "The Piazza" is focused particularly on the seeming reconciliation of the beautiful and sublime, the garden and the wilderness, in the American picturesque convention. Although in most respects the sketch is true to the topographical actualities of the Pittsfield area,[113] the range of hills to the east of the narrator's estate is invented. These "Hearth Stone Hills," accessible and inviting as their name suggests and associated with "the season's new-dropped lamb" and "Christmas dawn," offer a "goodly sight." "But," the narrator quips, "to the north is Charlemagne — can't have the Hearth Stone Hills with Charlemagne" (pp. 2-3). He muses, when approaching Marianna's hut, on the "gentle, nurturing heat" said to radiate from "hearth-stones in fairyland" (p. 9), but Marianna laments that her "chimney-place has been blocked up with snow, just like hollow stump" (p. 12). When he recommends mountain walks to relieve her lonely life of "sitting, sitting, restless sitting," she pointedly replies, "Better feel alone by hearth, than rock" (p. 14). Only the most blighted domesticity can be admitted in a realm so cruelly circumscribed by the exigencies of survival. Marianna's garden in the wilderness is as blighted as her sensibility:

> two hop-vines climbed two poles, and, gaining their tip-ends, would have then joined over in an upward clasp, but the baffled shoots, groping awhile in empty air, trailed back whence they sprung. (p. 14)

---

113. A map of the area is provided as the frontispiece of *Melville & Hawthorne in the Berkshires*, ed. Vincent. Marianna's tumbled cottage may be an imaginative adumbration of the ruins of the Williams College observatory of Greylock's summit.

The previous occupants of the mountain cottage have moved on to another and perhaps equally delusive garden in the wilderness: "They went West," remarks Marianna, "and are long dead" (p. 12).

While the terms with which "The Piazza" undermines aesthetic ideas suggest that Melville's ironies are primarily directed against native American conventions, allusions to Wordsworth foster an international range of reference. During the week of August 4, 1850, the week of the famous Pittsfield mountain excursion, Duyckinck had in his possession proof sheets of the Appleton edition of *The Prelude* "to read & use at leisure in the paper [*Literary World*]"; letters written to his wife during the week refer alternately to *The Prelude* and to the scenery surrounding Melville's estate.[114] As we may assume that Wordsworth's poem played no small part in the literary discussions among Duyckinck, Melville, Hawthorne, and Holmes during that auspicious week and as "The Piazza" looks back to Melville's experience in Pittsfield in the early 'fifties, it is not surprising to find reference in the sketch to "a Simplon pass among the clouds" (p. 5) above Greylock. In Book VI of *The Prelude*, the crossing of the Simplon Pass occasioned Wordsworth's magnificent apostrophe to the imagination as the power that opens the "invisible world" when "the light of sense goes out." The message of the "types and symbols of Eternity" that Wordsworth finds in nature is that "Our destiny ... Is with infinitude." Melville's sketch, which everywhere fosters a view of the imaginative life as illusion, reaches its climax "in a pass between two worlds" like the Simplon, but, unlike Wordsworth's pass, Melville's is "participant of neither" world (p. 10). Marianna's sublime mountain realm admits neither humane social life — the life of the hearth — nor transcendent ecstasy. What is more, it points up the disparateness rather than the compatibility of aesthetic and religious experience.

"The Piazza" is clearly calculated to disparage the mode of conflated religion and aesthetic, which, having been developed in the eighteenth century and refined by the Romantics, was revived and put to distinctively ideological use by American cultural nationalists. The pieties disparaged in the sketch are at once religious and aesthetic. The narrator notes that the lack of a piazza in such a grandly situated home as his

> seemed as much of an omission as if a picture-gallery should have no bench; for what but picture-galleries are the marble halls of these same limestone hills? — galleries hung, month after month anew, with pictures ever fading into pictures ever fresh. And beauty is like piety — you cannot run and read it; tranquillity and constancy, with, now-a-days, an easy chair, are needed. For though, of old, when

114. Mansfield, "Glimpses of Melville's Life," pp. 27-28. After describing "cleft two humped Saddleback" and the "mouldering rural grandeur" of Melville's property, Duyckinck writes of the "two voices" in Wordsworth, "one of the mountains, one of the Sea."

reverence was in vogue, and indolence was not, the devotees of Nature, doubtless, used to stand and adore — just as, in the cathedrals of those ages, the worshipers of a higher Power did — yet, in these times of failing faith and feeble knees, we have the piazza and the pew. (pp. 1-2)

Evinced here is the alienation from the present characteristic of Irving and Hawthorne, yet through his narrator Melville attacks the picturesque aestheticism his predecessors had commended as an anodyne for irritating obtrusions of the present. The terms of his attack are important insofar as they deride the passive state of aesthetic repose connected with the picturesque since its inception. He connects the "easy chair" and "indolence," Hawthorne's often confessed sin, with the "failing faith and feeble knees" of modern latitudinarianism. The soporiferous state conducive of the picturesque — the narrator relishes his "sleeping meadow" from a "poppy-bed" (p. 1) — is connected with a complacent faith in a benign God's immanence in nature. An urbane but jaded descendent of Rip Van Winkle and one who would accede to Hawthorne's prescription of an "age-long nap" for a world afflicted with "morbid activity,"[115] the narrator can combine aesthetic and pallid religious experience in the comforts of his piazza. The static, contrived prospect is an amphitheater of divine benignity in which the "old wars of Lucifer and Michael" seem "sham fights" (p. 6). Of course, a covert dimension of the sketch, indicated continuously by the sustained ironic tone and the often archaic, self-consciously ornate language, insinuates the reality of natural evil. The wars of Lucifer and Michael may be old, but they are nonetheless virulent. Battle lines now seem ill-defined; good and evil coalesce; white flowers are blighted by white worms.

The context of Melville's conceit of landscape as the theater of God is the broad and — in Melville's day — commonplace convention of nature as the art and Revelation of God. The spate of belletristic renderings of this convention might be typified by "Scenery and Mind," E.L. Magoon's contribution to the *Home Book of the Picturesque*:

> The book of Nature, which is the art of God, as Revelation is the word of his divinity, unfolds its innumerable leaves, all illuminated with glorious imagery, to the vision of his creature, man.[116]

The natural language of Greylock as book of nature bespeaks not divine immanence but God's complicity in a deception cosmic in scale. The mountain's summit, where the narrator discovers that illumination as well as vision are delusive, is blocked by a fence "banning a dark road, which, however, dark, led up ... Forbidding and forbidden ground," and

115. *Mosses from an Old Manse*, Centenary Edition (Columbus: Ohio State University Press, 1974), p. 29; subsequent citations refer to this edition.
116. *Home Book of the Picturesque*, p. 5.

the fallen apples found on the mountain slopes are "Eve's apples, seek-no-furthers" (p. 8). Remarking the delusiveness of optical phenomena and the related capacity of mountain scenery to "play at hide and seek," the narrator suggests not the immanence but the absence of God through syntactical ambiguity:

> a blue summit, peering up away behind the rest, will, as it were, talk to you over their heads, and plainly tell you, that, though he (the blue summit) seems among them, he is not of them (God forbid!), and, indeed, would have you know that he considers himself — as, to say truth, he has good right — by several cubits their superior ... (p. 4)

On the mountain, Jacks-in-the-pulpit, "like their Baptist namesake, preached but to the wilderness," and the eddies in a stream had "spun out empty chapels in the living rock" (p. 8).

American nationalists were especially inclined to read in the book of nature promise of a special covenant with God, and to this reading — or as Melville would have it, misreading — "The Piazza" is addressed chiefly through the delusive and ambiguous rainbow above Greylock. Melville intended this symbol to relate to covenant theology, for it appears after storm clouds wrap Greylock "like a Sinai, till one thinks swart Moses must be climbing among scathed hemlocks there" (p. 5). American nationalists, who celebrated God's grace in the American landscape and proclaimed his immediacy in the sublime of nature, took up the Puritan tradition of identifying America's destiny with the Israelites' errand in the wilderness. By the eighteen-fifties, the fusion of nationalist ideology, covenant theology, and natural sublimity had become so commonplace that Melville's readers could not fail to connect his rainbow with the Mosaic covenant as well as with the covenant of Genesis 9:8,12:

> And God spake unto Noah, and to his sons with him, saying ... This is the token of the covenant which I make between me and you, and every living creature that is with you, for perpetual generations: I do set my bow in the cloud, and it shall be for a token of a covenant between me and the earth ... and the waters shall no more become a flood to destroy all flesh.

As Poenicke has noted, "It is this special human pact with the sublime which Melville ... unrelentingly questions."[117] The "scathed hemlocks" of Greylocks's sublime summit are the signatures of an angry God. Significantly the only mark of the redemption of history through Christ is a "low cross-pile of silver birch" that seems to the narrator a "sequestered grave" (p. 9). The view from the piazza, we recall, cannot accommodate the "Hearth Stone Hills" with their "Christmas dawn" and "new-dropped lamb." To Melville's mind, wrathful Jehovah and the

117. "A View from the Piazza," p. 279.

Prince of Peace could no more be reconciled than pastoral nature and wilderness, nature's beauty and nature's sublimity.

In confronting the picturesque, Melville took up irony and parody as modes sufficiently complex to cope with the matrix of theological, epistemological, and ideological implications that had accreted to the aesthetic in America. The purview of "The Piazza" is extensive, encompassing matters as diverse as grail legend, natural theodicy, biblical traditions of wilderness, and the heroic conventions of fairytale and romance, but the relations of the sketch to two works in the conventional picturesque, Thoreau's *A Week on the Concord and Merrimack Rivers* and Hawthorne's Old Manse sketch, bring Melville's parodic intentions into sharp focus.

Breinig has noted affinities between "The Piazza" and *A Week*, which Melville borrowed from Duyckinck in 1850, but he makes no attempt to correlate the ascents of Mount Greylock in both works.[118] In some respects "The Piazza" may have been calculated to disparage aspects of Thoreau's digressive passage on Greylock in the "Tuesday" section of *A Week*. Thoreau seems to have ascended the mountain via the same route taken by Melville's narrator and "The Piazza" counters his fanciful notion that the road to the summit is such as a "pilgrim" might "enter upon who would climb to the gates of heaven." The experiences of Melville's narrator and those of Marianna stand in refutation of Thoreau's view that "It seemed as if he must be the most singular and heavenly-minded man whose dwelling stood highest up the valley."[119] Both Thoreau and the narrator of "The Piazza" encounter lone women in the course of their ascents, women who are each, in Thoreau's words, "full of interest in that lower world from which I had come." Unlike the mad Marianna, however, Thoreau's woman stands as the type of rustic womanhood, a vestige of American pastoral: she was

> a frank and hospitable young woman, who stood before me in a dishabille, busily and unconcernedly combing her long black hair while she talked, giving her head the necessary toss with each sweep of the comb, with lively, sparkling eyes, ... talking all the while as if she had known me for years, and reminding me of a cousin of mine. (pp. 191-192)

118. "The Destruction of Fairyland," pp. 263-264. On Duyckinck's loan of *A Week*, see Sealts, p. 101. Thoreau's passage on Greylock may well have been a topic of conversation during Melville's ascent of the mountain in 1851, for it is discussed in Duyckinck's report on that excursion ("An Ascent of Mount Saddleback," p. 2). The absence of close verbal parallels between "The Piazza" and Thoreau's passage does not preclude a parodic relation; Melville probably returned Duyckinck's copy of *A Week* in 1850, for Duyckinck's report accurately quotes the "Tuesday" digression.

119. *The Writings of Henry David Thoreau*, Walden Edition (Boston: Riverside, 1906; reprinted New York: AMS Press, 1968), I, 191; all quotations from Thoreau are drawn from this edition.

The ruined, picturesque mill that Thoreau merely notes in passing is developed by Melville into a Sisyphean symbol:

> a huge, cross-grain block, fern-bedded, showed where, in forgotten times, man after man had tried to split it, but lost his wedges for his pains — which wedges yet rusted in their holes; on, where, ages past, in step-like ledges of a cascade, skull-hollow post had been churned out by ceaseless whirlings of a flint-stone — ever wearing, but itself unworn. (p. 8)

Melville was appalled by what he saw as complacent egoism in the works of Emerson and Thoreau alike; the "Castaway" chapter of *Moby-Dick* was probably written as a rebuttal to the section on "Solitude" in *Walden*, and several months after the publication of the *Piazza Tales* Melville was sufficiently offended by Emerson's and Thoreau's peculiar views of friendship to attack their notion of the sufficiency of the self in *The Confidence-Man.*[120] The following remark in Thoreau's Greylock digression may well have inspired Melville's Marianna as counter argument: "Like most evil, the difficulty [of crossing wild terrain alone] is imaginary ... I am not alone if I stand by myself" (p. 193). To Thoreau's view that "The inhabitants of earth behold commonly but the dark and shadowy under side of heaven's pavement" (p. 199) Melville would seem to agree, but "The Piazza" coiunters Thoreau's notion that "a favorable angle" of vision may afford a glimpse of heaven itself. Melville's sketch seems to accede ironically to Thoreau's claim that every visit to a summit like Greylock's should, "as it were, generalize the particular information gained below, and subject it to more catholic tests" (p. 197); the summit visit of Melville's narrator exposes realities inimical to transcendental optimism. What might be regarded as Melville's final ironic accedence is not expressed in "The Piazza" itself. Of the view from Greylock's summit Thoreau remarked, "It was a favor for which to be for ever silent to be shown this vision" (p. 198); "The Piazza" was the last short fiction Melville wrote and the view from Greylock was the last natural landscape in the fiction he published.

If the parodic elements of "The Piazza" must remain conjectural in respect to Thoreau, there can be no doubt that the sketch deliberately and elaborately parallels "The Old Manse." For each of Hawthorne's images that carry the implication of transcendent faith, Melville provides a correlative image of inverted implication. The bitter sweet apples in "The Old Manse" become for Melville's narrator apples that taste of the ground. While Hawthorne's garden provides "the most bewitching sights

---

120. The significance of Thoreau's works for Melville is and will most likely remain a contentious problem; for a sober assessment covering all significant scholarship on the matter, see Hershel Parker, "Melville's Satire of Emerson and Thoreau: An Evaluation of the Evidence," *American Transcendental Quarterly* 7 (Summer 1970): 61-67.

in the world" (p. 14) and conveys "the idea of an infinite generosity and exhaustless bounty, on the part of Mother Nature," Melville's narrator plants in hope only to reap fruit blighted with death. Marianna's two hop-vines, which strove to be "joined over in an upward clasp," but, "groping awhile in empty air, trailed back whence they sprung" (p. 14), foster a sense of estrangement and disunity that counters the rather different symbolism of Hawthorne's grape-vines, which "twine themselves around shrub and tree" and "unite two trees of alien race in an inextricable twine, marrying the hemlock and the maple against their will ..." (p. 23). While for Hawthorne indolence and sleep bring fanciful inspriation and respite from the diseased world of actuality, Melville links indolence with delusion and, after associating sleep with death through allusion to *Hamlet*, defines the oppressive life of "ever wakeful" Marianna within the confines of "the bench, the bed, the grave" (pp. 13, 11). As the Old Manse is a "fairyland" in a "magic circle" (p. 33) the piazza offers a prospect of "fairy-land" (p. 6), but its "charmed ring" is delusive, a trick of perspective. Virtually all of Hawthorne's picturesque images foster confidence in the universal benevolence of nature, while good and evil interpenetrate in Melville's natural world. Reading nature as revelation, Hawthorne recalls a symbol of natural benevolence:

> Once, as we turned our boat to the bank, there was a cloud in the shape of an immensely gigantic figure of a hound, crouched above the house, as if keeping guard over it. Gazing at this symbol, I prayed that the upper influences might long protect the institutions that had grown out of the heart of mankind. (pp. 25-26)

Melville transforms this shadow into what mad Marianna imagines to be the shadow of her dead dog Tray. The hallucination cannot sustain even imagined security, for Tray's shadow is blotted by an immense satanic shadow; the narrator sees

> through the fairy window, a broad shadow stealing on, as cast by some gigantic condor, floating at brooding poise on outstretched wings, ... it wiped away into itself all lesser shades of rock or fern. (p. 12)

Like Melville's narrator, Hawthorne describes his home as a kind of waystation from which a "pilgrim" might travel "on his way to the Celestial City" (p. 28), but "The Piazza" demonstrates that earthly roads lead only to earthly hells. The delusive golden light on Greylock is in part a parodic adumbration of Hawthorne's "beacon fire of truth," a metaphor for the genius of Emerson: "Uncertain, troubled, earnest wanderers," writes Hawthorne,

> through the midnight of the moral world, beheld his intellectual fire, as a beacon burning on a hill-top, and, climbing the difficult ascent, looked forth into the surrounding obscurity, more hopefully than hitherto.

Hawthorne offers this light, along with the salutory influences of nature, as an anodyne for the "weary activity of brain, and torpor or passion of the heart, that now afflicts the universe" (p. 31). Melville's narrator, whose morbid sensitivity is attributed to an undefined illness and who opens his tale in a state of "weary convalescence" (p. 6), closes "The Piazza" by defining Hawthorne's "midnight of the moral world" as the world's true and chronic state. Melville had, in 1856, broader and more pressing concerns than Emerson's philosophy, however; the benighted conclusion of "The Piazza" is addressed not against Emerson but the general idea of the immanence of a benign God in nature. The conclusion's counterpoint might be Hawthorne's apostrophic passage on natural grace in "The Old Manse":

> A blessing is flung abroad, and scattered far and wide over the earth to be gathered up by all who choose. I recline upon the still unwithered grass, and whisper to myself: — 'Oh, perfect day! — Oh, beautiful world! Oh, beneficent God!' And it is the promise of a blissful Eternity; for our Creator would never have made such lovely days, and have given us the deep hearts to enjoy them, above and beyond all thought, unless we were meant to be immortal. This sunshine is the golden pledge thereof. It beams through the gates of Paradise, and shows us glimpses far inward.
> (p. 28)

This romantic conflation of aesthetic and religious experience is consistently undermined by "The Piazza" and finally damned in Melville's penultimate statement: "No light shows from the mountain" (p. 15).

CHAPTER II

THE VIEW FROM THE MAST-HEAD: *MOBY-DICK*

In part Melville's private allegory of romantic faith and the crisis of its loss, "The Piazza" is related to the author's career prior to 1852 chiefly through a richly developed conceit of the mountain excursion as sea-voyage, a conceit that is the obverse of Melville's seascape-as-landscape tropes especially abundant in *Typee* (1846), *Omoo* (1847), *Mardi* (1849), and *Moby-Dick* (1851). The narrator of "The Piazza" likens his horse to a yawl and refers to his quest as an "inland voyage to fairy-land" (p. 4). The imagery of his landscape is more often than not rendered in marine idiom and image; "Canute like, sitting here," the narrator remarks,

> One is often reminded of the sea. For not only do long ground-swells roll the slanting grain, and little wavelets of grass ripple over upon the low piazza, as their beach, and the blown down of dandelions is wafted like the spray, and the purple of the mountains is just the purple of the billows, and a still August noon broods upon the deep meadows as a calm upon the Line; the vastness and the lonesomeness are so oceanic, and the silence and the sameness, too, that the first peep of a strange house, rising beyond the trees, is for all the world like spying, on the Barbary coast, an unknown sail. (p. 4)

The generation of landscape metaphors through the analogy of sea and land would, of course, be natural to a mariner turned writer for whom sublimity was ineluctably associated with the sea, but the persistence of the conceit throughout "The Piazza" is surely intended to establish and analogical relationship between Melville's South Sea romances and the ascent of Greylock. The narrator reports that he

> wore a light hat of yellow sinnet, with white duck trowsers — both relics of my tropic sea-going. Clogged in the muffling ferns, I stumbled, staining the knees a sea-green. (p. 10)

These lines place in relation the Berkshire mountain quest and the earlier sea quests, and those which liken Marianna to "some Tahiti girl, secreted for a sacrifice, first catching sight, through palms, of Captain Cook" (p. 10) recall particularly the encounters of Tommo with Fayaway in *Typee* and Taji with Yillah in *Mardi*. Melville's matrix of retrospective allusions suggests that the aesthetic ideas that impell the narrator of "The Piazza" to Greylock's summit are in some sense apposite to those at work in the earlier romances.

A reconstruction of Melville's aesthetic ideas in *Typee* and *Omoo* must be tentative and inferential, for both works purported to be and are in fact non-fictional in essence and they are remarkably opaque in regard to symbolic meaning. As Charles Anderson has demonstrated, *Typee*, which explores a genuine earthly paradise, and *Omoo*, which shows what manner of hell civilization may make of paradise, are thoroughly moored in the actualities of South Sea life in the eighteen-forties.[1] The controversy that arose over the authenticity of *Typee* immediately upon its appearance stemmed less from inherent qualities of the book than from a critical milieu in which the distinction between fact and fiction in literature was thought to be necessarily absolute.[2] The more critical readers reasoned that no book so thoroughly romantic as *Typee* could be based, as Melville's forthright preface put it, on "unvarnished truth."[3] Varnish there is, to be sure, but it is applied with restraint. Through happenstance, Melville's desertion from the whaler *Acushnet* in 1841 led to his encounter with savages that fulfilled — indeed, exceeded — the most fanciful ideals of Rousseauistic primitivism. Not fictive products of a naive faith in the Noble Savage — the vogue for which was on the decline by the eighteen-forties — Melville's natives of Nukuheva were in fact as close to a state of prelapsarian innocence as could be conceived.

The enthusiastic reception of *Typee* in America must be in some measure attributed to the prominence of Edenic and wilderness myth in the national self-consciousness. Scholars have distinguished two primary paradisiacal ideals at work in the mythology of America from the earliest colonial period:

> From the beginning, the relationship between the immigrant farmer and the virgin soil of the New World testifies to the durable adaptibility of the ideal design of the garden in the wilderness. On the southern coast ... the garden seemed already there — seemed Edenic. On the northern coast and later in the continental interior, however, the garden had to be carved out of the wilderness: first by cutting back deciduous forest, then by penetrating the iron-like topsoil of the prairies, then by irrigating the "deserts" of the far West. For this reason and because, in Massachusetts, the Calvinist Puritans could not countenance the possibility of an

---

1. *Melville in the South Seas* (New York: Dover Publications, Inc., 1966), especially pp. 69-324.

2. See Martin, *The Instructed Vision*, especially "American Fiction and the Metaphysics of Actuality," pp. 57-106, and "The World Without and the World Within," pp. 107-150. The prefaces of Irving, Cooper, and especially Simms and Hawthorne suggest that an American writer might cross with impunity the gulf between fact and fiction only after making clear his intention to do so.

3. *Typee: A Peep at Polynesian Life* (Evanston and Chicago: Northwestern University Press and the Newberry Library, 1968), p. xiv. Subsequent citations from *Typee* refer to this edition.

Plate V.   Thomas Cole, *Expulsion from the Garden of Eden* (1827). Museum of Fine
Arts, Boston. M. and M. Karolik Collection.

earthly Eden for fallen man, the ideal design fo the garden became that of the Promised Land.[4]

With the incursion into the wilderness came the displacement of the mythology of the given new Eden by the mythology of a new, covenantal Canaan, a paradise not given but rather achieved through struggle, sacrifice, and violence. In spite of the demise of the former ideal, a dichotomous paradisiacal mythology continued to exert a strong appeal upon the American moral imagination at least through Melville's generation. As Slotkin has demonstrated,[5] from the early Puritan captivity narratives through the wilderness literature of the mid-nineteenth century, treatment of native Americans in American writing reflect a fundamental irresolution in regard to the two paradisiacal myths, and the attempts of American landscape painters to reconcile the wilderness and the garden were seldom without a similar ambivalence. *Typee*, reportorial as it may be, is marked by the same quality.

Melville is intent on distinguishing the South Sea paradise of *Typee* from the antedeluvian topography of Edenic myth. "Those who for the first time visit the South Seas," he notes,

are generally surprised at the appearance of these islands when beheld from the sea. From the vague accounts we sometimes have of their beauty, many people are apt to picture to themselves enamelled and softly swelling plains, shaded over with delicious groves, and watered by purling brooks, and the entire country but little elevated above the surrounding ocean. The reality is very different; bold rock-bound coasts, with the surf beating high against the lofty cliffs, and broken here and there into deep inlets, which open to the view thickly-wooded valleys, separated by the spurs of mountains clothed with tufted grass, and sweeping down towards the sea from an elevated and furrowed interior, form the principal features of these islands. (p. 12)

The Typee valley is a paradise, an "enchanted garden in a fairy tale" (p. 71), but, enclosed by a wilderness of rain forest and precipitous gorges, it is a paradise achieved through no small measure of pain and danger. Conflating the myths of Eden and Canaan, this topography would have special appeal for readers familiar with such exotically symbolic paintings as Cole's *Expulsion from the Garden of Eden* (1827) [Pl. V]. The stark chiaroscuro, dramatic — perhaps, melodramatic — contrast of

4. Conron, p. 113. See also Slotkin (pp. 3-24 and passim) who accedes to the view that Puritan New England fostered the idea of the Americas as a new Canaan while the middle Atlantic and Southern colonies retained a more Edenic conception of wilderness. Slotkin relates the Puritan idea to sexual and regenerative archetypes. George H. Williams has traced the "double meaning" suggested by wilderness to the biblical ideas of "(a) the wilderness as a place of redemptive, covenantal bliss, and (b) the wilderness as the place of testing and tutelage" (*Wilderness and Paradise in Christian Thought* [New York: Harper & Brothers, 1962], p. 15).
5. *Regeneration through Violence*.

Eden and wilderness, and biblical focus of Cole's painting all but conceal its formal kinship with countless landscapes of the Hudson River School. Like Tommo's incursion into the Typee valley, the secular landscapes of the Hudson River School symbolically abrogate Adam's exile through the image of a new Eden in the wilderness. In Cole's *Oxbow* a sinuous river replaces the impassable chasm that divides paradise and wilderness in the *Expulsion*.

Immediately after their hellish descent to the Typée valley Tommo and Toby encounter, not surprisingly, children of Eden:

> They were a boy and girl, slender and graceful, and completely naked, with the exception of a slight girdle of bark, from which depended at opposite points two of the russet leaves of the bread-fruit treet. An arm of the boy, half screened from sight by her wild tresses, was thrown about the neck of the girl, while with the other he held one of her hands in his; and thus they stood together, their heads inclined forward, catching the faint noise we made in our progress, and with one foot in advance as if half-inclined to fly from our presence. (p. 68)

Here and elsewhere in *Typee* Melville alludes to and parodies *Paradise Lost*.[6] Melville's passage parallels the encounter of Satan with Adam and Eve, and the implication is that Tommo, a representative of civilized man, is Satan. An abiding concern of *Typee* and *Omoo* is, of course, the inevitable doom of Polynesian innocence through contact with the avarice, disease, and self-consciousness of civilization. The Miltonic allusions serve to underscore *Typee*'s unremarkable lesson that, as D.H. Lawrence put it, "We can't go back."[7] Tommo comes to learn through the ennui that oppresses him in his paradise that it is knowledge itself that bars the gates to any earthly paradise.

While it offers abundant evidence of Melville's skills as a graphic artist — skills often remarked by his earliest reviewers — and a natural sense for the affective potentials of landscape description, *Typee* has no mature or structured aesthetic viewpoint. Tommo is, like the narrator of "The Piazza," a quester whose encounter with an apparent paradise proves delusive, but the allegory of loss of faith developed in the later tale surely refers to a stage of Melville's career later than that in which he composed his South Sea books. An archetype among the most common in romantic literature, the heroic quest that ends in disenchantment is at work in Melville's "Fragments from a Writing Desk," and we find in *Typee* and *Omoo* not the slightest trace of the aesthetic and epistemological issues that figure so importantly in "The Piazza." But *Typee* does reveal basic

---

6. See Henry F. Pommer, *Milton and Melville* (Pittsburgh: University of Pittsburgh Press, 1950), pp. 16, 30, 66-67, 113. For a more extended discussion of the Miltonic parallels, see Robert Stanton, "*Typee* and Milton: Paradise Well Lost," *MLN* 74 (May 1959): 407-411.

7. *Studies in Classic American Literature* (New York: Viking Press, 1961), p. 143.

creative patterns that bear importantly in the aesthetic dimensions of Melville's later work. First, at work in *Typee* is what might be called Melville's logic of the center, his tendency to image truth as a core behind layers of deceptive appearance.[8] Charles Feidelson has rightly noted that "the topography of *Typee* is metaphoric" and that it "shadows forth the pattern of Melville's world."[9] To arrive at the truth of primitive life, Tommo penetrates the maze-like topography of Nukaheva, a landscape in which precipitous gorges and cliffs are concealed beneath deceptive verdure. At the island's center he must penetrate another veil of appearances fostered by the dissembling natives before he comes to that dark center of Typee civilization, cannibalism. Not so much an idea as a habit of mind, the logic of the center predisposed Melville to anatomy, to microcosm, and to elaborately structured topographical conceits in his later work. A second Melvillian pattern in *Typee* that bears importantly on the aeshtetic dimension of his writings is the interpenetration of the horrific and the beautiful. Tommo's trek through a wilderness of rain forest to lost Edenic groves is a journey from darkness to light, yet his discovery of the ghastly intentions of his savage hosts establishes as meretricious the lush beauty of their world. From *Typee* through *Billy Budd*, Melville's work seldom fails to exploit aesthetic deception as a correlative of moral deception. In his world natural beauty more often than not masks moral ambiguity or evil.

While the aesthetic disillusionment allegorized in "The Piazza" is not to be found in *Typee* or *Omoo*, a topical reference in the tale suggests that its biographical relevance may in some way encompass *Mardi*. Referring to his substitution of the regal name Charlemagne for Mount Greylock and his preference for the northern prospect that includes the mountain, the narrator notes that

> It was not long after 1848; and, somehow, about that time, all round the world, these kings, they had the casting vote, and voted for themselves.[10]

Written just prior to the Pittsfield period to which "The Piazza" refers, *Mardi* offers only traces of the aesthetic concerns that figure importantly

8. The recurrent image of circle or enclosed center in Melville's work has been often noted. The most insightful discussions have been archetypal; see James Baird, *Ishmael: The Art of Melville in the Contexts of International Primitivism* (Baltimore: Johns Hopkins Press, 1956) and Martin Leonard Pops, *The Melville Archetype* (Kent, Ohio: Kent State University Press, 1970), especially pp. 1-25.

9. *Symbolism and American Literature* (Chicago: University of Chicago Press, 1953), p. 168.

10. *Piazza Tales*, p. 3. Neither the name of the peak nor the allusion to political unrest in Europe has been adequately explained. W.B. Stein ("Melville's Comedy of Faith") notes that the "cross-pile" of broken birch trees at the mountain's summit may be an ironic allusion to the miraculous cross in the sky seen by the mountain's namesake, the Christian hero Charlemagne.

in *Moby-Dick*, *Pierre*, and the shorter fiction of the 'fifties. Melville often takes up the sublime of nature in *Mardi*, but when he does so his idiom and metaphors are derivative. The mark of British romantic poetry is clear in his many seascape-as-landscape conceits:

> But lingering not long in those silent vales, from watery cliff to cliff, a sea-chamois, sprang our solitary craft, — a goat among the Alps!"

A debt to Byron is particularly evident; remarking the view from a ship's mast-head, Taji notes that

> this standing upon a bit of stick 100 feet aloft for hours at a time, swiftly sailing over the sea, is very much like crossing the Channel in a balloon. Manfred-like, you talk to the clouds: you have a fellow feeling for the sun. (p. 16)

Jocose in tone as they may be, these lines express an attitude toward transcendental experience that is not in the least satiric. They may look forward to the great chapter on the mast-head in *Moby-Dick*, but they lack the latter passage's penetrating assessment of the sublime. Yet *Mardi* is not without critical probings into the nature of aesthetic experience, as Taji's remarks on a landsman's experience of a calm suggest: to the landsman's

> alarmed fancy, parallels and meridians become emphatically what they are merely designated as being: imaginary lines drawn round the earth's surface. (pp. 9-10)

The "everlasting lull" of the sea evokes no Lockean train of divine associations or transcendental vision of cosmic unity but "horrible doubts" and associations that remain "nameless." Bereft of means of relating his experience of the calm to any normal conceptual framework, the landsman becomes "madly skeptical"; the vacuous prospect

> not only revolutionizes his abdomen, but unsettles his mind; tempts him to recant his belief in the eternal fitness of things; in short, almost makes an infidel of him. (p. 10)

A most prophetic passage, "A Calm" is Melville's first treatment of vacuity or sensory deprivation as a source of the horrific sublime.

"Of the Chondropterygii," a digression on the White Shark, is another prophetic passage in *Mardi* that insiuates doubt of the "eternal fitness of things," the beneficence of nature. "Of all sharks," remarks Taji,

> save me from the ghastly White Shark. For though we should hate naught, yet some dislikes are spontaneous; and disliking is not hating. And never yet could I bring myself to be loving, or even sociable, with a White Shark.

Antecedent of Moby Dick, the White Shark glides "like a spirit in the water, with horrific serenity of aspect" (p. 41). This monster, paradox-

11. *Mardi; and a Voyage Thither*, ed. Harrison Hayford, Herschel Parker, and G. Thomas Tanselle (Evanston and Chicago: Northwestern University Press and The Newberry Library, 1970), p. 37. All subsequent citations refer to this edition.

ically invested with beauty, inspires a "spontaneous" or instinctive aversion that no facile eighteenth-century theodicy or nineteenth-century transcendentalism can assuage. The irony of Taji's glib comment anticipates the dark theological currents of Melville's hunt for a greater sea-beast: "As well hate a seraph, as a shark. Both were made by the same hand" (p. 40).

As rich and illuminating as it may be in terms of Melville's subsequent career, *Mardi* cannot have been the point of reference for the allegory of loss of aesthetic faith in "The Piazza." To be sure, the book begins like the tale as a quest in nature, but as it progresses the sharp pictorial quality of its early chapters becomes blurred; initially naturalistic — Mardi was to have been a sequel to *Omoo* — its settings are subsequently idealized and finally abstracted in Melville's baffling metaphysical allegory. The book does not end with a failed quest but rather with a symbolic rebirth of the hero who announces his resolve to strike out anew "over an endless sea" (p. 654). *Mardi* fails as art because of Melville's inability to control its range. Neither we nor Melville could attribute its failure to a fallacious aesthetic for the simple reason that *Mardi* lacks a coherent, definable vision of nature. For present purposes, this is most clearly evinced in the remarks that follow the magnificent combat of whales in the thirteenth chapter:

> Had old Wouvermans, who once painted a bull bait, been along with us, a rare chance, that, for his pencil. And Gudin or Isabey might have thrown the blue rolling sea into the picture. Lastly, one of Claude's setting suns would have glorified the whole. Oh, believe me, God's creatures fighting, fin for fin, a thousand miles from land, and with the round horizon for an arena, is no ignoble subject for a masterpiece (p. 42).

Less than three years after the publication of *Mardi* Melville completed such a masterpiece, yet when he wrote this passage his vision was not sufficiently developed to render coherently what would be his greatest symbol. Here Melville struggles for focus, gropes among disparate styles for a manner adequate to his subject: form is mechanically imposed on content. In *Moby-Dick* form and content interfuse; vision is not only a function of meaning but meaning itself. To *Mardi* and the earlier South Sea books "The Piazza" bears but passing relevance; it is in *Moby-Dick* that the concerns of the tale are at work on a grand scale, for "The Piazza" is but an extraordinarily compressed redaction of the epic quest for the truth and human value of nature that is *Moby-Dick*.

Loomings in the Valley of the Saco: Epistemology

Surely one of the most complex of literary works, *Moby-Dick* may nevertheless be reduced to two fundamental questions to which it is addressed. The first is empirical: What is essential nature? The second, answerable only in relation to the first, is moral and in part aesthetic: What relation does nature bear to man? Prior to any serious engagement with either enquiry, Melville had necessarily to deal with two preliminary questions in the prolegomena that are his opening chapters. At what nexus between mind and matter — or, more simply, how — shall essential nature be known? And, what is the nature of our knowledge?

Ishmael takes up both preliminary epistemological questions in "Loomings," the initial chapter appropriately tagged by a seaman's term that refers to the indefinition of objects perceived at sea. He offers a word-painted landscape:

> But here is an artist. He desires to paint you the dreamiest, shadiest, quietest, most enchanting bit of romantic landscape in all the valley of the Saco. What is the chief element he employs? There stand his trees, each with a hollow trunk, as if a hermit and a crucifix were within; and here sleeps his meadow, and there sleep his cattle; and up from yonder cottage does a sleepy smoke. Deep into distant woodlands winds a mazy way, reaching to overlapping spurs of mountains bathed in their hillside blue.[12]

Like the prospect afforded by Melville's piazza, the valley of the Saco was a pradise for mid-century artists of the picturesque; there the American middle landscape subsisted in harmony with the sublime and beautiful, and the felicitous relation of man and nature seemed a given state rather than aesthetic ideal. Hawthorne, who shared Melville's deep misgivings about the prevailing naturalistic aesthetics of his times, used the valley of the Saco as setting in "The Greast Carbuncle" and "The Ambitious Guest," tales profoundly critical of the American conventions of the picturesque and the sublime.[13] Yet we need not know of the ironic use Melville's friend had made of the Saco setting to suspect that Ishmael's painting of the same locale is broached not to celebrate but to attack the pastoral vision upon which it is based. The fundamentally meretricious quality of that vision, its conventionality and staleness, is insinuated in Melville's language; meadow, trees, cattle, cottage, distant woodlands and mountain spurs are presented as stock-in-trade devices of a landscape convention that had become, by 1851, thoroughly commonplace.[14]

12. *Moby-Dick*, ed. Luther S. Mansfield and Howard P. Vincent (New York: Hendricks House, 1962), p. 2. All subsequent citations from *Moby-Dick* refer to this edition.

13. Melville borrowed *Twice-Told Tales*, which contains these stories, from Evert Duyckinck in the summer of 1849.

14. Oliver W. Larkin identifies the manner of Ishmael's painting as that of the landscapist Thomas Doughty (*Art and Life in America* [New York: Rinehart & Company, 1949], p. 201); if the painting had an actual antecedent, it might have been done by any number of American artists who took up the muted contrasts and hazy atmosphere of Claude Lorraine.

Like the enchanting view from "The Piazza," Ishmael's landscape lies "tranced," suggesting that its effects depend upon a deadening of the sensibility rather than heightened awareness. Both landscapes are static perspectives before which a removed percipient passively observes in a dream-like state. It is not nature but an image of nature that is observed. Just as the "Extracts" of recorded whaling lore and legend are dismissed as "solely valuable or entertaining, as affording a glancing bird's eye view of what has been promiscuously said, thought, fancied, and sung of Leviathan" (p. xxxix), so the Saco painting, a view of a landsman's view, is dismissed as an inadequate source of knowledge. Ishmael leaves the extracts and painting alike and goes to sea. So doing, he points up the relevance of the Saco painting and the extracts to the epistemological dimension of his quest. How is essential nature to be known? It may be known only through immediate sensational experience. The point is hammered home through the jocular digression on the proper mode of sea-going that concludes Melville's initial chapter. This passage, usually read as an index of Melville's democratic spirit, fosters the primacy of immediate over secondary experience. Like the water-gazers, who are "of week days pent up in lath and plaster — tied to counters, nailed to benches, clinched to desks" (p. 2), landsman Ishmael "grows hazy about the eyes" (p. 3). To clear his vision he goes to sea not as a passive passenger but as a common seaman exposed to the "pure air" of the forecastle deck:

> For as in this world, head winds are far more prevalent than winds from astern ..., so for the most part the Commodore on the quarter-deck gets his atmosphere at second hand from the sailors on the forecastle. He thinks he breathes it first; but not so. (p. 5)

The raw data of sense, the unbreathed air of the forecastle, is the true anodyne for a blurred or oblique vision of reality.

It is in the course of a brief critique of the Saco painting that the second preliminary epistemological question — What is the nature of knowledge? — is engaged. Having completed his word-painted canvas, Ishmael asks a complex and compelling question:

> But though the picture lies thus tranced, and though this pine-tree shakes down its sighs like leaves upon this shepherd's head, yet all were vain, unless the shepherd's eye were fixed upon the magic stream before him. Go visit the Prairies in June, when for scores on scores of miles you wade knee-deep among Tiger-lilies — what is the one charm wanting? — Water — there is not a drop of water there! Were Niagara but a cataract of sand, would you travel your thousand miles to see it? Why did the poor poet of Tennessee, upon suddenly receiving two handfuls of silver, deliberate whether to buy him a coat ... or invest his money in a pedestrian trip to Rockaway Beach? Why is almost every robust healthy boy with a robust healthy soul in him, at some time or other crazy to go to see? Why upon your first voyage as a passenger, did you yourself feel such a mystical vibration, when first

told that you and your ship were now out of sight of land? Why did the old Persians hold the sea holy? Why did the Greeks give it a separate deity, and own brother of Jove? Surely all this is not without meaning.

Through this massive catalogue of questions Melville shifts from the tranced New England landscape to the world's seas as the nexus between nature and mind where knowledge rather than a dream might be had. Yet all the accumulated weight of these ponderous questions comes to rest not in resolution but in epistemological paradox. "Surely all this is not without meaning," but "still deeper" is

> that story of Narcissus, who because he could not grasp the tormenting, mild image he saw in the fountain, plunged into it and was drowned. But that same image, we ourselves see in all rivers and oceans. It is the image of the ungraspable phantom of life; and this is the key to it all. (p. 3)

All "water-gazers," Ishmael suggests, are kin to Narcissus. All human perception involves the mirror image of self; nature is colored, perhaps even created, in perception. Ishmael's epistemological first principles would seem to be at the very least metaphysically incompatible. Narcissus is rightly deemed the "key to it all," for the subjectivity of perception is dramatized throughout *Moby-Dick*. Yet if perception is creative and the world it generates is a fiction, how might immediate sensational experience be a legitimate source of knowledge?

As one form of the clash between monism and idealism, the epistemological paradox of "Loomings" is as ancient as thought itself. Yet, however well read Melville may have been in ancient philosophy,[15] the informing context of his chapter is the epistemological subjectivity of modern romanticism. The subjectivity of English romantic literature, its presentation of the external world as stuff in part generated by mind, stems not so much from the rejection of materialism in favor of transcendental idealism as the convergence of two aesthetic and epistemological traditions in the late eighteenth century.[16] The first is the mechanistic tradition that began with Hobbes and Locke, developed through Addison, Hutcheson, Burke, Hartley, and the Common Sense school, and achieved the status of aesthetic and epistemological orthodoxy in Melville's critical milieu with the writings of Dugald Stewart and

15. See Merton M. Sealts, Jr., "Herman Melville's Reading in Ancient Philosophy" (Ph.D. dissertation, Yale, 1952) or Sealts's more accessible paper, "Melville's 'Neoplatonical Originals;'" *MLN* 67 (February 1952): 80-86.

16. The literature on this matter is vast; essential studies include M.H. Abrams, *The Mirror and the Lamp: Romantic Theory and the Critical Tradition* (New York: W.W. Norton & Company, 1953), Ernest lee Tuveson, *The Imagination as a Means of Grace: Locke and the Aesthetics of Romanticism* (Berkeley: University of California Press, 1960), and Walter Jackson Bate, *From Classic to Romantic: Premises of Taste in Eighteenth-Century England* (New York: Harper & Row, 1946).

Archibald Alison. The second tradition extends from Plato, Plotinus, and the oriental mystics Porphyry and Proclus through the mid-seventeenth-century Cambridge Platonists, Cudworth, More, and smith. Developed literarily in Spenser, Burton, and Brown and later philosophically in Berkeley, the English idealist tradition ultimately found its complement in the ideas of Kant and his followers, which were transferred to England by Coleridge, Carlyle and others.

As metaphysics the two traditions were as irremediably opposed in the late eighteenth century as they are today, for as metaphysics neither is subject to verification. As epistemologies, however, the two traditions all but converged in romantic subjectivism. In the darker moments of the verse of Wordsworth and Coleridge the uneasy reciprocity of ideal and actual might threaten to collapse, the ideal might dissolve into Descartes' mechanistic universe, but neither poet had much difficulty vacillating between what M.H. Abrams has called the constitutive epistemological analogues of mirror and lamp.[17] They could do so because the sensationalist line of aesthetics and epistemology had all but completely displaced the locus of aesthetic value from external objects to the mind itself:

> The late eighteenth-century British associationists like Alison had declared that beauty derived not so much from abstract harmonies of form, composition, or color as from the things that the human mind related through memory (which was remembered sensation) to the object seen, the emotional, intellectual (and hence also the historical) associations with which the mind from its experiences invested the object. Both associationism and Reynolds' neoclassic norms proceeded from the same empirical basis in Locke, but associationism as a perceptural theory focused on the nonrational action of the mind in connecting impressions. Locke himself had deplored such an irrational process, though he had acknowledged its importance; Hartley and his followers transformed it into a mechanistic rationalism; but Archibald Alison had rescued the idea from Hartleian necessitarianism, stressing implicitly the uniqueness of each aesthetic response and the sensibility of the individual perceiver.[18]

Of course, Alison's subjectivism was latent in the sensationalist line from its inception. Concurrent with the rise of the psychological approach to aesthetics came a growing awareness of the fallibility of the senses and the capriciousness of the associative mental processes. The persistent attempts and continuing failure of aestheticians to define taste and develop a means of cultivating it are symptomatic of the destabilizing effects the psychological had on aesthetic values. Hume, who was educated under Common Sense mechanists at Edinburgh, had only to develop the implications of associationism to arrive at a radically skeptical position from which all knowledge of external nature was mired in doubt.

17. Abrams, p. 31 and passim.
18. Roger B. Stein, *John Ruskin and aesthetic Thought in America* (Cambridge: Harvard University Press, 1967), p. 35.

It is impossible to fix with any precision the degree of Melville's knowledge of European epistemology and aesthetics prior to 1851, but evidence suggests that it was considerable both in depth and scope. He certainly knew more of the traditions of value and perceptual theory developed from Locke than have the majority of contemporary students of his work. First introduced to Locke through a textbook used at the Albany Academy and later through Ruskin's *Modern Painters*,[19] Melville was doubtless exposed repeatedly to the popularizations of Locke's ideas that were ubiquitous in the criticism of his day. Addison's *Spectator* papers seem to have been among his earliest readings, and sections in *Moby-Dick* and "The Piazza" suggest his close reading of Addison's rendering of Lockean perceptual theory in the papers on "The Pleasures of the Imagination."[20] He knew Akenside's poetic treatise of the same title,[21] and through it was exposed ot the aesthetic ideas of Shaftesbury, Hutcheson, and Addison as well. He personally owned an American edition of Burke's *Enquiry*, which he marked and annotated, and he borrowed and read Hartley's *Observations on Man* in 1848.[22] Although no record has survived of Melville's having owned or borrowed Hume's *Treatise of Human Nature*, evidence that he had a thorough command of Hume's ideas has been presented by Howard C. Horsford.[23] Melville's knowledge of the idealist tradition may also be substantially documented.

19. The text was Lindley Murray's *The English Reader: or, Pieces in Prose and Poetry, Selected from the Best Writers* (1819), which includes Lyttleton's imaginary dialogue between Locke and the French skeptic Bayle; see Merton M. Sealts, Jr., *Melville's Reading: A Checklist of Books Borrowed and Owned* (Madison: University of Wisconsin Press, 1966) — hereafter designated as "Sealts, *Checklist*" — entry no. 380. Part I, Section II of *Modern Painters* contains a concise exposition of Lockean epistemology and a reading of Parts I and II alone would have provided Melville with a respectable overview of eighteenth-century epistemology and aesthetics; on Melville's acquaintance with Ruskin's work, see Sealts, *Checklist,* entry nos. 430 and 431.

20. Sealts (*Checklist*, p. 8) sees a biographical relevance that is "by no means unlikely" in the recollections of boyhood reading in *Redburn* and *Pierre*; Redburn recalls a six-volume edition of the *Spectator* that he read in his father's library (*Redburn* [Evanston and Chicago: Northwestern University Press and The Newberry Library, 1969], p. 7). Poenicke ("A View from the Piazza," p. 269) points to the similarities between the quest in Melville's story and that of the knight in *Spectator* No. 413 who is deceived by the enchanting secondary attribute that is color.

21. See Sealts, *Checklist*, entry no. 8. In her edition of *The Confidence-Man* (New York: Hendricks House, 1954), p. 304, Elizabeth S. Foster notes that "Mark Akenside's volume had been in Melville's childhood home, a gift from his father to his mother during their courtship."

22. Sealts, *Checklist*, entry nos. 97 and 243, and Glen, "Melville and the Sublime in *Moby-Dick*," p. 165.

23. "The Design of the Argument in *Moby-Dick*," *Modern Fiction Studies* 8 (Autumn 1962): 233-251.

There is abundant evidence of his familiarity with Plato,[24] and allusions in *Mardi* indicate that he had read in *The Six Books of Proclus on the Theology of Plato* (1816), a translation of Plotinus by the English Platonist Thomas Taylor.[25] But the platonic cast of many passages in his works was primarily derived from modern idealist tracts, and in these he read deeply between 1848 and the commencement of *Moby-Dick*. In 1848 he purchased an American edition of *Biographia Literaria* and through it received his first exposure to German idealism.[26] Through Carlyle, whose *German Romance*, *On Heroes and Hero-Worship*, and *Sartor Resartus* he read in 1850,[27] Melville became further acquainted with the doctrine developed by Kant, Novalis, and Fichte that matter had not an absolute but a relative existence and that the self and nature were ontologically fused in human consciousness. Although he seems to have known no German, he may have gained knowledge of German idealism through means somewhat more direct than the interpolations of Coleridge and Carlyle. In London in the winter of 1849 he purchased and read a translation of Goethe's *Truth and Poetry*, and upon returning to America he seems to have read in Goethe's transcendentalist *Theory of Colours*.[28] He may have been lead to Goethe by the American philologist George J. Adler, in whose company he spent much of the cruise to England in the same year. A Kant enthusiast, Adler probably introduced Melville to the contents of the *Critique of Pure Reason* and *Critique of Aesthetic Judgment*; remarking his talks with Adler that lasted late into the nights at sea, Melville noted in his journal that Adler was "full of the German metaphysics" and that he constantly discoursed on Kant and Swedenborg.[29]

24. Reference to Plato is common in Melville's writings; Pierre recalls, among other books, a set of works on Plato in the library of his father (*Pierre: or, The Ambiguities* [Evanston and Chicago: Northwestern University Press and The Newberry Library, 1971], p. 249.

25. See Sealts, "Melville's 'Neoplatonical Originals'," pp. 80-86.

26. Sealts, *Checklist*, entry no. 154.

27. Ibid., entry nos. 121, 122, 123.

28. Ibid., entry no. 228. Although Eckermann's *Conversations of Goethe* does not appear in the Sealts *Checklist*, there is abundant evidence in *Moby-Dick* that Melville had read it; see Mansfield's and Vincent's notes to Moby-Cick, pp. 585, 638, 649, 678, 705, 714, 765, 784, 813. On his familiarity with Sir Charles Eastlake's translation of Goethe's *Farbenlehre*, see my note on "The Whiteness and Darkness of the Whale," *Extracts* 20 (November 1974): 1-2.

29. Leyda, *The Melville Log*, I, 319; entry in Melville's journal dated October 12. Melville seems to have been quite taken with Adler as well as his German philosophy, for both are frequently mentioned in the journal. Note the entry for October 22 (Leyda, I, 322): "We had an extraordinary time & did not break up till after two in the morning. We talked metaphysics continually, & Hegel, Schegel [sic], Kant & c were discussed under the influence of the whiskey."

Steeped as he was in both the sensationalist and the idealist traditions that comprised the European epistemological legacy, Melville had necessarily to fashion *Moby-Dick* as a quest that is at once outwardly and inwardly directed. Yet it is not the European legacy itself but the manner in which that legacy was transmuted in America and enlisted in the cause of cultural nationalism that accounts for the peculiar urgency with which epistemological issues are taken up and adumbrated in *Moby-Dick*.

In terms of epistemology, the period of American cultural history from the early eighteenth century through the third decade of the nineteenth century might be summed up as an unruffled hegemony of Lockean principles.[30] The clash between Lockean and Kantian perceptual theories in England antedated the furor over transcendentalism in America by nearly four decades because only after Americans had committed themselves to cultural nationalism were they forced to confront nature and their relation to it in a rigorously critical philosophical fashion. A viable epistemology, or, in Richard P. Adams's words, "the right relation between the subjective and the objective aspects of experience,"[31] became an even more pressing concern among Americans than it had been for the English romantics, for the creation of a national art that focused necessarily on man in nature seemed to demand a firm and convincing conception of the nature of knowledge of the external world. To foster such a conception they had to attempt a synthesis of self and sense, of intuition and experience, or, in the terms of "Loomings," of Narcissus and the Ishmaelian voyager.

To provide an epistemological basis for an original American art, this synthesis had in some sense to be "original" itself. The associationism of Kames, Price, and Alison would not do, for, while it provided a means of reconciling objective and subjective experience, it had the effect of distancing aesthetic experience from immediate sensation. And, as Irving, Cooper, Hawthorne, and dozens of lesser lights lamented, associationism seemed always at odds with the largely vacant and unhistoried American landscape. While the extremism of its idealist dimension was wholly unacceptable to the Lockean critical establishment of the 'thirties, Emerson's *Nature* reveals the inevitable contradictions that arose as Americans attempted to fuse the sensationist and idealist traditions. A mandate for "new thoughts" of "new men" in a "new land," *Nature* opens with a revolt not against Locke but against the past itself:

30. See Merle Curti, "The Great Mr. Locke: America's Philosopher, 1783-1861," *Huntington Library Quarterly* 11 (Spring 1937): 107-151.

31. *The American Novel and Its Tradition* (New York: Doubleday & Company, 1957), pp. 105-113.

Our age is retrospective ... The foregoing generations beheld God and Nature face to face; we, through their eyes. Why shoiuld not we also enjoy an original relation to the universe?[32]

These words seem to preclude a reading of the essay as disinterested enquiry and they establish as negative the essay's relationship to the mainstream of British aesthetic tradition. Assuming that man's relationship to nature and the conceptions by which he evaluates his experience of nature are moribund and intolerable, Emerson argues that Americans must not permit their vision of nature to be occluded by the perceptions of past generations. We must ourselves become eyes, become perception itself.

Emerson calls for a relationship to nature that is direct, concrete, immediate, but as he begins to assess the "values of nature, and to cast up their sum,"[33] it becomes unclear whether sensational experience has ontological validity in itself or is a fiction generated by mind. What does become clear is that Emerson's essay is a testament of faith rather than an analytic discourse. He exploits Hume's skepticism in order to dodge the question of the reality of matter; it makes no difference to him "whether Orion is up there in the heaven, or some God paints the image in the firmament of the soul," for, "Be it what it may, it is ideal to me so long as I cannot try the accuracy of my senses."[34] He confesses his "utter impotence to test the authenticity of the report of [his] senses, to know whether the impressions they make ... correspond with outlying objects," but employs this confession as licence to regard the "whole of nature" as "metaphor of the human mind."[35]

The phrase "original relation to the universe" reverberates throughout *Nature*, but its range of implication shifts radically as Emerson evolves his aesthetic. Initially he seems to imply that an "original" relation to nature should be one in which no Old World associations obtrude between percipient and the raw data of sensation; Americans should learn to behold "God and nature face to face." But as he propounds his doctrine of the primacy of mind over matter his call for an "original relation" becomes a call for new Adams who might originate a new universe by perceiving and naming nature in new ways. The radical subjectivity of such a program — not to mention the stupendous egoism of its assumptions — could only elicit a storm of controversy in a nation devoted, since the time of the Puritan divines, to Locke, to the empirical

32. *The Complete Works of Ralph Waldo Emerson*, ed. Edward Waldo Emerson (Boston: Houghton, Mifflin and Company, 1903), I, 3. All subsequent quotations from Emerson are drawn from this edition.
33. *Works*, I, 5.
34. *Works*, I, 48.
35. *Works*, I, 32, 47.

verifiability of ideas, and to the primacy of experiential knowledge. That *some* natural facts are signs of spiritual facts most of Melville's contemporaries could agree, for such a view was sanctioned by the Puritan tradition of reading natural facts as types of God's grace or wrath as well as by the mainstream of eighteenth-century British aesthetic tradition. But to argue that nature was but a metaphor of the human mind seemed nothing less than heresy. Even before the transcendentalists formulated their doctrines the American critical concensus was firmly aligned against idealism. Timothy Walker, for example, championed the Lockean position of New England and Knickerbocker critics alike when he attacked Carlyle in 1831: "We doubt the good influence of [Carlyle's] Mysticism. We deny the evil tendencies of Mechanism ... Give us Locke's Mechanism."[36]

Melville came of age as a writer in the midst of the battle of contending perceptual theories, and it is not surprising to find in *Moby-Dick* a striking metaphoric rendering of the elusive balance of Kant and Locke that so preoccupies his contemporaries. In Chapter 73, Ahab orders Stubb and Flask to kill a right whale so that its head, chained to the larboard side of the *Pequod*, might counterbalance the weight of the sperm whale's head that threatens to capsize the ship. The perilously balanced, over-burdened ship becomes an image of the life of the mind in America:

> As before, the Pequod steeply leaned over towards the sperm whale's head, now, by the counterpoise of both heads, she regained her even keel; though sorely strained, you may well believe. So, when on one side you hoist in Locke's head, you go over that way; but now, on the other side, hoist in Kant's and you come back again; but in very poor plight. Thus, some minds for ever keep trimming boat.

Ishmael's instinctive response to this endless "trimming" is revolt, an anti-intellectual response to an unresolvable metaphysical dilemma: "Oh, ye foolish! Throw all these thunder-heads overboard, and then you will float light and right" (p. 326). But Melville could no more dispose of the antinomy of Kant and Locke than could his age. Both thunderheads remain chained to the *Pequod* for eight chapters of elaborate craniological comparisons that serve as a subtle epistemological conceit. As sperm and right whale "present the two extremes of all the known varieties of the whale" (p. 327), so Kant and Locke represent the two extremes of epistemological theory. Ishmael's study of the two heads is at once "practical cetology" (p. 327) and comparative epistemology.

---

36. *North American Review* 33 (July 1831), p. 224; cited by Harry H. Clark, "Changing Attitudes in Early American Criticism," *The Development of American Literary Criticism*, ed. Floyd Stovall (Chapel Hill: University of North Carolina Press, 1955), p. 67.

Most of Melville's literary compatriots of the 'forties aligned themselves firmly against the "German metaphysics" that they associated with
the growing tide of American idealism,[37] and one would expect their
biases to be relfected in Ishmael's comparative epistemology. Yet, in spite
of the many passages in *Moby-Dick* that disparage idealism, Ishmael's
craniological comparison of the two whales consistently fosters the
superiority of the Kantian whale head:

> In the first place, you are struck by the general contrast between these heads. Both
> are massive enough in all conscience; but there is a certain mathematical symmetry
> in the Sperm Whale's which the Right Whale's sadly lacks. There is more character
> in the Sperm Whale's head. As you behold it, you involuntarily yield the immense
> superiority in him, in point of pervading dignity. (p. 327)

American neo-Kantians took the Lockeans' pattern of "deducing mind
from matter, or tracing the origin of ideas to nerves, vibrations, and
vibratiuncles,"[38] to be a debasement of mind, and their ideas may in some
fashion lie behind the ignoble image of the Right Whale's head congered
by Ishmael:

> As in general shape the noble Sperm Whale's head may be compared to a Roman
> war-chariot ...; so, at a broad view, the Right Whale's head bears a rather inelegant
> resemblance to a gigantic galliot-toed shoe. (p. 331)

Comparing the expressions of the two whale heads, Ishmael takes the
"broad brow" of the Sperm Whale "to be full of a prairie-like placidity,
born of a speculative indifference to death." "But mark the other head's
expression," he continues,

> See that amazing lower lip, pressed by accident against the vessel's side, so as firmly
> to embrace the jaw. Does this whole head seem to speak of an enormous practical
> resolution of facing death?

The Lockean Right Whale Ishmael takes "to have been a Stoic," while he
remarks that the Kantian Sperm Whale seems to have been "a Platonian,
who might have taken up Spinoza in his latter years" (p. 334). Yet, while
the Kantian is the more imposing of the thunderheads, the epistemology
of which it is emblemmatic is no less imprisoned in the world of sensory
data than the Lockean epistemology imaged by the Right Whale. What is

37. On the critical positions of New York literary circles in the thirties and forties
see: Perry Miller, *The Raven and the Whale: The War of Words and Wits in the Era of
Poe and Melville* (New York: Harcourt, Brace and Company, 1956); John Stafford,
*The Literary Criticism of "Young America": A Study in the Relationship of Politics and
Literature, 1837-1850* (New York: Russell and Russell, 1967); and John Pritchard,
Literary Wise Men of Gotham: Criticism in New York, 1815-1860 (Baton Rouge, La.:
Louisiana State University Press, 1963).
38. J.F. Clarke as cited by Perry Miller, *The Transcendentalists: An Anthology*
(Cambridge: Harvard University Press, 1950), pp. 47-48.

"least dissimilar" in the two whale heads is "the two most important organs, the eye and the ear" (p. 327), and these are "all out of proportion" to "the magnitude of the head" (p. 328):

> Is it not curious, that so vast a being as the whale should se the world through so small an eye, and hear the thunder through an ear which is smaller than a hare's? But if his eyes were broad as the lens of Herschel's great telescope; and his ears capacious as the porches of cathedrals; would that make him any longer of sight, or sharper of hearing? Not at all. — Why then do you try to "enlarge" your mind? Subtilize it. (p. 330)

Here, as elsewhere in *Moby-Dick*, Ishmael sounds the depths of the epistemological paradox of his age. Like many of his contemporaries, Melville is ever anxious to place into stable and convincing relation subjective and objective experience, or, in Ishmael's terms, to trim ship between the compelling world views of Locke and Kant. Yet he is acutely aware at once that the only test of experiential and intuitive knowledge is sensation and that the knowledge attainable through the senses is as limited as it is subject to the distortions of a percipient's perspective and temperament.

As a quest for a comprehensive vision of nature, *Moby-Dick* is composed of multiple points of view that are anatomized as they are presented. In relation to Melville's overall method, the much-discussed symbol of Ahab's doubloon is synecdochic. The crew's perspectives on the coin stand as a microcosm of man's perspectives on nature, for, as Ishmael defines it, the doubloon is "the white whale's talisman" (p. 427). Elaborately demonstrated in the catalogue of readings of the doubloon's significance is the interpenetration of self and non-self, of mind and fact, that comprises all perception. For the sublimely egotistical Ahab, the "round gold is but the image of the rounder globe" (p. 428) and the earth is but an image of self; he reads the coin's details as ciphers of his own personality:

> The firm tower, that is Ahab; the volcano, that is Ahab; the courageous, the undaunted, and the victorious fowl, that, too, is Ahab; all are Ahab. (p. 428)

Starbuck's reading reveals at once Christian belief, a conventional aesthetic of nature compatible with that belief, and fear that fact shall in some manner unsettle both. "'Let me read'," he muses,

> A dark valley between three mighty, heaven-abiding peaks, that almost seem the Trinity, in some faint earthly symbol. So in this vale of Death, God girds us round; and over all our gloom, the sun of Righteousness still shines a beacon and a hope. If we bend down our eyes, the dark vale shows her mouldy soil; but if we lift them, the bright sun meets our glance half way, to cheer.

Starbuck suggests belief in a divine reciprocity between a percipient and a book of nature that bears largely glad tidings. "Yet, oh, the great sun is no fixture," he remarks, and if, at midnight, we would fain snatch some sweet solace from him, we gaze for him in vain! This coin speaks wisely, truly, but still sadly to me. I will quit it, lest Truth shake me falsely. (p. 429)

Stubb, armed with an almanack and Bowditch's navigation handbook, reads the doubloon as an allegorical sermon of constellations "writ high in heaven." "The sun goes through it every year, and yet comes out of it all alive and hearty. Jollily he, aloft there, wheels through toil and trouble; and so, alow here, does jolly Stubb" (p. 430). Even Stubb, who strives to avoid thought at all costs, refers to matters epistemological, as he remarks of books and, by implication, nature that they "... give us the bare words and facts, but we come in to supply the thoughts" (p. 430). Fine counterpoint to the speculations of Ahab, Starbuck, and Stubb is Flask's materialist point of view:

> I see nothing here, but a round thing made of gold ... So, what's all this staring been about? It is worth sixteen dollars, that's true; and at two cents the cigar, that's nine hundred and sixty cigars.

We are presented with the responses of the savages Queequeg and Fedallah through Flask; his view refracts two new views: "There's another rendering now; but still one text. All sorts of men in one kind of world, you see" (p. 431).

Consistent with their respective "renderings" of the doubloon are the whalemen's views of their prey. We may only infer what Ahab thinks of the whale as specie, but his view of Moby Dick in particular is clear within limits. He takes the White Whale to be either the agent or principal of all the evil endured by man, yet, in spite of the enormous sweep of this definition, the whale's significance is somehow encompassed within Ahab's soul; he is driven by the conviction that the White Whale has deliberately and malevolently assaulted him. Starbuck is possessed of a "deep natural reverence" for all things. "Outward portents and inward presentiments are his" (p. 112) for he is one who balances experiential and intuitive knowledge. He is inclined to superstition, "but to that sort of superstition, which in some organizations seems rather to spring, somehow, from intelligence than from ignorance" (p. 112). He will have no man in his boat who is unafraid of the whale, but regards the species as well as Moby Dick as merely brutish — if dangerous — beasts. Cheerful and thoughtless Stubb sees the whale as little more than a delectable dish. The equally thoughtless Flask sees the "wondrous whale" as "but a species of magnified mouse, or at least water-rat" (p. 116).

The elaborate catalogue of viewpoints of whale and doubloon seems best summed up in mad Pip's conjugation: "I look, you look, he looks; we look, ye look, they look." The line is repeated four times and finally capped with a phrase that posits, in the words of William Ellery

Sedgwick, the "solipsism of consciousness":[39] "And I, you, he; and we, ye, and they, are all bats" (p. 432). Many Melvillians have subsequently taken up Sedgwick's lead and assumed that all viewpoints in *Moby-Dick* are ultimately views of self. Merlin Bowen takes the import of Pip's conjugation to be the "impassable" quality of the "gulf between the mind and its object,"[40] a solipsistic position that he implies is also Melville's. R.W. Watters fosters a similar reading as he argues that matter in *Moby-Dick* has of necessity "innumerable meanings" because it is "a blank existence upon which form or meaning is projected by the observer."[41] Milton R. Stern tempers the evident solipsism of Melville's book by insisting on the "independent actuality" of matter in it; the *Pequod*'s crew may be kin to Narcissus, he rightly points out, but their perspectives on the external world are unremittingly subjected to the test of experience.[42]

Perhaps the least contentious method of resolving the problem of multiple point of view in *Moby-Dick* is to define the meaning of its central symbol as, in Stern's words, the "totality of all meanings"[43] perceived in it. Yet there is abundant evidence of a hierarchy of viewpoints within the composited perspectives of the book. Even as Melville establishes perceptual relativism through the catalogued perspectives on whales and on the doubloon, he suggests the relative merits of each of the crew-members' perspectives by arranging them in descending order of importance as well as by assigning to them different intensities of scrutiny. To Ahab's vision he devotes one long chapter and many portions of separate chapters. To the visions of Starbuck, Stubb, and Flask he devotes one chapter, attending to them in that order so as to suggest their descending order of significance. The feudal arrangement discussed in the two chapters on "Knights and Squires" is an arrangement of authority as well as of power; last in the hierarchy of authority are the ignorant and inarticulate savages who are mere squires to kingly Ahab's knights. The same ordering of viewpoints is followed in "The Doubloon," indicating that the successive "renderings" of the coin's meaning are ranked in descending order of authority. Those who see Melville's epistemology as solipsistic would do well to remember that Pip, spokesman for absolute perceptual relativity, confronts the emblematic doubloon last and that he does so only after he has been maddened by the experience of being cast

39. *Herman Melville: The Tragedy of Mind* (Cambridge: Harvard University Press, 1945), p. 112.

40. *The Long Encounter: Self and Experience in the Writings of Herman Melville* (Chicago: University of Chicago Press, 1960), p. 122.

41. "The Meanings of the White Whale," *University of Toronto Quarterly* 20 (January 1951): 163.

42. "Some Techniques of Melville's Perception," *PMLA* 73 (June 1958), p. 255.

43. "Some Techniques of Melville's Perception," p. 164.

away at sea. As Edward H. Rosenberry has wisely remarked, "On all questions of significance [in *Moby-Dick*] the prior question becomes: Seen by whom, in what mood, and in what light?"[44]

Of course all of the multifarious points of view in *Moby-Dick* are filtered through Ishmael's sensibility; his vision must in some sense be the book's. In the first rigorous attempt to come to terms with the epistemological issues of *Moby-Dick*, Paul Brodtkorb, Jr., takes Ishmael's many moods to be the key to the book's complex of viewpoints. Brodtkorb connects the "fact of Ishmael's mutability" to the idea — derived from Kant directly or via Coleridge — that "subject stands in some partially constitutive relation to object."[45] The point of Ishmael's subjective rendering of experience is by no means new, for F.O. Matthiessen noted quite early that "Melville had gone farther than Emerson in his realization that what you find in nature, whether you consider a phenomenon angelic or diabolic, depends — as Coleridge knew in the 'Ode to Dejection' — greatly on your own mood."[46] What is new in Brodtkorb's study is his attempt to "take subjectivity into systematic account throughout one book."[47] He attempts to explain Ishmael's inconsistencies, especially his vacillation among the views that Moby Dick is divine, demoniacal, or merely naturalistic, in terms of mood as a primary determinant of the quality of experience. In spite of its often insightful explicatory passages, his reading has the effect, in Robert Zoellner's words, "of cutting the entire novel loose from any controlling or normative reality outside of Ishmael's mental processes."[48] Like Edgar A. Dryden, who sees Ishmael's world as "purely verbal" and "a fanciful world of his own creation,"[49] Brodtkorb slights *Moby-Dick*'s crucially important battery of episodes in which natural forces obtrude tellingly into the subjective reveries of Ishmael and others; far from fostering mood as the cornerstone of experience, such episodes present the subjective state of the percipient as a component of experience as dangerous as it is significant.

44. *Melville and the Comic Spirit* (Cambridge: Harvard University Press, 1955), p. 116.

45. *Ishmael's White World: A Phenomenological Reading of "Moby-Dick"* (New Haven: Yale University Press, 1965), p. 12.

46. *American Renaissance: Art and Expression in the Age of Emerson and Whitman* (New York: Oxford University Press, 1941), p. 406.

47. Brodtkorb, p. 154.

48. *The Salt-Sea Mastodon: A Reading of "Moby-Dick"* (Berkeley: University of California Press, 1973), p. 273.

49. *Melville's Thematics of Form: The Great Art of Telling the Truth* (Baltimore: Johns Hopkins Press, 1968), pp. 87, 99; on the topic of subjectivity in general, see "Ishmael as Teller," pp. 83-113.

In *The Salt-Sea Mastodon*, Robert Zoellner bases his brilliant if contentious reading of *Moby-Dick* squarely on the epistemological dimension of Melville's book. Unlike Dryden and Brodtkorb, who envision Ishmael's voyage as all but exclusively a voyage within, Zoellner recognizes the persistent manner in which the subjectivism of *Moby-Dick* is balanced by "an unmistakable empirical coloration" that "would seem to have its source in Lockean sensationalism."[50] He sees the significance of the whale ship trimmed between Kantian and Lockean whaleheads as reverberating throughout the novel:

> The Kantian thunderhead may go overboard with the Lockean, so that Ishmael may ride light and right as befits a sailor, but a conceptual residue remains to shape the great metaphors in which he tells his story.[51]

There are abundant reasons to accept Zoellner's thesis that in *Moby-Dick* Melville worked toward a synthesis of Lockean and Kantian epistemology; as has been discussed, the reconciliation of Locke and Kant — which, as Zoellner notes, are "counter-words for the broad philosophical polarities represented by 'empiricism' versus 'idealism,' or that which is 'imaginative' contrasted to that which is 'real'"[52] — was an abiding intellectual concern in Melville's day. But Zoellner's idea that Melville works toward this synthesis through elaborately defined and clearly distinguishable "Ahabian and Ishmaelian epistemologies"[53] is questionable at the very least. The theories of knowledge expressed by Ahab and Ishmael alike bear the unmistakable marks of both sides of the Kant-Locke antinomy. So far as they may be inferred from the text, their epistemologies are in important respects the same. The two differ not so much in terms of intellectual ideas as in the relative confidence each places in intellection itself as a legitimate ground of action. Maniacal Ahab takes his idea of the natural world to be an index of a cosmic affront that must be avenged at any cost. Skeptic Ishmael vascillates

50. Zoellner, p. 8.
51. Zoellner, p. 9.
52. Ibid.
53. Ibid. Zoellner argues that "the difference between Ahab ... and Ishmael ... is epistemological. They do not agree on the relationship between perceiver and perceived. This disagreement lies at the root of any attempt to establish a definitive interpretation of *Moby-Dick*. If Ahab is right, then Ishmael is wrong; if Ishmael is right, then Ahab is wrong" (p. 11). This "precise investigative trajectory," as Zoellner terms it (p. 11), seems all too simple to be reconciled with Melville's symbolic method and pervasive ambiguity. The approach may stem from an unqualified acceptance of Ishmael as a consistently maintained persona as well as from the assumption that the catastrophic conclusion of the book carries with it Melville's implied damnation of Ahab's point of view. Ahab's monomania and totalitarian rule are doubtless condemned, but in no way does Melville — or Ishmael, for that matter — imply that Ahab's epistemology is erroneous.

between his allegiance to heart and to mind; while he recognizes the legitimacy of Ahab's metaphysics, his moral instincts and concern for the practival exigencies of survival preclude his full acceptance of Ahab's radical intellectualism.[54]

Ahab's epistemology is most elaborately set forth in the famous quarter-deck scene. Responding to Starbuck's allegation that Moby Dick is merely a "dumb brute" that assaults only "from blindest instinct," Ahab defines the whale as nexus between noumenal or intuited reality and the phenomenal or sensationally apprehended world:

> All visible objects, man, are but as pasteboard masks. But in each event — in the living act, the undoubted deed — there, some unknown but still reasoning thing puts forth the mouldings of its features from behind the unreasoning mask. If man will strike, strike through the mask! How can the prisoner reach outside except by thrusting through the wall? To me, the white whale is that wall, shoved near to me. Sometimes I think there's naught beyond. But 'tis enough. He tasks me; he heaps me; I see in him outrageous strength, with an inscrutable malice sinewing it. That inscrutable thing is chiefly what I hate; and be the white whale agent, or be the white whale principal, I will wreak that hate upon him. (p. 162)

The general outline of Ahab's epistemology may be deduced from this passage. He believes that knowledge is both intuitive and sensational; that the world apprehended by the senses is often illusory and perhaps malevolently deceptive; that essential or noumenal reality reveals itself, "sets forth the mouldings of its features," in active natural phenomena, and, therefore, that essential nature may be ascertained not through passive contemplation but through active engagement with natural forces. All of these principles are also voiced by Ishmael.

We have in Ishmael the semblance of an objective observer, but the terms with which he suggests his objectivity indicate an epistemology apposite to Ahab's: "Doubts of all things earthly," he remarks, "and intuitions of some things heavenly; this combination makes neither believer nor infidel, but makes a man who regards them both with equal eye" (p. 372). This and similar passages have been used to interpret

---

54. Arguing that Ishmael thoroughly rejects Ahab's vision, Zoellner points out that the fighting Quaker with "greatly superior natural force" and a "globular brain" who is a "mighty pageant creature fit for noble tragedies" (p. 71) is not necessarily Ahab; but if Ishmael did not have Ahab in mind in these lines, we are left with the absurd inference that he was describing two other quaker seamen, Bildad and Peleg. These comic characters — possibly distilled from Melville's readings in Smollett or Dickens — could hardly be described as framed for tragedy. Zoellner's premise that *Moby-Dick* is a sustained assault on Ahab's vision is not uncommon in the scholarship; it is, for example, the abiding assumption of Vincent's *The Trying-Out of "Moby-Dick"* and it seems to be behind Newton Arvin's otherwise perplexing comment that "Illumination, not darkness and terror, is Moby Dick's great boon to humanity (*Herman Melville*, p. 188).

Ishmael as disinterested witness in the *Pequod's* tragedy as well as a perceptual norm against which Ahab's aberrant vision is to be judged.[55] But Melville's subtly modulated syntax suggests important limits to Ishmael's objectivity. His skepticism extends to both experiential and intuited knowledge. Like Ahab, he structures his metaphysic through Locke's primary qualities and secondary attributes of matter. His analytic of color in "The Whiteness of the Whale" extends Ahab's idea of the sensationally apprehended world as pasteboard mask, and, like Ahab, he seeks out rends in the veil of the phenomenal world through which the noumenal world he intuits might be confirmed or denied.

Ishmael may be "object-oriented," as Zoellner has argued, but he is also as "event-oriented"[56] as Ahab. He does not so much create, as Dryden would have it, a "fanciful world"[57] as he struggles to convey what he terms "the real living experience of living men" (p. 179). As Ahab sees truth emerge only in "the living act, the undoubted deed" (p. 162), so Ishmael tellingly argues that "the only mode in which you can derive even a tolerable idea of [the whale's] living contour, is by going a whaling yourself" (pp. 265-266). His persistent disparagement of landsmen and their misconceptions of the sea received at second hand suggests that he, like Ahab, finds a distanced, contemplative or purely intellective relation to nature a wholly inadequate basis of comprehension. Ishmael goes to sea, in Peleg's words, "'to find out by experience what whaling is'" (p. 71), and he takes the fact that he has "had to do with whales with these visible hands" (p. 123) as exclusive warrant to speak the truth of the experience of whales and whaling. To be sure, Ishmael does not attempt, as does Ahab, to strike through the pasteboard of phenomenal nature to noumenal truth, but like his captain he reads certain *dynamic* aspects of nature — "the muffled rollings of a milky sea; the bleak rustlings of the festooned frosts of mountains; the desolate shiftings of the windrowed snows of prairies" (p. 193) — to be obtrusions of a terrifying noumenal world. Perhaps the ultimate mark of Ishmael's belief that the truth of nature lies somehow in its dynamism is the extraordinary kinaesthetic effect of his language. The sense of "violent, chaotic physical motion"[58]

55. As common as it is basically sound, the interpretation of Ishmael's vision as normative in function is most fully developed by Beongcheon Yu, "Ishmael's Equal Eye: The Source of Balance in *Moby-Dick*," *ELH* 32 (March 1965): 110-125. See also R. Dilworth Rust, "Vision in *Moby-Dick*," *Emerson Society Quarterly* 33 (Fall 1963): 73-75 for a catalogue of vision-as-perception metaphors in *Moby-Dick*. The effort to forge a radical distinction between the visions of Ahab and Ishmael in the work of Yu, Brodtkorb, and Zoellner seems motivated by a desire to portray Melville's conception of nature as less dark and demoniacal than his text suggests it was.

56. *Salt-Sea Mastodon*, p. 27.

57. *Melville's Thematics of Form*, p. 89.

58. D.H. Lawrence, *Studies in Classic American Literature* (New York: Viking Press, 1961), p. 152.

that Lawrence remarked in *Moby-Dick* is effected through pervasive and calculated use of verbal nouns and adjectival adverbs. Through these devices Ishmael creates of a retrospective tale a dynamic, sensual experience.[59]

Ahab takes the dynamism of Moby-Dick — the "living act" — to be the expression of the inscrutable malice he intuits as the essence or noumenon of the universe. For Ishmael as well the meaning of the whale is inextricably bound up in the whale's power and the expression of that power in action. As the pseudo-scientific chapters elaborately demonstrate, a dead whale is no whale; essence transcends object; the meaning of the whale transcends the total of its physiological components.[60] Ishmael can hardly be said to accept "the merits of science,"[61] for the whole thrust of his cetological chapters — fully a fourth of the book — is that the meaning of the whale eludes reductionist anatomizing. As Ahab casts his quadrant into the sea with the cry: "Science! Curse thee, thou vain toy!" (p. 494), Ishmael gives up his effort to phrenologize the whale's brow, remarking that "Physiognomy, like every other human science, is but a passing fable" (p. 345).

While Ahab, man of action, finds his sphere of action in the phenomenal world of Locke, he certainly does not, as Zoellner alleges, see "perception as unidirectional input."[62] He is as acutely aware as Ishmael of the narcissistic, self-reflective component of perception. As a political adept, he imposes his view of nature and of Moby Dick upon the crew of the *Pequod* by manipulating the light by which they perceive the external world. Convinced that truth of the natural world is eternally interfused with truth of self, he reads the soubloon in a manner consistent with Ishmael's vision of life as in large measure a voyage within:

---

59. Newton Arvin remarks that "Almost unanalyzable is the effect these [verbal nouns] have of uniting the dynamism of the verb and the stasis of the substantive" (*Herman Melville* [New York: William Sloane Associates, 1950], p. 163). The effect has been brilliantly analyzed by Morton L. Ross, "*Moby-Dick* as an Education," *Studies in the Novel* 6 (Spring 1974)þ: 62-75.

60. Cf. Zoellner's view that "The physiological facts of the whale" are presented by Ishmael for the purpose of "de-mythification" and that Ishmael's "naturalistic whale" is a counter to Ahab's "transcendental whale" (pp. 154, 146). Within the confines of such a reading, the question of who "mythologizes" the whale becomes problematical. As Zoellner himself notes, "It is astonishing to discover what a small portion of Ahab's speaking lines are devoted to comment on Moby Dick, or even on whales in general" (p. 146). Ishmael's cetological digressions magnificently demonstrate that naturalism is a woefully inadequate instrument of definition. His game is no more circumscribed by flesh and blood than Ahab's.

61. Yu, p. 118.

62. *Salt-Sea Mastodon*, p. 11.

this round gold is but the image of the rounder globe, which, like a magician's glass, to each and every man in turn but mirrors back his own mysterious self. Great pains, small gains for those who ask the world to solve them; it cannot solve itself. (p. 428)

The problem of self again looms large in the design for an ideal man that Ahab proposes to the carpenter:

I'll order a complete man after a desirable pattern. Imprimis, fifty feet high in his socks; then chest modelled after the Thames tunnel; then, legs with roots to 'em, to stay in one place; then, arms three feet through the wrist; no heart at all; brass forehead, and about a quarter of an acre of fine brains; and let me see — shall I order eyes to see outwards? No, but put a sky-light on top of his head to illuminate inwards.[63] (pp. 466-467)

Such an image could be construed only by a man convinced that perception is both a giving and a receiving, a compound of self and sensation. Like Ishmael, who protests the possibility of truly enlarging the mind within the prison of the senses, Ahab is in revolt against the confines of the phenomenal world. That revolt certainly does not mark his epistemology as "simplistically sensational."[64] His maniacal hunt is motivated not by the phenomenal world — of which his attitude is generally disdainful — but by a thing "inscrutable," a noumenal reality upon the intuition of which he places his confidence. In point of fact, the only simplistically sensational remark in Melville's book is voiced by Ishmael, who describes the Sperm Whale's brow — a correlative of Ahab's pasteboard mask — as "dead, blind," and "impregnable, uninjurable wall" (pp. 335, 336).

If neither Ahab nor Ishmael locates a stable nexus of sensation and intuition, the equipoise of Kant and Locke, both express the conviction that such a nexus exists. Ahab's belief that knowledge consists of the interpenetration of sensation and intuition is implicit in his apostrophe on transcendental correspondence:

O Nature, and O Soul of man! how far beyond all utterance are your linked analogies! Not the smallest atom stirs lives in matter, but has its cunning duplicate in mind. (p. 310)

The vast construct of *Moby-Dick*, comprised of the interpenetration of metaphysics and the tar, oil, and blubber of sensational experience,

63. Ahab's pattern suggests a debt to Mary Shelley's *Frankenstein*; see Sealts, entry no. 467, and Vincent's note in *Moby-Dick*, p. 813. Zoellner rightly notes that the skylight in Ahab's giant recalls Locke's concept of the mind as *camera obscura* (p. 269), but the giant's *inwardly* directed eyes *invert* Lockean epistemology. Cf. Ishmael's Lockean image: "Man may ... be said to look out on the world from a sentry-box with two joined sashes for his window" (p. 328).

64. Zoellner, p. 5.

stands itself as testimony to Ishmael's like conviction. "Some certain significance lurks in all things," he reasons,

> else all things are little worth, and the round world itself but an empty cipher, except to sell by the cartload, as they do hills about Boston, to fill up some morass in the Milky Way. (p. 358)

The relation between the epistemologies or, more broadly speaking, points of view of Ahab and Ishmael has been a contentious problem in Melville scholarship and it will most likely remain such primarily because Melville chose not to provide evidence with which to categorize either point of view finally and precisely. Among the many ambiguities of perhaps our most ambiguous literary genius, this is surely the crux, for out of scholarly attempts to mitigate or resolve it have evolved most of the major readings of *Moby-Dick* and of the Melville canon generally. Although few have been willing to accede to Charles Anderson's curt dismissal of the "sailor metaphysics"[65] in *Moby-Dick*, even the most sensitive students of Melville's work have occasionally failed to resist the temptation of attributing his perceptual ambiguity — in large measure an epistemological problem — to his limitations as thinker. Both Luther S. Mansfield's judgment that Melville was "not an original or systematic philosopher"[66] and Richard Chase's view that as thinker he was "an inspired amateur"[67] have a certain literal cogency, but their pertinence is all but wholly lost when it is considered that the same words might be as legitimately applied to Emerson or Thoreau. Not to be tedious, we fairly expect intellectual inspiration in a writer, and systematic philosophy is of course no necessary component of great art. If the sort of apologic typified by the remarks of Mansfield and Chase diminish the seriousness with which Melville's ideas are received, another technique of treating the philosophical dimension of *Moby-Dick* — that of conceiving its abstractly intellectual aspects as a distinct creation super-added to an earlier conceived whaling adventure — may have the same effect.[68] Metaphysics,

---

68. The theory that *Moby-Dick* is comprised of two separately conceived and composed narratives seems to have begun with Charles Olson, *Call Mè Ishmael* (San Francisco: City Lights Books, 1947), p. 35. It was further advanced by George R. Stewart in "The Two *Moby-Dicks*," *American Literature 25 (January 1954): 417-488*, and most recently elaborated by James Barbour, *"The Composition of Moby-Dick,"* *American Literature* 47 (November 1975): 343-360. No doubt the book evolved through two or more stages and took an ultimate form rather different from that which Melville initially conceived, but the likelihood of its being, from the beginning, a metaphysical romance, is suggested by the fact that before the alleged second stage of composition Evert Duyckinck saw it as "romantic, fanciful & literal ... something quite new in literature" (letter to George Duyckinck, August 7, 1850; repr. in Leyda, *The Melville Log*, I, 385).

or, in Melville's words, "ontological heroics,"[69] seem to have been a vital element from the earliest chapters on, and if they took the form of contradiction, that contradiction was endemic to Melville's age.[70] The clash between sensationalist and intuitionist epistemologies was resolved — or, rather, abated — only late in his century when faith in romantic idealism died.

Seeking, nevertheless, a consistency of thought where it may not obtain, some students of *Moby-Dick* have developed interpretive traditions by postulating a dramatic tension between the points of view of Ahab and Ishmael. The difficulties of such an approach are immediately evident in the facility with which its proponents assign different — indeed, diametrically opposed — perceptual roles to the characters. Yu and Zoellner see Ishmael's perceptual orientation as normative, according equal significance to sense and intuition; but, while Yu follows the common interpretation of Ahab as mad transcendentalist who mistakes his vision of the world for its reality,[71] Zoellner portrays him as a sort of debased Lockean whose vision is mechanistically sensational.[72] That such radically different readings of Ahab may be cogently supported by selections from the text itself suggests that no definitive reading of *Moby-Dick* can rest on the distinction between Ahabian and Ishmaelian visions; as Melville provided no firm basis for such a distinction, to insist that the book's meaning rests upon it carries with it the implication that *Moby-Dick* is grievously flawed. But far more important than the differences in the readings of Yu and Zoellner is the common ground of their assumption that Ishmael's viewpoint somehow triumphs while Ahab's

69. From a letter to Hawthorne, dated June 29, 1851, in reference to the ideas that prepossessed Melville during the composition of *Moby-Dick* (*The Letters of Herman Melville*, ed. Merrill R. Davis and William H. Gilman [New Haven: Yale University Press, 1960], p. 133; henceforth referred to as "*Letters*"). It should be noted, however, that Melville did not, as Zoellner (p. 268) alleges, refer to metaphysical ingredients in *Moby-Dick* in a letter to Richard Bentley dated June 5, 1849; the letter refers to the *absence* of metaphysics in *Redburn*.

70. On epistemological contradiction in Emerson, see Drummond, pp. 72-84. A chronic problem in transcendental writing, it also surfaces frequently in Hawthorne, who wrote in his prefaces of the difficulty of adjusting his inward eye to a proper focus with outward experience. Lawrence Holland has noted that Hawthorne's prefaces celebrate a process rather than explore a theory (*The Expense of Vision* [Princeton, N.J.: Princeton University Press, 1964], pp. 155-182); Melville, whose predilection for doubt was obsessive, could not rest content in such a celebration.

71. "Ishmael's Equal Eye," pp. 118-125.

72. *Salt-Sea Mastodon*, especially pp. 2-12. But see the perplexingly contradictory portrait of "Ahab: The Ugly Narcissus," pp. 91-117. Ahab remarks in soliloquy: "Oh! how immaterial are all materials! What things real are there, but imponderable thoughts?" (p. 520); this could hardly be the view of a man whose epistemology is simplistically sensational.

epistemology is damned by Melville as the book develops.[73] The idea is untenable for several reasons, not the least of which is the fact that as a first-person narrative presence Ishmael all but wholly disappears quite early in the book; his disappearance may indicate, as Alan Lebowitz has persuasively argued, that he "has in a sense been subsumed into Ahab's character."[74] Further, as James Barbour has pointed out,[75] the correspondence of Melville in the late stages of *Moby-Dick*'s composition includes many passages that suggest Melville's sympathies lay squarely with Ahab's defiant stance and that evince clearly the tenor of Ahab's words. One such letter, written to Hawthorne in the spring of 1851, is particularly damaging to the theory that Melville worked out his message in *Moby-Dick* by fostering the ascendancy of an equal-eyed Ishmael over and against a blind or myopic Ahab:[76]

> We think that into no recorded mind has the intense feeling of the visable truth ever entered more deeply than into this man's. By visable truth, we mean the apprehension of the absolute condition of present things as they strike the eye of the man who ... declares himself a sovereign nature (in himself) amid the powers of heaven, hell, and earth. He may perish; but so long as he exists he insists upon treating with all Powers on an equal basis.[77]

This passage — jestingly designated an excerpt from the "'Pittsfield Secret Review' " — refers to Hawthorne; as such it is a striking example of the way Melville seems to have unaccountably misrepresented his friend, transforming him and his work into an ideal of what he himself wished to achieve personally and professionally. No writer has been more prone to inadvertant self-revelation than Melville, and an astonishing shift in pronouns following the above lines is case in point; "If," Melville continues,

> any of those Powers choose to withhold certain secrets, let them; that does not impair my sovereignty in myself; that does not make me tributary.

---

73. Matthiessen argued that Ahab's death is the fit end of a man whose "unregenerate will ... stifles his soul" (*American Renaissance*, p. 457); doubtless the salvation of Ishmael and doom of Ahab imply judgment, but it is restricted to the psychological plane, bearing no necessary relevance to the metaphysical or epistemological levels of the book.
74. *Progess into Silence: A Study of Melville's Heroes* (Bloomington and London: Indiana University Press, 1970), p. 144.
75. "The Composition of *Moby-Dick*," especially pp. 351-355.
76. Zoellner has skirted extra-textual evidence through the "root assumption ... that every word of *Moby-Dick* ... comes from Ishmael rather than Melville" (p. xi); the books so abounds in minutely described scenes in which Ishmael has no part that this assumption hardly warrants comment. Applied to Melville, the formalist theory of persona is wholly anachronistic.
77. Tentatively dated April 16, 1851; *Letters*, pp. 124-125.

If Melville is writing at once of Hawthorne and himself, the idiom and tenor of his letter indicate that he is also writing about the nearly completed *Moby-Dick*. The phrase, "... he insists upon treating with all Powers on an equal basis," is clearly a verbal echo of the passage in which Ishmael claims to regard things heavenly and earthly with an equal eye. Yet, compounding complexity, the concluding passage of Melville's letter indicates that his true subject is not so much Hawthorne or himself or Ishmael as the vision of Ahab. Still ostensibly referring to Hawthorne, Melville continues

> He says NO! in thunder; but the Devil himself cannot make him say *yes*. For all men who say *yes*, lie; and all men who say no, — why, they are in the happy condition of judicious, unincumbered travellers in Europe; they cross the frontiers into Eternity with nothing but a carpet-bag, — that is to say, the Ego.

The entire passage resonates perfectly with the words and character of Ahab, who, after defining matter as pasteboard mask and vowing to strike through it, exclaims to Starbuck:

> Talk not to me of blasphemy, man; I'd strike the sun if it insulted me. For could the sun do that, then could I do the other; since there is ever a sort of fair play herein ... But not my master, man, is even that fair play. Who's over me? Truth hath no confines. (p. 162)

Thus it seems that the theory that Ahab's vision is damned necessarily carries with it the absurd implication that through his book Melville also damns his own deepest convictions. While it is true, as Richard Chase has said, that *Moby-Dick* is profoundly dialectical,[78] its dialectic is not so much at play between narrator and tragic hero as within each. To be sure, Ahab, as befits a romantic hero, is the more extreme of the two; he is by turns obsessed with and oblivious to sensationally apprehended matter. But Ishmael, too, is as heavily freighted as the *Pequod* with the dialectic of sensation and intuition, and, matching his pen with Ahab's harpoon, he probes both poles of the axis of reality.

In *Moby-Dick* Melville had more important game than the relative merits of two perceptual traditions; the ultimate justification for the epistemological lucubrations of the book is their vital relation to its moral dimension. The quest in vision within *Moby-Dick* is an essential adjunct of its quest for a sound moral significance — which is to say, aesthetic significance — in nature. Read properly in context, two profoundly important passages in the book, both of which have been employed to differentiate Ahab's vision from Ishmael's, offer proof that their aesthetic visions do not differ at all in principle.

In "The Gilder," Chapter CXIV, the *Pequod* cruises upon the exquisitely calm pacific. Ishmael remarks of this calm that it is conducive of a

---

78. *The American Novel and Its Tradition*, pp. 105-113.

"certain filial, land-like feeling towards the sea" that makes the sailor regard it "as so much flowery earth":

> The long-drawn virgin vales; the mild blue hill-sides; as over these there steals the hush, the hum; you almost swear that play-wearied children lie sleeping in these solitudes, in some glad May-time, when the flowers of the woods are plucked. (p. 486)

The inverse of Melville's landscape-as-seascape conceit in "The Piazza," this passage is nevertheless unmistakably the same vision of pastoral enchantment that lured the narrator of the later tale to Greylock's summit. Upon the lines that follow have been based the theory that Ishmael's vision is epistemologically balanced:

> And all this mixes with your most mystic mood; so that fact and fancy, half-way meeting, interprenetrate, and form one seamless whole.

While they doubtless convey the idea of correspondential unity between "fact and fancy," these lines can only divorce Ishmael's aesthetic position from Ahab's if they are quoted — as has often been the case — out of context. After the usual Melvillian pattern, a joyous vision of nature is followed immediately by qualifying paragraphs vital to meaning; I have italicized the critical terms:

> Nor did such soothing scenes, *however temporary*, fail of at least *as temporary an effect* on Ahab. But if these secret golden keys did seem to open in him his own secret golden treasuries, yet did his breath upon them prove but tarnishing. (p. 486)

Such a natural "effect" is as temporary for Ishmael as it is for Ahab, and as such it is largely irrelevant to what both regard to be the essential and chronic condition of the natural world. The point is made clear in Ishmael's brilliant apostrophe to the ephemerality of beauty and the sense of eternal exile that attends man's consciousness of it:

> Oh, grassy glades! oh, ever vernal endless landscapes in the soul; in ye, men yet may roll, like young horses in new morning clover; and for some few fleeting moments, feel the cool dew of the life immortal on them. Would to God these blessed calms would last. But the mingled, mingling threads of life are woven by warp and woof: calms crossed by storms, a storm for every calm. (p. 486)

A romantic progress of the soul is concluded in exile:

> There is no steady unretracing progress in this life; we do not advance through fixed gradations, and at the last one pause: — through infancy's unconscious spell, boyhood's thoughtless faith, adolescence' doubt (the common doom), then skepticism, then disbelief, resting at last in manhood's pondering repose of If ... Where lies the final harbor, whence we unmoor no more? In what rapt ether sails the world, of which the weariest will never weary? Where is the foundling's father hidden? Our souls are like those orphans whose unwedded mothers die in bearing them: the secret of our paternity lies in their grave, and we must there to learn it. (pp. 486-487)

Starbuck's response rings true with his rendering of the doubloon, and it drives home Melville's point that the moment of transcendent vision is a fleeting illusion. Praying that "teeth-tiered sharks" and "cannibal ways" be forever banned from the "bride's eye" of the calm, he asks the impossible: "Let faith oust fact; let fancy oust memory; I look deep down and do believe" (p. 487).

Noting that Ahab's breath may tarnish the sun's gildings, Ishmael, ever conscious of the reciprocity of perception, also repeatedly points up the fact that this extraordinary man may himself constitute a kind of sun,[79] thus radically recreating the world as it is perceived by others. Ahab is surely the type of the "original" literary character of which Melville wrote in *The Confidence-Man*: like a "Drummond light," he sheds his characteristics upon his surroundings in a manner "akin to that which in Genesis attends upon the beginning of things."[80] It is quite true, as Zoellner has argued, that Ahab's is a dark, "intellectual light" that he employs to force Pequod's crew to share the "nightmare world which is the projection of his own moral constitution."[81] But Ahab's world is certainly not a mere projection. The famous "Candles" chapter, in which Ahab terrifies the crew through the illusion of his mastery of lightning, surely functions not to discredit Ahab's vision but to demonstrate the roots of his political power. The aesthetic vision Ahab fosters dramatically — "I am darkness leaping out of light" (p. 500) — Ishmael accedes to and fosters through exposition; he, no less than Ahab, is obsessed with the noumenal darkness that whelms phenomenal light. The essential congruence of their aesthetic visions is again set forth in "The Try-Works," a chapter which, like "The Gilder," has often been used to set the Ishmaelian world against Ahab's.

In "The Try-Works," Ishmael's world comes to be, "in some enchanted way" (p. 422), wholly illumined and therefore originated by the hellish fire of the try-works. That fire is doubtless the correlative of Ahab's intellectual light; shooting her "red hell further and further into the blackness of the sea and the night," the *Pequod*,

> freighted with savages, and laden with fire, and burning a corpse, and plunging into that blackness of darkness, seemed the material counterpart of her monomaniac commander's soul. (p. 421)

The reddened "fiend shapes ... capering half in smoke and half in fire,"

---

79. We might expect that Ahab would see a "sort of fair play" in striking the sun (p. 162), for in the mythic stratum of the book the sun is his correlative; see H. Bruce Franklin's reading of Ahab and Moby Dick as Osiris and Typhon in *The Wake of the Gods: Melville's Mythology* (Palo Alto, Calif.: Stanford University Press, 1963), pp. 53-98).

80. *The Confidence-Man: His Masquerade*, ed. Elizabeth S. Foster (New York: Hendricks House, 1952), p. 271.

81. *Salt-Sea Mastodon*, p. 22.

beget "kindred visions" in Ishmael, who at the same time yields to an "unaccountable drowsiness" (p. 421). Conscious suddenly of "something fatally wrong," he is shocked out of his lurid reverie by the obtrusion of the benighted phenomenal world:

> Uppermost was the impression, that whatever swift, rushing thing I stood on was not so much bound to any haven ahead as rushing from all havens astern.

Finally aware that he has, in his semi-conscious state, turned the ship into the wind and nearly capsized her, he reads a moral lesson into his experience:

> Look not too long in the face of the fire, O man! Never dream with thy hand on the helm. Turn not thy back to the compass; accept the first hint of the hitching tiller; believe not the artificial fire, when its redness makes all things look ghastly. To-morrow, in the natural sun, the skies will be bright; those who glared like devils in the forking flames, the morn will show in far other, at least gentler, relief; the glorious, golden, glad sun, the only true lamp — all others but liars!

This would seem to be Ishmael's wholesale rejection of a dangerous and illusory world illumined by Ahab's unnatural intellectual fire. But it remains such only if removed from the vital context of the qualifying paragraph that folows. Here Ishmael, having cast his lot with the "glad sun, the only true lamp" and the natural world it lights, turns back upon his choice and finds, as had Ahab, the blackness of darkness in essential nature:

> Nevertheless the sun hides not Virginia's Dismal Swamp, nor Rome's accursed Campagna, nor wide Sahara, nor all the millions of miles of deserts and of griefs beneath the moon. The sun hides not the ocean, which is the dark side of this earth, and which is two thirds of this earth. So, therefore, that mortal man who hath more of joy than sorrow in him, that mortal man cannot be true — not true, or developed. (p. 422)

Aesthetics of the National Epic

As a "vision quest"[82] *Moby-Dick* is a richly dialectical fabric of contending viewpoints of which the antipodes of Kantian and Lockean epistemologies are but broadly inclusive categories. As a quest in aesthetics the book is similarly dialectical. The urgency with which Melville explores and anatomizes aesthetics of nature, setting view against counterview, rises, no less than the urgency of his epistemological dialectic, from the nationalist literary milieu in which he wrote. The

82. The phrase is M. Scott Momaday's as cited by Zoellner, p. 266.

American vision of nature had necessarily to figure vitally in a book rightly designated an "American national epic."[83]

Perry Miller has done much to clarify Melville's position among the literary cliques and factions of New York prior to the writing of *Moby-Dick*: Melville had

> ... little development until he was twenty-five; when the feverish growth did come, it was in New York, and within the camp of the nationalists. He received his education — such as it was — from [Evert Augustus] Duyckinck and [Cornelius] Mathews, who were clear that the glory to be won was not imitation of Lamb or Hazlitt or even Dickens, but "originality." This to be incarnated in a big book, crowded with epic figures, American figures, sprung from the native soil, big as the mountains, large as the lakes, oratorical as Niagara. It could not be done in the novel, not by Jane Austen, Bulwer, or Thackeray. Cooper had pointed the direction, but had fallen by the wayside when he turned to realistic satire ... The great American book had to be big and it had to be a romance.[84]

As early as the turn of the century, Americans had hailed wilderness as the foundation of the Republic's future cultural distinction, yet, as of the decade prior to the publication of *Moby-Dick* only Cooper had satisfactorily explored what the nationalists regarded as America's paramount symbol. In the eighteen-forties English literary tastes were turning away from the romantic mode of Scott and Byron towards Austen, Thackeray and Dickens, towards the novel of manners and of society. Fervid nationalists, especially those in the Duyckinck circle, feared that young American talents would follow the new English mode and thereby abrogate the potential for a distinctively American literature. For to turn to the novel of Dickens, as thousands of American readers had done, was of necessity to forsake treatment of the diminishing wilderness.

Through the 'thirties and 'forties cultural nationalists employed the idiom of the sublime of nature to foster the idea, current since the Puritan emigration, of America's millennial mission in the New World.[85] The Old Testament rhetoric of sublimity became the natural expressive vehicle of nationalism, for nowhere did America's destiny seem more manifest than in its awesome wilderness. Melville's position in regard to American millennialism and the part nature played in it was a compound of belief and doubt. He had written into *Redburn* an apostrophe to the idea of an American Eden:

83. Slotkin, *Regeneration through Violence*, p. 538.

84. *The Raven and the Whale: The War of Words and Wits in the Era of Poe and Melville* (New York: Harcourt, Brace and Company, 1956), pp. 256-257.

85. On the idea of American millennialism the most helpful studies are Ernest Lee Tuveson, *Redeemer Nation: The Idea of America's Millennial Role* (Chicago: University of Chicago Press, 1968) and Charles L. Sanford, *The Quest for Paradise: Europe and the American Moral Imagination* (Urbana: University of Illinois Press, 1961).

We are the heirs of all time, and with all nations we divide our inheritance. On this Western Hemisphere is a future which shall see the estranged children of Adam restored as to the old hearthstone Eden.[86]

And the millennialist ideal surfaces again in *White-Jacket*:

> We are the pioneers of the world; the advance guard, sent through the wilderness of untried things, to break a new path in the New World that is ours.[87]

The unabashed confidence with which this and other popular ideas are rendered in these two hastily composed works may in some measure account for Melville's low opinion of them.[88] A possibly more reliable index of Melville's view of the relation between nature and American destiny is available in the Vivenza sections of *Mardi* wherein he engages, in obscure allegory, the darker implications of patriotic naturalism; America may represent no break from the cycles of history, he suggests, for if its greatness is founded on wilderness as a kind of moral resource the inevitable demise of that resource will bring cultural decadence.[89] This vaguely expressed misgiving in *Mardi* is developed into the profoundly ambiguous millennialism of *Moby-Dick*. Here Melville's doubts are expressed through the conflict among Ahab's several mythic identities.[90] A king-like man who has spent forty years in exile at sea, Ahab leads his crew of Israelites through the watery wilderness in search of a dragon-leviathan. While he is Christ-like — his hunt begins on December 25 and he wears, metaphorically, a cross on his brow and the Iron Crown of Lombardy on his head — and hunts the beast of Revelations, he becomes, paradoxically, the Anti-Christ or beast that he hunts. And his tragedy is narrated by one who assumes the mask of Ishmael, an outcast in the wilderness who is specifically excluded from Jehovah's covenant. But our subject is not Melville's mythological reflections on the problem of nature and nation but his approach to that problem through the aesthetics of nature.

---

86. *Redburn: His First Voyage* (Evanston and Chicago: Northwestern University Press and The Newberry library, 1969), p. 169; all subsequent citations from *Redburn* refer to this edition.

87. *White-Jacket*, p. 151.

88. The two books were written between May and mid-September, 1849. Of them Melville wrote to his father-in-law on October 6: "They are two *jobs*, which I have done for money ... [My] only desire for their 'success' ... springs from my pocket, & not from my heart" (*Letters*, pp. 91-92).

89. *Mardi*, pp. 523-535. For a perceptive gloss of this difficult passage, see Miller, *Errand into the Wilderness*, p. 206. Melville's anxiety was common among the nationalists; it is massively at work in Cole's allegorical oils, "The Course of Empire."

90. For a brilliant summation of the matter, see Michael T. Gilmore, "Melville's Apocalypse: American Millennialism and *Moby-Dick*," *ESQ* 21 (Third Quarter 1975): 154-161.

94

The fundamental ambivalence of the earliest moral assessments of the wilderness — whether it might passively offer up a new Eden or, through human conquest, become the setting of a new Canaan — persisted through the eighteenth and early nineteenth centuries. It is residually but potently at work in the arts of Melville's generation wherein it was transmuted into the aesthetic polarity of pastoral and sublime nature. As has been discussed, nationalist writers and literati of the 'thirties and 'forties sought to end this bifurcated vision through the conflation of sublimity and pastoral in the American picturesque. But either of the two aesthetic visions might be employed independently to foster the idea of nationalist millennialism. The Puritan notion of the errand into the wilderness as a sublime spiritual trial and apocalyptic combat with Anti-Christ was current well into the eighteenth century, as the following passage from one David Austin, a biblical scholar, attests:

> Behold, then, this hero of America, wielding the standard of civil and religious liberty over these United States! — Follow him, in his strides, across the Atlantic! — See him, with his spear already in the heart of the beast! — See tyranny, civil and ecclesiastical, bleeding at every pore! See the votaries of the tyrants; of the beasts; of the false prophets, and serpents of the earth, ranged in battle array, to withstand the progress and dominion of him, who hath commission to break down the usurpations of tyranny — to let the *prisoner out of the prison-house*; and to set the vassal in bondage free from his chains — to level the mountains — to raise the valleys, and to prepare an highway for the Lord.[91]

Behind this Longinian rhetoric may be discerned the emergent shadows of such popular and mythic American heroes as Davy Crockett, Daniel Boone, and Andrew Jackson, as well as the fictive hunter-heroes of Cooper, Bird, and Simms. Though blind to the political and spiritual ambiguities of which Melville was so acutely aware, Austin seems also to have anticipated that demoniacal huntsman, Ahab.

The literary circle of George and Evert Duyckinck, the clique in which Melville matured as a writer, seems to have been particularly alive to the sublime of nature and to its potential enlistment in the cause of cultural nationalism. A major figure in this "Young America" group was Cornelius Mathews, an avid nationalist who, on the Berkshire mountain excursion with Melville, the Duyckincks, and others in August, 1850, had read aloud Holmes's patriotically naturalistic poem, "Monument Mountain." In 1839 Mathews published *Behemoth: A Legend of the Mound Builders*, a novel concerning the struggle of an ancient race of American savages to kill an enormous mastodon. Miller rightly assessed *Behemoth* to be "about as ridiculous a fanfaronade as the age produced,"[92] but the

91. "The Downfall of Mystical Babylon; or a Key to the Providence of God, in the Political Operations of 1793-1794," in *The Millennium* (Elizabethtown, 1794), p. 353; cited by Tuveson, *Redeemer Nation*, p. 117.
92. *The Raven and the Whale*, p. 82.

book is a valuable index to aspects of the Duyckinck circle that bear pertinently on *Moby-Dick*. While Mathews' tale is based on an Indian legend that Jefferson mentioned in *Notes on Virginia*, his savages antedate Indian civilization. Their struggle is as ageless and primordial as the symbolic beast that plagues them. The mastodon is immeasurably vast; attacked by the Mound-Builders, its "bulk dilated, till it came between them and heaven, and filled the whole circuit of the sky."[93] There are too many suggestive ties between *Behemoth* and *Moby-Dick* to be catalogued here, but the important aesthetic connection may be made clear through Evert Duyckinck's assessment of Mathews' book as the first American literary venture in the "physical sublime."[94] That this judgment conspicuously excludes the novels of Cooper suggests that Duyckinck meant "physical sublime" to refer to the sublime of animate nature, the capacity of an animal to evoke the ideas of infinite power and extension. The phrase recurred in his sober assessment of Melville's works in an 1855 review that reveals the occasional acuteness of Duyckinck's literary instincts: "In the character of Ahab and his contest with the whale [Melville] has opposed the metaphysical energy of despair to the physical sublime."[95]

In *Behemoth* Mathews attempts to generate something approximating national myth. His novel stands as an ineptly rendered but telling index of the manner in which the nationalist literati of Melville's generation could transmute biblical, Miltonic, and aesthetic tradition to forge a distinctively American sublime. Lost in the past, the savages in *Behemoth* are heroes not in time but in space.[96] If their prey is sublime, so too is their hunt. Hugh Blair, whose *Lectures on Rhetoric and Belles Lettres* was widely used as a textbook in American academies, had done much to foster among Americans a taste for the primitive or, as it was then known, "Ossianic sublime" that invests Mathews' savages. This was by

93. *The Various Writings of Cornelius Mathews* (New York: G.P. Putnam & Sons, 1843), p. 102.
94. Duyckinck as cited by Miller, *The Raven and the Whale*, p. 82. Affinities between Mathews' book and *Moby-Dick* have been discussed by Miller, pp. 82-83, and, more rigorously, by Curtis Dahl, "Moby Dick's Cousin Behemoth," *American Literature* 31 (March 1959): 21-29.
95. *Cyclopaedia of American Literature* (New York: Charles Scribner, 1855), II, 673. Miller (*The Raven and the Whale*, pp. 29, 42, 282, and passim) notes that the frequency with which references to the sublime recur in New York criticism during the 'forties is matched only by the frequency with which the term "vraisemblance" appears; the fact would seem to suggest a dichotomized aesthetic that illuminates the Kant-Locke antinomy as well as the tension between metaphysics and the technics of whaling in *Moby-Dick.*,
96. On space in the American romance, see R.W.B. Lewis, "The Hero in Space: Brown, Cooper, Bird," *The American Adam* (Chicago: University of Chicago Press, 1955), pp. 90-109.

no means a difficult process, because, as Tuveson has demonstrated, Americans had traditionally regarded their redemptive mission in the wilderness as founded on elemental or primitive racial qualities of the sort celebrated in Anglo-Saxon and eighteenth-century Celtic literature.[97]

The Puritans had habitually read their history allegorically, casting themselves as a new Anglo-Saxon Israel in deadly struggle against a Romish Anti-Christ. The same self-conception was adumbrated by eighteenth- and nineteenth-century Americans who came to see themselves as a Germanic race whose mission of conquest and redemption on the New World was primordially ordained. To cite but one typical example, in 1854 an American senator took up the question of the recognition of Texas in terms that link racial and national destiny with the sublime:

> Just in its origin, valiant and humane in its conduct, sacred in its object, the Texan revolt has illustrated the Anglo-Saxon character, and given it new titles to the respect and admiration of the world. It shows that liberty, justice, valor — moral physical and intellectual power — discriminate that race wherever it goes. Let our America rejoice, let Old England rejoice, that the Brassos and Colorado, new and strange names — streams far beyond the Western bank of the Father of Waters — have felt the impress, and witnessed the exploits of a people sprung from their loins, and carrying their language, laws and customs, their *magna charta* and its glorious privileges, into new regions and far distant climes.[98]

Buried beneath this jingoistic rhetoric are the morally ambiguous aspects of the American mission that troubled the more incisive among American thinkers. These ambiguities are for the most part reducible to the question of the relation between conquest and moral redemption, of violence and peaceful mission, in American destiny. As such they are recognizable in the tension between the pastoral and sublime visions of nature, a tension to which Melville was ever alive. To the pastoral vision of American destiny he gave voice in *White-Jacket,* which is marked with the hope that all peoples "shall yet come and lie down under the shade of our ark, without bloody hands being lifted."[99] In *Moby-Dick* he could find no stable basis for the pastoral vision, no foundation for faith that mind and matter, man and nature, were sufficiently harmonized to admit the realization of an earthly paradise. But more importantly, he anatomized the sublime, hunting down its elusive meaning in its most refined and essential form. And in the process the peaceful ark of *White-Jacket* became supplanted by the image of America as an horrific death-ship, "freighted with savages, and laden with fire, and burning a corpse, and

97. *Redeemer Nation*, especially pp. 137-186.

98. Thomas Hart Benton, *Thirty Years View* (New York, 1854), I, 675; as cited by Tuveson, *Redeemer Nation*, p. 151.

99. *White-Jacket*, p. 151.

plunging into ... blackness of darkness" (p. 421). What Miller has called the "long eclipse"[100] of *Moby-Dick* is in some measure to be explained by the fact that what Melville found in his hunt could hardly be received with joy by the America that had embraced the sublime of nature as the mark at once of national distinction and divine promise.

The anatomy of aesthetics of nature in *Moby-Dick* is best approached through Melville's "Hawthorne and His Mosses," an essay that takes its place with Emerson's "American Scholar" and "Divinity School Address" as one of the great documents of American cultural nationalism. The essay might be said to be massively framed by *Moby-Dick*, for Melville interrupted the composition of his masterpiece to write his review of *Mosses from and Old Manse*.

To write as brilliant a parody of the picturesque as the Piazza sketch, Melville had to be intimately acquainted with the mode, and "Hawthorne and His Mosses" stands as testimony of his mastery of it. Structurally the essay is governed by the essential assumption of pastoral that human life exists in correspondential relation to the cycles of nature. Out of this assumption Melville generates the essay's sustained conceit of organic fertilization as spiritual inspiration. Masking himself as a "Virginian Spending July in Vermont,"[101] he casts his discovery of Hawthorne's genius in terms of the discovery of a hidden landscape prospect:

It is curious how a man may travel along a country road, and yet miss the grandest, or sweetest of prospects, by reason of an intervening hedge, so like all other hedges, as in no way to hint of the wide landscape beyond. So has it been with me concerning the enchanting landscape in the soul of this Hawthorne. (p. 536)

The "perennial green" of Hawthorne's work comes to the narrator at the hands of a gay mountain girl who, having given him Dwight's picturesque. *Travels in New England*, now exchanges for them Hawthorne's *Mosses*. The exchange is likened to one of raspberries for moss, a conceit that points up the brisk, matter-of-fact quality of Dwight's travelogue and the picturesque quality of suspended decay in Hawthorne's more profound work. The narrator takes the "verdantly bound" volume, "garnished with a curious frontispiece in green, — nothing less, than a fragment of real moss," and reads it while reclined in "new mown clover":

the hill-side breeze blowing over me through the wide barn door, and soothed by the hum of the bees in the meadows around, how magically stole over me this Mossy Man! (p. 537)

---

100. *The Raven and the Whale*, p. 3.
101. "Hawthorne and His Mosses," in *Moby-Dick*, Norton Critical Edition, ed. Harrison Hayford and Herschel Parker (New York: W.W. Norton & Co., 1967), p. 535; all subsequent page numbers refer to this edition. The essay first appeared in *The Literary World*, Nos. 185, 186 (August 17, 24, 1850).

This elaborate, perhaps over-wrought, pastoral reaches its climax in a startlingly revealing image:

> already I feel that this Hawthorne has dropped germinous seeds into my soul. He expands and deepens down, the more I contemplate him; and further, and further, shoots his strong New-England roots into the hot soil of my Southern soul. (p. 548)

A considerable portion of Melville's essay is expended in stumping for a nationalist literature, and in this section he made his unreasoned claim that Hawthorne might be Shakespeare's better. Here he exploits the set phrases of patriotic naturalism: Hawthorne is

> one of the new, and far better generation of your writers. The smell of your beeches and hemlocks is upon him; your own broad prairies are in his soul; and if you travel away inland into his deep and noble nature, you will hear the far roar of his Niagara. (p. 546)

One might find the smell of beeches and hemlocks in Hawthorne's subtle, and meditative tales, but few could find a roaring Niagara in his soul. Such extravagance might in some measure be explained by the fact that Melville is celebrating a great "shock of recognition" (p. 547). Yet what he had come to recognize was not Hawthorne but himself. "From my twenty-fifth year I date my life," he would write to Hawthorne; "Three weeks have scarcely passed, at any time between then and now, that I have not unfolded within myself."[102] We have in "Hawthorne and His Mosses" the record of a splendid unfolding, one that bears vitally on the aesthetics of nature in *Moby-Dick* as well as the issue of patriotic naturalism in Melville's career.

It is not surpising that Melville focuses on the play of light and shadow in his review of Hawthorne, for the device was important to the latter's work and a requisite of all picturesque art. His summation of atmosphere in Hawthorne is as accurate as perhaps can be made:

> Hawthorne's melancholy rests like an Indian Summer, which, though bathing a whole country in one softness, still reveals the distinctive hue of every towering hill, and each far-winding vale.

However, Melville dismisses this picturesque quality of Hawthorne as a matter of secondary importance; it is, he remarks, "the least part of genius that attracts admiration" (p. 539):

> For spite of all the Indian-summer sunlight on the hither side of Hawthorne's soul, the other side — like the dark half of the physical sphere — is shrouded in a blackness, ten times black. (p. 540)

Brightness is given short notice in the essay:

> You may be bewitched by [Hawthorne's] sunlight, — transported by the bright gildings in the skies he builds over you; — but there is the blackness of darkness

102. Dated June 1 (?), 1851; *Letters*, p. 130.

beyond; and even his bright gildings but fringe, and play upon the edges of thunder-clouds. (p. 541)

Pastoral beauty, imaged as sunlight and brightness, would sem to be an ephemeral, secondary attribute of reality all but wholly blotted by an essential blackness of darkness in nature, as Melville fosters the impression that the power of blackness in Hawthorne marks that writer's "intuitive Truth," his "short, quick probings at the very axis of reality" (p. 541). We know in Ahab another who probes that axis and who, in the "Gilder" chapter, dismisses the sun's "gildings" and the delusion of cosmic unity they may foster.[103]

Melville attributes the "black conceit that pervades" (p. 541) Hawthorne to a moral conviction rooted in Calvinist theology:

> Whether Hawthorne has simply availed himself of this mystical blackness as a means to the wondrous effects he makes it to produce in his lights and shades; or whether there really lurks in him, perhaps unknown to himself, a touch of Puritanic gloom, — this, I cannot altogether tell. Certain it is, however, that this great power of blackness in him derives its force from its appeals to that Calvinistic sense of Innate Depravity and Original Sin, from whose visitations, in some shape or other, no deeply thinking mind is always and wholly free. (p. 540)

At work as he wrote these words on the greatest quest for the human — which is to say, moral — significance of nature to be written by an American, Melville is quick to connect the Calvinistic vision to its proper worldly test; "In certain moods," he remarks, "no man can weigh this world, without throwing in something, somehow like Original Sin, to strike the uneven balance" (pp. 540-541). The same uneven balance prepossesses Ahab as well as Ishmael, for whom the sun's gildings cannot reach the blackness of darkness at the axis of things, the "millions of miles of deserts and of griefs beneath the moon" (p. 422). Melville did not of course simply give voice, through his protagonists and through the mask he assumes in the Hawthorne essay, to a vision the darkness of which is a merely personal if abiding conceren. For in probing the moral axis of nature he probed the dilemma at the heart of the relation of American nature to American cultural nationalism. The context of *Moby-Dick* and "Hawthorne and His Mosses" is the effort of Melville's contemporaries in the pictorial and literary arts to meld the beautiful and the sublime, or, to borrow Melville's figure of balanced light and

---

103. Readings of *Moby-Dick* that are based on a theoretical clash between Ishmaelian and Ahabian visions of nature cannot accommodate without difficulty the apparent sameness of Melville's vision in "Hawthorne and His Mosses" and Ahab's vision throughout *Moby-Dick*. If Ahab's aesthetic is essentially Melville's and Ishmael's vision is a norm against which Ahab is judged, then we are left with the untenable conclusion that Melville's narrator attacks the fundamental convictions of his creator.

darkness in nature, to shift the fulcrum of nature's moral axis in such a way that the universe should seem inbued with divine and beneficent light. To that effort Melville's work stands as a dark and compelling reaction.

The link Melville fosters between the Hawthorne's darkness and the conception of innate depravity suggests that Melville's theologically derived ideas may in some sense be antecedent to his aesthetic vision of nature.[104] He seems to have been well read in the Puritan divines, whence he may have derived the conviction that man, exiled from Eden, is eternally damned to affliction and trial in a worldly wilderness. Such a view would fix his idea of the relation between American nature and the nation's destiny within the mythos of Canaan rather than Eden. Passages in *Moby-Dick* indicate his abiding interest in Gnostic dualism and the Manichean heresy, ideas that no doubt gave support and a measure of structure to his intuition that nature's essence is, as he put in in the Hawthorne essay, "blackness, then times black" (p. 540).[105] But Melville may have derived the terminology of his dissenting view of nature from eighteenth-century aesthetic discourse. We can expect that he read with quickened interest sections XIV through XVIII in Part Four of his edition of Burke's *Enquiry*, which are headed, successively, "Locke's opinion concerning darkness, considered," "Darkness terrible in its own nature," "Why Darkness is terrible," "The effects of Blackness," and "The effects of Blackness moderated."[106] But whatever the specific sources of Melville's vision may have been, the adumbration of darkness as the fundamental quality of the natural world in "Hawthorne and His Mosses" shows the limited degree to which Melville could accept and celebrate patriotic naturalism. The aesthetic tension of patriotic naturalism, the dialectic of pastoral beauty and natural sublimity, becomes the "uneven balance" of the Mosses essay. Even as Melville celebrates Hawthorne's genius through metaphors generated from the American landscape, he paradoxically suggests that picturesque beauty is meretricious and that "no deeply thinking mind" can be free of the conviction that man's life in nature is ultimately a tragic exile. The same tension is grandly at work in *Moby-Dick*, a book suffused with patriotic naturalism

104. The definitive study of Melville's theological ideas remains William Braswell, *Melville's Religious Thought: An Essay in Interpretation* (Durham, N.C.: Duke University Press, 1943; reprinted New York: Pageant Book Co., 1959).

105. See Thomas Vargish, "The Gnostic Mythos in *Moby-Dick*," *PMLA* 81 (June 1966): 272-277. On Pierre Bayle's *An Historical and Critical Dictionary* (Sealts, *Checklist*, entry no. 51) as the likely source of Melville's knowledge of Gnostic and Manichean doctrine see Millicent Bell, "Pierre Bayle and *Moby-Dick*," *PMLA* 66 (September 1951): 626-648.

106. For a discussion of the relevance of these sections of the *Enquiry* to *Moby-Dick* see below, pp. 139-140 and 160-161.

yet dedicated to the proposition that, in Ishmael's words, "unless you own the whale" — *ne plus ultra* of animate nature — "you are but a provincial and sentimentalist in Truth" (p. 336).

The apparently unqualified nationalism of *Moby-Dick* stems largely from its profusion of references to the American landscape. In this sea story, seascape tropes are generated more often than not from such American topographical features as the prairie, the Alleghany Mountains, Niagara Falls, the Mississippi and Hudson Rivers, the peaks of the Catskills, and the northwest woods. Under Melville's imaging pen, not only the sea but the technics and lore of whaling as well are ineluctably stamped with the national character and culture of America. The whaleboat, frequently likened to a birch-bark canoe, floats as often on an imagined prairie as on the sea. From it the whaleship may seem to be

> struggling forward, not through high rolling waves, but through the tall grass of a rolling prairie; as when the western emigrants' horses only show their erected ears, while their hidden bodies widely wade through the amazing verdure. (p. 486)

The harpoon of a whaleboat is conveniently positioned so as to enable the harpooner to snatch it up "as readily from its rest as a backwoodsman swings his rifle from the wall" (p. 288). Inventors of the "drugg," a whaling device, American Indians are among the earliest of whalemen, antedated only by such a mythic whaler as Hercules, whom Ishmael calls "that antique Crockett and Kit Carson" (p. 361). The best harpooners are, inevitably, American Indians, and the chief harpooner on the *Pequod* is the Gay Head Indian, Tashtego. Queequeg, though no Indian, is conceived by Ishmael as a kind of "George Washington cannibalistically developed" (p. 49). Whaling, a most savage hunt, is natural to the nation of savage spirit. Captain Peleg is at home in a wigwam erected on the deck on the *Pequod*, a ship named for an Indian nation. And the ship itself, a "thing of trophies, a cannibal of a craft" (p. 67), is festooned with whale bone as an Indian warrior is hung with scalps. If Melville's hunt and huntsmen are eminently American, so too, in a special sense, is the whale itself. Through countless metaphors, allusions, and analogies, Melville establishes the connection between the whale, sublimest of creatures, and the sublime American landscape. The whale's brow, to Melville's eye, is a veritable prairie; his stomach is as large as Kentucky's Mammoth Cave; his teeth are like stumps in the Michigan forest; his throat extends like the Erie Canal; his kingship in the sea is as the buffalo's in the Great Plains. Seldom seeking topographical images outside American borders, Melville may occasionally turn to South America or the Near East. As we might expect in a book created by a nationalist, references to European and British topography are conspicuously few in number.

Remarking the abundance of references to the American wilderness and frontier culture in *Moby-Dick*, Edwin Fussel has concluded that Melville's

> ... controlling metaphor — the image in which the other images swim, or upon which they float, or try to float — is the ocean (pre-eminently the Pacific) as American West.[107]

Melville lived and wrote within the period of America's most ambitious frontier expansion and, considering the circle of nationalist literati in which he matured as a writer, it is predictable that American expansion should figure importantly in *Moby-Dick*. But he did not, through some perverse obliquity of mind, fashion a sea story that is in fact an allegory of the West, and Fussell's reading may too narrowly restrict the referential range of wilderness in Melville's book. For Ishmael the Western frontier seems a thing of the past, and he boasts that American whalemen have a vital part in an imperial destiny that is not merely continental but global. The Nantucket whalemen, he notes early in the romance, are unrivalled conquerors:

> And thus have these naked Nantucketers, these sea hermits, issuing from their ant-hill in the sea, overrun and conquered the watery world like so many Alexanders; parceling out among them the Atlantic, Pacific, and the Indian Oceans. Let America add Mexico to Texas, and pile Cuba upon Canada; let the English overswarm all India, and hang out their blazing banner from the sun; two thirds of this terraqueous globe are the Nantucketer's. (pp. 62-63)

Melville's methods are primarily not allegorical but symbolical, and as his romance unfolds the symbolic range of the sea expands until it stands as a metaphysical frontier in which America's destiny is spiritual and intellectual as well as territorial.[108]

Like Tommo and Taji, who jump ship to escape the tedium and oppression of ship-board life and who plunge into primitive worlds, Ishmael leaves behind an oppressive landsman's world to find essential existence. The pattern suggests how fully immersed Melville was in the tide of American romantic primitivism.[109] In *Walden*, that New World

107. *Frontier: American Literature and the American West* (Princeton: Princeton University Press, 1965), pp. 261-262.

108. Vexed by "over doleful chimearas [sic]" as *Moby-Dick* passed through the press in the summer of 1851, Melville wrote a letter to Hawthorne that evinces the wide referential range of the frontier as symbol; "... men like you and me and some others, forming a chain of God's posts around the world, must be content to encounter now and then, and fight them the best way we can. But come they will, — for, in the boundless, trackless, but still glorious wild wilderness through which these outposts run, the Indians do sorely abound, as well as the insignificant but still stinging mosquitoes" (dated 29 June 1851, *Letters*, p. 132).

109. The best study of the general subject of primitivism in Melville's works remains James R. Baird, *Ishmael: The Art of Melville in the Contexts of International Primitivism* (Baltimore: Johns Hopkins University Press, 1956; reprinted New York: Harper Torchbooks, 1960). The specifically American context has yet to be studied.

pastoral and complement of Melville's quest in the sublime, Thoreau went to the woods to "live deliberately, to front only the essential facts of life," and to "reduce it to its lowest terms."[110] In *Moby-Dick* Melville leaves the New England landscape behind and substitutes outward quest for Thoreau's retirement, but the seaward gesture is motivated by the same compulsion toward the primordial essence of life. For Ishmael "mediation and water are wedded for ever" (p. 2), and

> all deep, earnest thinking is but the intrepid effort of the soul to keep the open independence of her sea; while the wildest winds of heaven and earth conspire to cast her on the treacherous, slavish shore. (p. 105)

The crew Melville sets afloat on the sea of independence is thoroughly invested with the primitivist racial myth that the nationalists of Melville's day had revived.

In its elitist aspect, the nationalist racial myth fostered the view that the Puritan migration was but the latest phase of the triumphant ascendance of the Goths of northern Europe. This savage, rugged race, it was alleged, had triumphed over decadent Roman religion and culture, and spread westward, ultimately colonizing New England. Perhaps the most articulate spokesman of the idea in Melville's day was George Perkins Marsh, a philologist who published a discourse on the subject in 1846. Marsh believed that the "Gothic mind attained its most perfect development, in the character of the great sect to which the pilgrims belonged."[111] He held that the primitive grandeur and stern moral fiber of the Goths had been sustained and nurtured in the harsh climate and topographic sublimities of northern Europe, and that these racial qualities had been similarly preserved among the Puritans in New England. For the Puritans, according to Marsh, the New World wilderness was the physical correlative of Miltonic and Old Testament sublimity, and an awesome and ever-present reminder of "the promise and menaces of the old and new covenant."[112] There is no evidence that Melville knew of Marsh's work, but it is clear that he shared the latter's essential ideas.[113] Ahab seems the perfect embodiment of Marsh's Goth. Ishmael's apostrophe to his captain —

110. *Writings*, II, 100-101.

111. *Address, delivered before the New England Society of the City of New York, Dec. 24, 1844* (New York, 1846); cited by Poenicke, "A View from the Piazza," p. 277, to whose discussion of Marsh I am indebted. For more information on Marsh's ideas, see Samuel Kliger, *The Goths in England: A Study in 17th and 18th Century Thought* (Cambridge: Harvard University Press, 1952), pp. 106 ff., and Tuveson, *Redeemer Nation*, p. 143.

112. Marsh, *Address*, p. 24.

113. Climatological determinism of a sort similar to Marsh's was a common adjunct to patriotic naturalism; see, for example, E.L. Magoon's "Scenery and Mind," *The Home Book of the Picturesque*, pp. 1-48.

Oh, Ahab! what shall be grand in thee, it must needs be plucked at from the skies, and dived for in the deep, and featured in the unbodied air! (p. 145)

— suggest the real difficulties the nationalists faced in finding a foundation for individual heroic stature within a society devoted to egalitarian ideals. A viable solution lay in the sublimites of the native landscape: Ahab's maniacal obsession did not subside, says Ishmael,

> but deepeningly contracted; like the unabated Hudson, when that noble Northman flows narrowly, but unfathomably through the Highland gorge. (p. 161)

A regal but somehow simple man might be elevated through the primitive, Ossianic sublime:

> But Ahab, my Captain, still moves before me in all his Nantucket grimness and shagginess; and in this episode touching Emperors and Kings, I must not conceal that I have only to do with a poor old whale-hunter like him; and, therefore, all outward majestical trappings and housings are denied me. (p. 145)

Or, the nationalist might take up the racial myth of Marsh; anatomizing those whaling captains who are "fighting Quakers, ... Quakers with a vengeance," Ishmael notes that

> there are instances among them of men, who, named with Scripture names — a singularly common fashion on the island [of Nantucket] — and in childhood naturally imbibing the stately dramatic *thee* and *thou* of the Quaker idiom; still, from the audacious, daring, and boundless adventure of their subsequent lives, strangely blend with these unoutgrown peculiarities, a thousand bold dashes of character, not unworthy a Scandinavian sea-king, or a poetical Pagan Roman. And when these things unite in a man of greatly superior natural force, with a globular brain and a ponderous heart; who has also by the stillness and seclusion of many long night-watches in the remotest waters, and beneath constellations never seen here at the north, been led to think untraditionally and independently; receiving all nature's sweet or savage impressions fresh from her own virgin, voluntary, and confiding breast, and thereby chiefly, but with some help from accidental advantages, to learn a bold and nervous lofty language — that man makes one in a whole nation's census — a mighty pageant creature, formed for noble tragedies. (p. 73)

From this discourse on the American hero Ahab emerges as the very type of the Goths, who, Marsh argues,

> ... were wont to recognize the voice of God, in the dusky terrors of the wintry tempest, the bellowing of the troubled ocean, the avalanche, the torrent, the thunder reechoing from the flanks of the mountain, required not to be told that there needs no anointed interpreter between Earth's children and their Heavenly Father.[114]

Out of the immediate experience of nature — "out of unhandselled

114. Marsh, *Address*, p. 26; as cited by Poenicke, p. 278.

savage nature,"[115] Emerson wrote — emerges the American hero.

Ahab may be "one in a whole nation's census," but that whole census had also to be accommodated in the nationalist racial myth. Racial elitism had to be reconciled with the fact of America's racial heterogeneity; Gothic Ahab had to be matched with the "Anacharis Clootz deputation from all the isles of the sea" (pp. 118-119) that comprises the crew of the American whaleship. Melville had more than once given voice to the idea that the melding of the races in America would bring about a return to the primordial nature of man. "You cannot spill a drop of American blood without spilling the blood of the whole world," he wrote in *Redburn*;

> Our ancestry is lost in the universal paternity; and Caesar and Alfred, St. Paul and Luther, and Homer and Shakespeare are as much ours as Washington, who is as much the world's as our own. We are the heirs of all time, and with all nations we divide our inheritance. On this Western Hemisphere all tribes and people are forming into one federated whole; and there is a future which shall see the estranged children of Adam restored as to the old hearthstone of Eden.[116]

The sense in which the multi-racial crew of the *Pequod* is itself a kind of composite portrait of Adamic man is but one of many manifestations in the book of the idea of America as wholly new yet — paradoxically — at the same time ageless. The whaling voyage is at once a thoroughly American industrial venture and a Bronze Age epic; it is laced both with references to prosaic contemporary affairs and to such mythic heroes as Alexander, Perseus, and Tamerlane.[117]

Melville's observation that his whalemen were "nearly all Islanders" (p. 118) is appropriate in a book governed by a conceit of the sea as a wilderness in which Americans act and think "untraditionally and independently" (p. 73). Islanders all, they are "*Isolatoes* too," for Ishmael, "not acknowledging the common continent of men," sees his fellow crewmen each as "living on a separate continent of his own." Though "federated along one keel" (p. 118), the whalemen are all Ishmaels, wanderers in a wilderness that is both literal and metaphorical. Nantucket, the island from which pre-historic whalemen first embarked, is

115. "The American Scholar," *Works*, I, 99-100. Cf. Ishmael's statement that "Long exile from Christendom and civilization inevitably restores a man to that condition in which God placed him, i.e., what is called savagery. Your true whale-hunter is as much a savage as an Iroquois. I myself am a savage; owing no allegiance but to the King of the Cannibals; and ready at any moment to rebel against him" (p. 270).

116. *Redburn: His First Voyage*, ed. Harrison Hayford, Hershel Parker, and G. Thomas Tanselle (Evanston and Chicago: Northwestern University Press and the Newberry Library, 1969), p. 169. All subsequent citations refer to this edition.

117. On the simulation in *Moby-Dick* of an archaic and heroic age see Arvin, *Herman Melville*, pp. 156-161.

not so much a settlement as the ultimate frontier encampment; it is "away off shore, more lonely than the Eddystone lighthouse," and "all beach without a background" (p. 61). Invested with primitive grandeur, the port, its whalemen, and the whaling enterprise are presented in the sublime rhetoric of superlatives. "Ahab is introduced as the largest of large men," Alan Lebowitz observes, "the foremost of whaling men who are themselves pre-eminent among sailors, who, in turn, according to the opening chapter, are the chief thought-divers of humanity."[118] Theirs are the longest of sea voyages, and their prey are the largest of beasts. The sperm whales, chosen victims of American whalemen, are, according to Melville, the largest of whales, and Moby Dick, greatest of sperm whales, is "the grand hooded phantom of them all" (p. 6). Compared to the supreme dangers of whaling, the landsman's difficulties are pallid, "For what are the comprehensible terrors of man compared with the inter-linked terrors and wonders of God!" (p. 107).

The comparison of the landsman's life with that of the whaleman is but one of a multitude of manifestations of the land-sea antinomy at work throughout Melville's book. The antinomy is established in the opening pages of the book, which are set in an island frontier of the sea, the "insular city of the Manhattoes, belted round by wharves as Indian isles by coral reefs" (p. 1). Here, prior to taking his reader to the remoter frontier of Nantucket, Ishmael disparages pastoral world of the Saco Valley and celebrates the hoards of "water-gazers" who "cherish very nearly the same feelings towards the sea" (p. 1) as he. Yet, while the *Pequod* may sail the seas of full half the globe, Melville's book never breaks with its conceptual moorings in the land-sea antinomy and the tension between a pastoral and sublime vision of nature it establishes. Out of this antinomy are generated the topographical conceits with which Melville fosters his own dark vision against the optimistic naturalism of his day. Ingeniously structured, these conceits — or "furious trope[s]," as Ishmael calls them (p. 182) — contribute importantly to the aesthetic themes of Melville's book.

In fashioning seascape metaphors with topographical images from the land, Melville took up a venerable technique of maritime literature. The device is especially pervasive in the sea tales of Cooper, for whom a placid sea is more often than not an undulating prairie and storm wrought waves are ranges of endless mountain peaks. The waves that "seemed real hills'[119] in *Redburn* and the longboat that climbs waves in *Mardi* like a

118. *Progress into Silence: A Study of Melville's Heroes* (Bloomington: Indiana University Press, 1970), p. 10.
119. *Redburn*, p. 379.

chamois hunter climbs the Alps are unremarkable vestiges of the mode. But in *Moby-Dick* Melville elaborated his seascape as landscape tropes, forging of them complex conceits that carry subtle and incisive aesthetic statements.

The meaning of the sea in *Moby-Dick* is presented through Melville's characteristically negative definition; it is the condition of "landlessness" (p. 105). The land, upon which all men are islanders and "isolatoes," is "safety, comfort, hearthstone, supper warm, blankets, friends, all that's kind to our mortalities."[120] Consistently presented by Melville in the imagery of domesticity and a felicitous, pastoral existence, the land is nevertheless "treacherous," "slavish," and "pitiful" (p. 105). It offers Ishmael, who goes to sea as "a substitute for pistol and ball" (p. 1), only a kind of life-in-death. Life on land is deceptive, ephemeral, its beauties attributes and therefore illusions. As all roads in Manhattan lead to the sea, all men are inclined to the sea, Melville's topographical analog for the "axis of reality." The sea approximates space itself. Like the "blackness of darkness" that forms the "uneven balance" with light in the Hawthorne essay, the sea is "the dark side of this earth, ... which is two thirds of this earth" (p. 422). Yet in it "resides the highest truth, shoreless, indefinite as God" (p. 105). To seek out that essential, perhaps noumenal truth is at once the romantic quest and the romantic agony; "Better it is," remarks Ishmael,

> to perish in that howling infinite, than to be ingloriously dashed upon the lee, even if that were safety! For worm-like then, oh! who would craven crawl to land! Terrors of the terrible! is all this agony so vain? (p. 105)

Melville is ever quick to salute his countrymen as the best of frontiersmen. In the digressive "Town-Ho's Story" he celebrates Steelkilt through a gargantuan topographical conciet that suggests the full metaphoric range of his concept of frontier:

> "This lakeman, in the land-locked heart of our America, had yet been nurtured by all those agrarian freebooting impressions popularly connected with the open

120. Melville was inclined to connect pastoral landscapes with femininity and sublime seascapes with masculinity. Note, for example, the famous "Agatha" letter to Hawthorne in which Melville places his imagined heroine among sheep at the brink of a sea-cliff: "Here [There?], in strange & beautiful contrast, we have the innocence of the land placidly eyeing the malignity of the sea" (dated August 13, 1851; *Letters*, p. 156). Melville's tableau suggests his familiarity with a commonplace convention of American seascape. In discussing the "differentiation of male and female space" in American art, Roger B. Stein has pointed out that in seascape "The American woman was to be mostly cut off from the possibilities of venturing outward ... The woman was to be the guardian of the land while the man ventured into dark and stormy seas" (*Seascape and the American Imagination* [New York: The Whitney Museum and Clarkson N. Potter, Inc., 1975], pp. 12-13).

ocean. For in their interflowing aggregate, those grand fresh-water seas of ours, — Erie, and Ontario, and Huron, and superior, and Michigan, — possess an ocean-like expansiveness, with many of the ocean's noblest traits; with many of its rimmed varieties of races and climes. They contain round archipelagoes of romantic isles, even as the Polynesia waters do; in large part, are shored by two great contrasting nations, as the Atlantic is; they furnish long maritime approaches to our numerous territorial colonies from the East, dotted all round their banks; at intervals, they yield their beaches to wild barbarians; for leagues and leagues are flanked by ancient and unentered forests, where the gaunt pines stand like serried lines of kings in Gothic genealogies; ... Thus, gentlemen, though an inlander, Steelkilt was wild-ocean born, and wild-ocean nurtured." (pp. 242-243)

Melville metaphorically transmutes one sector of the American west into an oceanic wilderness. Such an environment, he suggests, fosters the sort of savage independence characteristic of Ahab. The American landscape may function as a kind of probationary training ground for marine frontiersmen. Musing on the national significance of the Erie Canal, Ishmael argues that

to many thousands of our rural boys and young men born along its line, the probationary life of the Grand Canal furnishes the sole ransition between quietly reaping in a Christian cornfield and recklessly ploughing the waters of the most barbaric seas. (pp. 249-250)

The immediacy of the American's relation to the land thus facilitates his transition from pastoral felicity ("reaping in a Christian cornfield") to the whaleman's confrontation with the "howling infinite" of sublime nature.

Melville may endlessly boast of the capacity of Americans to create Christian cornfields and endure barbaric seas, but he by and large resists any implication that the two realms are in any ultimate sense similar or that the pastoral and the sublime are reconcilable. The troughs of waves may *seem* to be "long-drawn virgin vales" or "grassy glades" and their crests may *seem* to be "blue hill-sides" (p. 486), but they appear benignantly so only in "holiday weather" (p. 122) and rare, "blessed calms" (p. 486). The beautiful calm of the sea's surface is, literally speaking, superficial; it is a landsman's illusion, as Ishmael reflects in describing the pause before the breaching of a struck whale:

As the three boats lay there on that gently rolling sea, gazing down into its eternal blue noon; and as not a single groan or cry of any sort, nay, not so much as a ripple or a bubble came up from its depths; what landsman would have thought, that beneath all that silence and placidity, the utmost monster of the seas was writhing and wrenching in agony. (p. 354)

Melville often evokes momentary visions of peace and placidity in nature but he almost unfailingly checks any implication of natural harmony and beneficence that might be inferred from these visions through ominously impending or finally emergent violence and horror.[121]

The chapters entitled "Brit" and "Squid" comprise one of the most sustained of Melville's seascape-as-landscape conceits, and as they typify the pattern he follows when employing the device, the chapters warrant close attention. Melville opens "Brit" and establishes his conceit by exploiting the land-like appearance of the sea when its surface is blanketed by the yellow-hued organic substance upon which the right whale feeds. Of the "vast meadows of brit" Ishmael remarks that "For leagues and leagues it undulated round us, so that we seemed to be sailing through boundless fields of ripe and golden wheat":

> On the second day, numbers of Right Whales were seen, who ... with open jaws sluggishly swarm through the brit, which, adhering to the fringing fibres of what wondrous Venetian blind in their mouths, was in that manner separated from the water ... As morning mowers, who side by side slowly and seethingly advance their scythes through the long wet grass of marshy meads; even so these monsters swam, making a strange, grassy, cutting sound; and leaving behind them endless swaths of blue upon the yellow sea. (p. 272)

For Ishmael it is chiefly the "sound they made as they parted the brit" that made the whales seem mowers, for

> their immense magnitude renders it very hard really to believe that such bulky masses of overgrowth can possibly be instinct, in all parts, with the same sort of life that lives in a dog or a horse. (p. 273)

To man "all creatures of the land" may seem "of their kind in the sea," but only because through "the continual repetition" of ocean travel "man has lost that sense of the full awfulness of the sea which aboriginally belongs to it." Turning to the "unspeakably unsocial and repelling" reality of marine life, Melville sets out to restore the aboriginal reality of the sea, that "everlasting terra incognita," to the mind of his reader. In so doing he demolishes the apparent sameness of sea and land established in the pastoral trope that opened the chapter. "Wherein differ the sea and the land, that a miracle upon one is not a miracle upon the other?" he asks:

> Preternatural terrors rested upon the Hebrews, when under the feet of Korah and his company the live ground opened and swallowed them up for ever; yet not a modern sun ever sets, but in precisely the same manner the live sea swallows up ships and crews. (p. 274)

121. Leo Marx sees the interrupted pastoral or violated idyll as an important recurrent pattern in American literature (*The Machine in the Garden*; on the pattern in Melville see pp. 277-319). Marx sees the agency of interruption chiefly as the "counterforce" of industrial technology. Industrialism and the image of the machine have an important presence in *Moby-Dick* (see Stephen C. Ausband, "The Whale and the Machine: An Approach to *Moby-Dick*," *American Literature* 47 [May 1975]: 197-211), but neither has much to do with the violated idylls of the book. Melville's "counterforce" is nearly always in nature itself.

"But not only is the sea such a foe to man who is an alien to it," he continues.

> but it is also a fiend to its own offspring ... sparing not the creatures which itself hath spawned. Like a savage tigress that tossing in the jungle overlays her own cubs, so the sea dashes even the mightiest whales against the rocks, and leaves them there side by side with the split wrecks of ships. No mercy, no power but its own controls it.

The sea is a "Noah's flood ... not yet subsided; two thirds of the world it yet covers." We must consider, says Ishmael, the "universal cannibalism of the sea; all whose creatures prey upon each other, carrying on eternal war since the world began." Consider this, he says,

> and then turn to this green, gentle, and most docile earth; consider them both, the sea and the land; and do you not find a strange analogy to something in yourself? For as this appalling ocean surrounds the verdant land, so in the soul of man there lies one insular Tahiti, full of peace and joy, but encompassed by all the horrors of the half known life. God keep thee! Push not off from that isle, thou canst never return! (pp. 274-275)

This passage might seem to be fashioned simply to heighten the sense of mortal danger that invests Ishmael's story, but it also carries important aesthetic and epistemological implications. To liken the self to an "insular Tahiti" and cast the external world as encompassing "horrors" of a "half known life" is to preclude any such beneficent harmony of self and nature as was postulated in the optimistic naturalism of Melville's day. In *Nature* Emerson had essayed the fusion of self with "all that is separate from us, all which Philosophy distinguishes as the NOT ME."[122] Melville's figure of the sea — a realm in which man is "alien" — as the "NOT ME" of the universe, fixes the gulf between self and nature as morally and epistemologically immense.

In "Squid," the chapter that follows "Brit," Melville further adumbrates the alienation of man from nature. Restoring the metaphoric vision of the sea as verdant landscape, he presents the *Pequod* "wading through the meadows of brit," her masts waving to a "languid breeze, as three mild palms on a plain" (p. 275), on a gorgeously pacific sea. It was

> one transparent blue morning, when a stillness almost preternatural spread over the sea, however unattended with any stagnant calm; when the long burnished sun-glade on the waters seemed a golden finger laid across them, enjoining some secresy; when the slippered waves whispered together as they softly ran on ...

Into this scene of peace obtrudes the giant squid, a weirdly horrific anticipation of the White Whale; this

> great white mass lazily rose, and rising higher and higher, and disentangling itself from the azure, at last gleamed before our prow like a snow-slide, new slid from the hills.

122. *Works*, I, 4.

This "unearthly, formless, chance-like apparition of life" with no percep-
tible face or front ..., no conceivable token of either sensation or
instinct" (p. 276), emerges from the noumenal depths of the sea,
breaching its empherally calm surface and dispersing its beauties.

"A Squeeze of the Hand" is perhaps the only passage in *Moby-Dick* in
which the beauty and serenity of the natural world remain unmitigated by
horror. Here Ishmael squeezes the lumps out of sperm:

> As I sat there at my ease, cross-legged on the deck ... under a blue tranquil sky; the
> ship under indolent sail; and gliding so serenely along; as I bathed my hands among
> those soft, gentle globules of infiltrated tissues, woven almost within the hour; as
> they richly broke to my fingers, and discharged all their opulence, like fully ripe
> grapes their wine. (p. 414)

Approaching a state of transcendental consciousness, Ishmael laces his
writing with the inevitable and telling traces of pastoral idiom:

> ... I snuffed up that uncontaminated aroma, — literally and truly, like the smell of
> spring violets; I declare to you, that for the time I lived as in a musky meadow ...

Washing his hands and heart of the "horrible oath" he had taken to assist
in the slaying of the White Whale, Ishmael reaches an ecstatic sensation
of union with nature and man:

> Squeeze! squeeze! squeeze! all the morning long; I squeezed that sperm till a
> strange sort of insanity came over me; and I found myself unwittingly squeezing my
> co-laborers' hands in it ... Such an abounding, affectionate, friendly, loving feeling
> did this avocation beget; that at last I was continually squeezing their hands, and
> looking up into their eyes sentimentally; as much as to say, — Oh! my dear fellow
> beings, why should we longer cherish any social acerbities, or know the slightest ill-
> humor or envy! Come; let us squeeze hands all round; nay, let us all squeeze
> ourselves into each other; let us squeeze ourselves universally into the very milk
> and sperm of kindness. (pp. 414-415)

The diffusion of the self in this passage is suggestive of Emerson, but the
transcendental experience it celebrates is less visionary than erotic.[123] In
this respect Melville would seem to have anticipated Whitman. In any
case, the sense of biologistic unity with nature that emerges in this
passage also surfaces in "The Grand Armada," the chapter in which
Ishmael's whaleboat is dragged into the midst of a shoal of mating
whales; "We glided between two whales," he reports,

---

123. One might say homo-erotic; the chapter that follows "A Squeeze of the Hand"
opens with a description of the "grandissimus" or phallus of the whale. Yet this
passage concludes with Ishmael's idea that all "attainable felicity" lies with "the wife,
the bed, the table, the saddle, the fire-side, the country" (i.e., with a conventional
conjugal life). Leslie A. Fiedler sees a "peculiar American Form of innocent
homosexuality" in *Moby-Dick* (*Love and Death in the American Novel* [New York:
Criterion Books, 1960], p. 531), but his narrow perspective lacks the reasonable
balance of Newton Arvin's reading of the "oneiric" level of the book (*Herman
Melville*, pp. 170-182).

into the innermost heart of the shoal, as if from some mountain torrent we had slid into a serene valley lake. Here the storms in the roaring glens between the outermost whales, were heard but not felt. In this central expanse the sea presented that smooth satin-like surface, called a sleek, produced by the subtle moisture thrown off by the whale in his more quiet moods. (pp. 384-385)

Of this scene is fashioned another of Melville's seascape-as-landscape tropes. Though "surrounded by circle upon circle of consternations" the whales "serenely revelled in dalliance and delight" (p. 385);

But even so, amid the tornadoed Atlantic of my being, do I myself still for ever centrally disport in mute calm; and while ponderous planets of unwaning woe revolve round me, deep down and deep inland there I still bathe me in eternal mildness of joy.

Within the shoal the mating and nursing whales seem "domesticated" by "some spell," and they regard the whalemen with "wondrous fearlessness," "confidence," and peace. Yet what seemed to Ishmael a genuine state of repose at the center of the whale's existence proves to be a temporary, "becharmed panic," a "stationary fright" (p. 388). The "entranced" (p. 387) scene of peace and harmony breaks into chaos, the "tornadoed Atlantic" that is the chronic condition of nature.

There can be no doubt that as a seaman Melville had himself experienced the state of transcendental consciousness, so vivid is evocation of it in *Mardi's* first chapter. Once mounted high on the mast-head his narrator reports that

To and fro, and all over the towers of this Nineveh in the sky, flew troops of birds. Watching them long, one crossed my sight, flew through a low arch, and was lost to view. My spirit must have sailed in with it; for directly, as in a trance, came upon me the cadence of mild billows laving a beach of shells, the waving of boughs, and the voices of maidens, and the lulled beatings of my own dissolved heart, all blended together.[124]

During the composition of *Moby-Dick*, however, he began to examine the idea of the transcendental dissolution of self with doubt and a measure of hostility. Writing to Hawthorne in June of 1851 about the personal unfoldings that he was experiencing, he lampooned the idea as he found it in Goethe:

In reading some of Goethe's sayings, so worshipped by his votaries, I came across this, *"Live in the all."* That is to say, your separate identity is but a wretched one, — good; but get out of yourself, spread and expand yourself, and bring to yourself the tinglings of life that are felt in the planets Saturn and Venus, and the Fixed stars. What nonsense! Here is a fellow with a raging toothache. "My dear boy," Goethe says to him, "you are sorely afflicted with that tooth; but you must *live in the all*, and then you will be happy!" As with all great genius, there is an immense deal of

124. *Mardi*, p. 8.

flummery in Goethe, and in proportion to my own contact with him, a monstrous deal of it in me.[125]

But as though to temper this disparaging reflection, Melville appended a postscript to his letter:

N.B. This "all" feeling, though, there is some truth in. You must often have felt it, lying on the grass on a warm summer's day. Your legs seem to send out shoots into the earth. Your hair feels like leaves upon your head. This is the *all* feeling, but what plays the mischief with the truth is that men will insist upon the *universal application of a temporary feeling or opinion.*[126]

Throughout *Moby-Dick* Melville insists on the ephemerality of the "all feeling"; it is only "for that time" that Ishmael spent squeezing sperm that he "lived in a musky meadow" (p. 414) and it is only in a rare and brief-lived calm, amid "the beauty and brilliancy of the ocean's skin," that one "forgets the tiger heart that pants beneath it; and would not willingly remember, that this velvet paw but conceals a remorseless fang" (p. 486).

The "all feeling" may, as in the "Squeeze of the Hand" and "The Grand Armada," provide a brief respite from the insularity of the self, from the estrangement from the "tornadoed Atlantic" of nature, but it may also carry the gravest of liabilities. For the cabin-boy Pip the price of experiencing the all is madness. Abandoned at sea on a "beautiful, bounteous, blue day," Pip finds himself, no less than "the sun, another lonely castaway," lost amid the "intolerable," "awful lonesomeness" of space. "The intense concentration of self in the middle of such a heartless immensity, my God! who can tell it?" exclaims Ishmael (p. 412). Recovered to the ship, the boy is an idiot:

The sea had jeeringly kept his finite body up, but drowned the infinite of his soul. Not drowned entirely, though, Rather carried down alive to wondrous depths, where strange shapes of the unwarped primal world glided to and fro before his passive eyes; and the miser-merman, Wisdom, revealed his hoarded heaps; and among the joyous, heartless, ever-juvenile eternities, Pip saw the multitudinous, God-omnipresent, coral insects, that out of the firmament of waters heaved the colossal orbs. He saw God's foot upon the treadle of the loom, and spoke it; and therefore his shipmates called him mad. (p. 413)

"So man's insanity is heaven's sense," concludes Ishmael, and in so doing he touches upon what is perhaps the ultimate source of man's alienation. The noumenal reality of nature, "the unwarped primal world," seems to

125. *Letters*, pp. 130-131. Davis and Gilman (*Letters*, p. 131n) note that the precise source of the phrase from Goethe has not been found. "Und im Ganzen, Guten, Schonen / Resolut zu leben," a phrase in Goethe's "Generalbeichte," was translated by Carlyle as "To live .. in the Whole" (*Critical and Miscellaneous Essays* [Boston, 1839], III, 205).

126. *Letters*, p. 131; emphasis added in concluding sentence.

man's reason "absurd and frantic." Knowing the noumenon, man is left "indifferent as his God."

The implications of "The Castaway" chapter are clearly inimical to the faith in the "all feeling" fostered by Concord as well as European transcendentalists, and they also effectively counter the faith the nationalists had invested in the sublime as the mark of a special covenant between God and Americans. But the most damning critique of the transcendental experience as well as the cult of the sublime is Melville's chapter on "The Mast-Head." After the manner of his favorite seventeenth-century essayists, Melville fashions this chapter as an anatomy of sublime promontories and the phenomenology of the sublime. Through it he exposes the egregious glossing of vital distinctions between mind and matter that attends the transcendental vision.

The context of Ishmael's discourse on mast-head standing is the immense tide of interest in optical phenomena and vision generally that rose in the early eighteenth century and crested in the cult of the sublime and picturesque of the romantic age. At the very start of the anatomy of the mast-head it is clear that we are to take the mast-head as but one type of the countless methods man has employed to expand — literally and metaphorically — his vision. In keeping with his abiding inclination to trace all things to their remotest origins, Ishmael begins at the beginning:

> Now, as the business of standing mast-heads, ashore or afloat, is a very ancient and interesting one, let us in some measure expatiate here. I take it, that the earliest standers of mast-heads were the old Egyptians; because, in all my researches, I find none prior to them. For though their progenitors, the builders of Babel, must doubtless, by their tower, have intended to rear the loftiest mast-head in all Asia, or Africa either; yet (ere the final truck was put to it) as that great stone mast of theirs may be said to have gone by the board, in the dread gale of God's over the wrath ; therefore we cannot give these Babel builders priority over the Egyptians. And that the Eqyptians were a nation of masthead standers. is an assertion based upon the general belief among archaeologists, that the first pyramids were founded for astronomical purposes; a theory singularly supported by the peculiar stair-like formations of all four sides of these edifices; whereby with prodigious long upliftings of their legs, those old astronomers were wont to mount to the apex, and sing out for new stars; even as the look-outs of a modern ship sing out for a sail, or a whale just bearing in sight. (p. 151)

Shifting the focus of this delightful digression from the mast-head standers of the land to those of the sea, Ishmael develops what is ostensibly a celebration of the prospect afforded by the mast-head. As such his digression is basically apposite to such prospect writings as Willis' "View from West Point" (1840), Hawthorne's "Sights from a Steeple" (1831), Parson's *Book of Niagara Falls* (1836), Thoreau's "Ktaadn" (1864), and scores of less finished peformances in the mode. As though parodying a traveling essayist's critique of a Catskill mountain hostelry, he laments that the whaleship's mast-head "should be so sadly destitute of anything approaching a cosy inhabitiveness, or adapted to breed a comfortable localness of feeling"[127] (p. 153). Behind this disarming humor, Ishmael moves his reader toward the hostile environment of Greylock's sublime summit:

> To be sure, in cold weather you may carry your house aloft with you, in the shape of a watch-coat; but properly speaking the thickest watch-coat is no more of a house than the unclad body; for as the soul is glued inside of its fleshly tabernacle. and cannot freely move about in it, nor even move out it, without running great risk of perishing (like an ignorant pilgrim crossing the snowy Alps in winter); so a watch-coat is not so much of a house as it is a mere envelope, or additional skin encasing you. (pp. 153-154)

The amusing digressiveness of this passage all but coneals its satiric barb. Idealists may postulate that the physical universe is but the garb of the Oversoul, but the individual soul, glued within its watch-coat the body, is not thereby relieved of the constant struggle for survival.

Ishmael warns the reader of the "bewitching effect" of the masthead promontory, of the "sublime uneventfulness" of the infinite "watery pastures" (p. 155) that entrances the mind at such a height. Numbering himself among the masses of water-gazers, he confesses that he kept a poor watch at the mast-head:

> With the problem of the universe revolving in me, how could I — being left completely to myself at such a thought-engendering altitude, — how could I but lightly hold my obligations to observe all what-ships' standing orders? (pp. 155-156)

With the mast-head as stage, Melville places in opposition visionary transcendentalism and the practical exigencies of survival, as Ishmael admonishes ship-owners against employing any dreamy young Idealist, "given to unseasonable meditativeness; and who offers to ship with the Phaedon instead of Bowditch in his head" (p. 156). (In the *Phaedon* Plato argued for the immortality of the soul on the grounds that the mind is capable of divorcing itself from physical sensation; Bowditch authored a prosaic seaman's manual.) Ishmael warns that the

> ... sunken-eyed young Platonist will take you ten wakes round the world, and never make you one pint of sperm the richer. Nor are these monitions at all unneeded. For nowadays, the whale-fishery furnishes an asylum for many romantic, melan-

---

127. Cf. Evert Duyckinck's lamentation of the discomforts of Greylock's summit and the disrepair of the Williams College Observatory near the mountaintop ("An Ascent of Mount Saddleback," *Literary World* 9 [August 30, 1851]: 162-163). Melville's satire on "improved mast-heads" had as its specific target William Scoresby — lampooned as "Fogo von Slack" and "Doctor Snodhead" in *Moby-Dick* — who had included a digression on improved crow's nest in his *Account of the Arctic Regions* (Sealts, *Checklist*, entry no. 450). On the complicated use of other sources in the Mast-Head chapter see Vincent, *The Trying Out of "Moby-Dick*," pp. 146-160.

choly, and absent-minded young men, disgusted with the carking cares of earth, and seeking sentiments in tar and blubber. (p. 156)

The interpenetration of the life of the mind and the "tar and blubber" of sensational experience pervades *Moby-Dick* so thoroughly as to be its informing theme. Yet as Ishmael develops his anatomy of the transcendental sublime he exposes the mortal dangers inherent in it; the transcendental melding of mind and matter, the "all feeling" of the letter to Hawthorne, is temporary and frightfully delusive. Delving into the psychological dynamics of the sublime, Ishmael argues that a Platonist mounted on the mast-head may become so

... lulled into such an opium-like listlessness of vacant, unconscious reverie by the blending cadence of waves with thoughts, that at lest he loses his identity; takes the mystic ocean at his feet for the visible image of that deep, blue, bottomless soul pervading mankind and nature ... In this enchanted mood, thy spirit ebbs away to whence it came; becomes diffused through time and space ... (pp. 156-157)

"But while this sleep, this dream is on ye," he continues,

move your foot or hand an inch; slip your hold at all; and your identity comes back in horror. Over Descartian vortices ye hover. And perhaps, at midday, with one half-throttled shriek you drop through that transparent air into the summer sea, no more to rise for ever. Heed it well, ye Pantheists! (p. 157)

That the deluded Platonist falls to his death through specifically Cartesian space suggests Melville's subtly intelligent grasp of the history of the ideas with which he deals. He surely knew that Descartes' theory of vortices had been wholly supplanted by Newtonian physics,[128] but he also knew that Cartesian dualism had been the formidable and tenacious barrier against which idealistic monists — most notably Kant, Coleridge, and Emerson — had necessarily pitted themselves. He had read, in the eighth chapter of his edition of *Biographia Literaria*, the passage in which Coleridge designated Descartes as the father of modern philosophical dualism; "To the best of my knowledge," wrote Coleridge,

Des Cartes was the first philospher who introduced the absolute and essential heterogeneity of the soul as intelligence and the body as matter ... The soul was a thinking substance and the body was a space filling substance.[129]

He also knew — directly and through the *Biographia* — of David Hartley's attempts in his *Observations on Man* to mitigate Cartesian

128. His source of information on Cartesian physics was very probably Ephraim Chambers' *Cyclopaedia: or, An Universal Dictionary of Arts and Sciences* ... (London: Knapton, 1728) (Sealts, *Checklist*, entry no. 128); precisely the sort of arcane compendium of which Melville was especially fond, the *Cyclopaedia* contains a wealth of information on the theory of vortices and Cartesianism generally, and Chambers offers incisive comparisons of Cartesian and Newtonian physics (s.v. "Vortex," "Cartesianism," "Gravity," "Fluid," and "Newtonian Physics").

129. *Biographia Literaria*, ed. J. Shawcross (oxford: Oxford University Press, 1907), I, 88. all subsequent passages from *Biographia Literaria* are drawn form this edition.

dualism through the associationist theory of the relation between mind and matter. Through the broaching of the Cartesian vortex Melville thus fostered incisively critical implications on both metaphysical and epistemological fronts; the fall from the masthead exposes at once the disunity of the soul and the body's exigencies of survival and also the horrific possibility that the material world is itself primarily a spiritless, mechanistic void.[130]

The most subtly subversive effect of the aesthetic argument in *Moby-Dick* rises from the way Melville compounds his attack on the American convention of the sublime with an attack on conventional notions of natural beauty. Perhaps even more elusive in meaning than the sublime, the concept of the beautiful had become, in his day, all but empty of specificity. It may well be that Locke had set in motion a progressive destablization of the term through his designation of the traditional requisites of natural beauty as secondary — and illusory — attributes rather than qualities of matter. In any case, when they were not referring to women, or to the good, or to a tempered form of sublimity, Melville's contemporaries wrote of the experience of the beautiful in nature as an attributive process of mind. "After all," wrote the painter Cole, "beauty is in the mind. A scene is rather an index to feelings and associations."[131] Melville was fully capable of a graceful suffusion of beauty in landscape or seascape description, but the conventionally pastoral idiom he tends to employ as vehicle always taints natural beauty with a hint of meretriciousness. The "little flock of sheep," the "farmer's banded children" who go "a-nutting"[132] in "The Piazza" are, no less than the calms in *Moby-Dick* that seem "some glad May-time, when the flowers of the woods are plucked" (p. 486), purposefully overwrought vestiges of Spenserian or sentimental pastoral. They establish a kind of fairyland purposefully set up for destruction.[133] But perhaps the most potent dimension of Melville's assault on naive naturalistic aestheticism rises from the manner in which he justaposes or fuses beauty with horror and thereby renders it ambiguous if not insidious. The sea upon which Pip is abandoned is, like the sea from which the horrid squid emerges and

---

130. "The physical principle of Cartesianism is this, that *nothing exists but substances*; which appears a dangerous principle to the divines" (Chambers, *Cyclopaedia*, s.v. "Cartesian Philosophy").

131. Thomas Cole as cited by Louis Legrand Noble, *The Life and Works of Thomas Cole*, ed. Elliot S. Vesell (Cambridge: Belknap Press of Harvard University Press, 1964), p. 145.

132. *Piazza Tales*, p. 6.

133. On this subject as it pertains to "The Piazza" see Breinig, "The Destruction of Fairyland," pp. 254-283; the function of pastoral imagery in *Moby-Dick* has yet to be studied.

into which the Platonist falls, invested with exquisite, almost supernatural beauty. The "most dreaded creatures of the sea," Ishmael several
times remarks, "glide under water, unapparent for the most part, and
treacherously hidden beneath the loveliest tints of azure"; the shark, one
of nature's "most remorseless tribes," is marked by a "dainty embellished
shape," a "devilish brilliance and beauty" (p. 274).[134] In discussing the
whale's tail as a mortal weapon, Ishmael celebrates the "graceful flexion
of its motions; where infantileness of ease undulates through a Titanism
of power"; it is from their graceful ease that the tail's motions "derive
their most appalling beauty" (p. 373).

Beauty that "appalls" — the term and its cognates are among
Melville's favorites — is not conventional beauty but the sublime, and it
is toward this aesthetic that Melville's romance unremittingly drives.
Foreshadowing their response to the White Whale, the crew of the
Pequod face the giant squid with eyes askance and curse the "appalling
beauty of the vast milky mass, that ... glistened like a living opal in the
spangling sun" (p. 257). Ishmael, of course, tirelessly subverts any stable
moral signification of the beautiful as he delves in his cetological
anatomizing past apparent qualities of nature toward its sublime,
noumenal essence. For him Moby Dick is all that appalls in the universe,
and it is the whale's whiteness — that chromatic correlative of noumenal
reality — that "above all things appalled" (p. 185). Ishmael's cerebral
quest is developed in apposition to Ahab's active quest; together the two
pierce through the world of appearances, the level of attributive beauty,
to the noumenal, qualitative level of matter. Ahab's quest, no less than
Ishmael's, is developed in terms of aesthetic categories of experience. "I
leave a white and turbid wake," Ahab muses in "The Sunset," "pale
waters, paler cheeks, where'er I sail. The envious billows sidelong swell to
whelm my track; let them; but first I pass." The sun, whose "gold brow
plumbs the blue," sets "by the ever-brimming goblet's rim";

> Oh! time was, when as the sunrise nobly spurred me, so the sunset soothed. No
> more. This lovely light, it lights not me; all loveliness is anguish to me, since I can
> ne'er enjoy. Gifted with the high perception, I lack the low, enjoying power;
> damned, most subltly and malignantly! damned in the midst of Paradise! (p. 165)

Ahab's "low, enjoying power" and "high perception" correspond,
analogically, to the beautiful and the sublime. Beyond his white and
blighting wake lies the apparent "paradise" of color and beauty, the
"ever-brimming goblet" of earth. Ahead, bereft of the secondary attri-

134. The beauty of the shark seems to have held speical fascination for Melville; he
digressed in *Mardi* on the shark's "horrific serentiy of aspect" (p. 41), developed that
aspect into the metaphoric "sharkishness" of the natural world in *Moby-Dick* (pp.
148, 250-252, and passim), and, late in his career, devoted to it "The Maldive Shark,"
a fine lyric.

butes of matter, lies pure inhuman sublimity. Which is to say, ahead lies
Moby Dick.

There is, to be sure, a full measure of beauty associated with Moby
Dick, but it is an insidiously ambiguous beauty. The "Spirit Spout," the
gorgeous and portentous talisman of the whale, seems to lure the
whaleship toward its prey; there reigns aboard the *Pequod*

> a sense of peculiar dread at this flitting apparition, as if it were treacherously
> beckoning us on and on, in order that the monster might turn round upon us, and
> rend us at last in the remotest and most savage seas.

These "apprehensions" derived

> a wondrous potency from the contrasting serenity of the weather, in which,
> beneath all its blue blandness, some thought there lurked a devilish charm, as for
> day and days we voyaged along, through seas so wearily, lonesomely mild, that all
> space, in repugnance to our vengeful errand, seemed vacating itself of life before
> our urn-like prow. (p. 232)

The frightfully ominous and ambiguous beauty of the spirit spout plays
upon Ahab's mind so that he becomes prepared "to connect the ideas of
mildness and repose with the ... particular whale he sought" (p. 276). And
it is in fact amid an exquisitely mild and beautiful sea that the White
Whale breaches. In "The Chase — First Day" the sea "seemed drawing a
carpet over its waves; seemed a noon-meadow, so serenely it spread."
Moby Dick's "dazzling hump was distinctly visible, sliding along the sea
as if an isolated thing, and continually set in a revolving ring of finest,
fleecy, greenish foam." As he parted each swell "on each bright side, the
whale shed off enticings." His "serenity," his "quietude," is "the vesture
of tornadoes" but he is "Yet clam, enticing calm ..." (pp. 539-540). This
peculiar concatenation of mildness and might is rendered in what must
surely be one of the finest paragraphs in the language:

> A gentle joyousness — a mighty mildness of repose in swiftness, invested the
> gliding whale. Not the white bull Jupiter swimming away with ravished Europa
> clinging to his graceful horns; his lovely, leering eyes sideways intent upon the
> maid; with smooth bewitching fleetness, rippling straight for the nuptial bower in
> Crete; not Jove, not that great majesty Supreme! did surpass the glorified White
> Whale as he so divinely swam. (p. 539)

Not merely god-like but unsurpassed by gods, this beast is so superlative
as to be definable only in terms of what he is not. Transcending
comparison, it transcends language. But however unlimited, its significance somehow unspeakably transcends the sublime of nature that
American romantics — especially nationalist romantics — had hailed as
the expression of God and the mark of His special covenant with man:

> And thus, through the serene tranquilities of the tropical sea, among waves whose
> hand-clappings were suspended by exceeding rapture, Moby Dick moved on, still
> withholding from sight the full terrors of his submerged trunk, entirely hiding the

wrenched hideousness of his jaw. But soon the fore part of him slowly rose from the water; for an instant his whole marbleized body formed a high arch, like Virginia's Natural Bridge, and warningly waving his bannered flukes in the air, the grand god revealed himself, sounded, and went out of sight. (p. 540)

More than the leviathan of Job, with whom no covenant may be made, and infinitely more than Jonah's whale, that merely chastening agent of Jehovah, this beast seems the cipher neither of a beneficent nor indifferent universe but rather of a universe insidiously malevolent.

Two Seascapes: The Moral and Horrific Sublime

In the heart of the cetological sections of *Moby-Dick*, Ishmael devotes an entire chapter to the peaking of the whale's flukes as "perhaps the grandest sight to be seen in all animated nature":

Out of the bottomless profundities the gigantic tail seems spasmodically snatching at the highest heaven. So in dreams, have I seen majestic Satan thrusting forth his tormented colossal claw from the flame Baltic of Hell. But in gazing at such scenes, it is all in all what mood you are in; if in the Dantean, the devils will occur to you; if in that of Isaiah, the arch-angels. (p. 375)

Often misread as evidence of Ishmael's alleged epistemological solipsism, this passage is concerned not so much with the subjectivity of experience as it is with the emotive and moral ambivalence of the sublime. The tendency of the sublime to break down or resolve itself into one of two emotive states, the one horrific and the other marked by the sense of portentous moral presence or of the immanence of an omnipotent God, is a striking index of the aesthetic's abiding instability. Marjorie Nicolson's definition of the experience of the sublime as a species of awe that is "compounded of mingled terror and exultation"[135] points out the psychological source of that instability, for awe is the brief-lived meeting of two ultimately antipodal emotive states, terror and exultation. Unlike the static emotive state traditionally regarded as the effect of ideal beauty, the state effected by sublimity is kinetic yet, paradoxically, held in unstable arrest as the mind is torn between loathing and desire, or — and in this is suggested the important relation of sublimity to tragedy — fear and pity. This unstable meeting of conflicting emotion is precisely that which Melville engaged in that oxymoric phrase, "appalling beauty." The sustaining link between the romance and the anatomy in *Moby-Dick*, between Ahab's active hunt and Ishmael's intellectual hunt, is the apposition of killing and knowing, of harpoon and pen.[136] As anatomist,

135. *Mountain Gloom and Mountain Glory*, p. 143.

136. The complex question of genre in *Moby-Dick* has spawned a great deal of commentary; more important discussions of the matter include Herbert S. Donow, "Herman Melville and the Craft of Fiction," *Modern Language quarterly* 25 (Spring

121

Ishmael is as heavily and variously armed as Ahab, and, considering Melville's creative milieu and personal interests, it is not surprising to find painting among Ishmael's most important instruments of definition. What Sharon Furrow has called Melville's "highly developed pictorial sense"[137] was no doubt refined by his strong and abiding interest in the plastic arts. The study of painting, Leon Howard has said, was "one of his favorite hobbies,"[138] and the notes and markings in his extensive library of art books demonstrates, according to the foremost student of his marginalia, that "he was eager to learn how plastic artists could, for example, impart movement to still forms with the play of color or light and darkness."[139] His interest was no doubt abetted by the New York literati with whom he associated between 1846 and 1851. There were at least six painters — Sanford Gifford, Daniel Huntington, Charles Lanman, William Sidney Mount, William Page, and R. W. Weir — connected rather closely with the Duyckinck brothers,[140] whose *Literary World* ran a sophisticated column of art criticism in nearly every number. Evert Duyckinck served on the board of the American Art-Union, and at the gala opening of the Union's 1847 season he introduced Melville to Mount and to the poet Bryant, who was himself intimately acquainted with several American landscapists. Both at home and, as his journals indicate, abroad, Melville became an inveterate haunter of galleries. His fondness for the sort of dramatic chiaroscuro typified by the work of Salvator Rosa was probably stimulated by readings in the British Gothic novel, but he seems to have achieved, by the mid-eighteen-fifties, a remarkable catholicity of taste; "At the Hostelry," an unpublished verse narrative he probably wrote after his second trip to Europe in 1856, comments briefly but with more than amateurish insight on Giotto, Leonardo, Claude Lorraine, Salvator Rosa, Jan Steen, Vandyck, Franz Hals, Tintoretto, Teniers, Van der Velde, Van Tromp, De Ruyter,

1964): 181-186; Joel Porte, *The Romance in America* (Middletown, Conn.: Wesleyan University Press, 1969), pp. 152-192; Seelye, *Melville: The Ironic Diagram*, pp. 1-73; Arvin, *Herman Melville*, pp. 51-60; and Paul McCarthy, "Elements of Anatomy in Melville's Fiction," *Studies in the Novel* 6 (Spring 1974): 38-61.

137. "The Terrible Made Visible: Melville, Salvator Rosa, and Piranesi," *ESQ* 19 (Fourth quarter 1973): 237.

138. *Herman Melville*, p. 330.

139. Walker Cowen, "Melville's Marginalia," (unpublished Ph.D. dissertation, Harvard University, 1965); as cited by Hershel Parker, ed., *The Recognition of Herman Melville* (Ann Arbor: University of Michigan Press, 1967), p. 343.

140. For this information I am indebted to Professor A. John Roche III of the University of Rhode Island, who is the author of a forthcoming biography of Evert Duyckinck.

122

Watteau, Constable, Durer, and other continental masters.[141]
American painters of Melville's generation who were especially anxious to exploit the sublime of nature in the cause of cultural nationalism were alive to the antipodal emotive effects of the aesthetic. They, no less than their British contemporaries, saw Salvator Rosa as the master of the terrifying sublime and Claude as the master of the gentler, gorgeous sublime that effected exultation.[142] Such American landscapists as Cole, Durand, and Allston were inclined to be suspicious of Rosa's horrific sublime, for they were acutely aware of the difficulty of reconciling the terrors of nature with the idea that the sublime of nature signalled forth God's special covenant with Americans. They were also aware, however, that the covenant symbolized in American nature was comprised, as George P. Marsh put it, of both "promises and menaces,"[143] and for the latter they saw Rosa's horrific topographies as an appropriate expressive vehicle. What came to be referred to as the "false sublime" of merely terrifying, Rosa-like landscapes might be redeemed and rendered "true" or "moral sublime" if terror was imaged as the awesome warning, the "menace," of a just but angry God.[144]

Melville fully grasped the implications of the debate over the horrific and the moral sublime, for that debate is dramatized in the opening chapters of *Moby-Dick*. In the New Bedford church of Father Mapple and in the Spouter-Inn, two buildings that function metaphorically as elaborate portals or entries through which the reader passes into the world of *Moby-Dick*, Ishmael encounters paintings that function iconographically as visions of the moral and of the horrific sublime.

The New Bedford chapel in which Ishmael attends services prior to

141. On Melville and Rosa see Furrow, pp. 237-248. Newton Arvin has suggested that Melville was introduced to Rosa through the Gothic novels in which he had read deeply prior to the writing of *Moby-Dick*; see "Melville and the Gothic Novel," *New England Quarterly* 22 (March 1949), p. 36. Frank Jewett Mather, Jr., who visited the apartment in which the Melville's lived in their later years, reported that the walls were hung with prints by Rosa as well as Claude; see "Herman Melville," *The Review* 1, No. 14 (August 16, 1919): 299.

142. See Sanford, *The Quest for Paradise*, especially pp. 138-145. Sanford notes that "influential American critics" who used the terminology of the Salvatorean and Claudian sublime included Rufus Griswold, Margaret Fuller, Henry Tuckerman, Ralph Waldo Emerson, Gulian C. Verplanck, James J. Jarves, Hugh S. Legare, Edgar Allan Poe, Hugh Swinton Legare, George T. Tucker, Charles Lanman, and Richard H. Dana (p. 141n). The terminology was employed by art and literary critics alike in this age devoted to the credo *ut pictura poesis*.

143. *Address* ..., p. 24; as cited by Poenicke, "A View from the Piazza," p. 277.

144. Representative of this American moral sublime are Cole's *The Expulsion from the Garden of Eden*, Trumbull's *The Last Family Who Perished in the Deluge* and Allston's *Elija in the Desert* and *The Deluge*.

Plate VI. Thomas Cole, *The Voyage of Life*: *Manhood* (1840). Munson-Williams-Proctor Institute, Utica, New York.

Plate VII. Thomas Cole, *The Voyage of Life: Old Age* (1840). Muson-Williams-Proctor Institute, Utica, New York.

shipping aboard presents an orthodox Christian view of the terrors of the sea as trial of faith. The painting that graces its wall dramatizes in chiaroscuro the promise of Christian salvation from the chaotic sea of a fallen world. It depicts

> ...a gallant ship beating against a terrible storm off a lee coast of black rocks and snowy breakers. But high above the flying scud and dark-rolling clouds, there floated a little isle of sunlight, from which beamed forth an angel's face; and this bright face shed a distinct spot of radiance upon the ship's tossed deck, something like that silver plate now inserted into the Victory's plank where Nelson fell. "Ah, noble ship," the angel seemed to say, "beat on, beat on, thou noble ship, and bear a hardy helm; for lo! the sun is breaking through; the clouds are rolling off — serenest azure is at hand." (pp. 38-39)[145]

This typical rendering of the moral sublime may have had an actual antecedent in a canvas "representing a ship in stiff breeze off a lee shore" that hung, reported John Ross Dix,[146] in the seaman's chapel in Boston. In any case, the painting's baldly allegorical devices were already commonplace when Melville took them up. Two of them need no more comment than is provided in Ishmael's gloss. "Yes, the world's a ship on its voyage out, and not a voyage complete," he remarks. The pulpit like the prow of the ship is "this earth's foremost part" and from it "the storm of God's quick wrath is first descried" (p. 39). A third device — the bright spot of distant azure in the stormy sky — is related to its painterly origins by the words of the painter Cole: "In the pure blue sky is the highest sublime," he wrote: "There we look into the uncurtained, solemn serene — into the infinite — toward the throne of the Almighty."[147]

"The Voyage of Life," Cole's massive, panoramic series in oil, strikingly evinces the tendency of American landscapists to move from the objective to the ideal and on to the allegorized moral sublime. Melville may have had the series in mind when he composed the chapel painting, for he most likely saw them on exhibit in the New York Art-Union. They trace the progress of the soul from a platonic cave through the turbulent waters of life. No matter how wild, dark, and ominous Cole's landscape becomes, the soul is beckoned on to distant azure by the divine light of a ministering angel. The chapel painting shares with *The Voyage of Life: Manhood* [Pl. VI] and *The Voyage of Life: Old Age* [Pl. VII] the promise of God's ultimate intervention in the chaos that is

---

145. Thomas C. Carlson has pointed out that the tetrameter and trimeter rhythms of the imagined angel's pronouncement are those of the ballad as well as of Protestant hymns; see "Ishmael as Art Critic: Double Metrical Irony in *Moby-Dick*," *Extracts* 20 (November 1974): 2-3.

146. *Pulpit Portraits ... of Distinguished Divines* (Boston, 1854); as cited by Allan MacDonald, "A Sailor Among the Transcendentalists," *New England Quarterly* 8 (September 1935): 307-319.

147. Cole as cited by Noble, *The Life and Works of Thomas Cole*, p. 282.

124

earth, and so corresponds to the Christian stoicism of Father Mapple's sermon.

Like the painting that is its emblem, Mapple's sermon is an apologia for natural evil; the apparent chaos of nature is the instrument with which God redeems sinful man as He redeemed Jonah. Yet the view from the chapel is, Melville demonstrates throughout *Moby-Dick*, no less an illusory perspective than the view from "The Piazza." Ishmael's rescue notwithstanding, the denouement of Melville's voyage of life is met not in salvation but in catastrophe, and the measure of "serenest azure" that is at hand in the book seems as much the work of an insidiously conspiring God as the of emblem his mercy. Even as Melville presents Father Mapple's Christian theodicy he insinuates its inadequacy. Mapple's sermon is formally an exegesis of the Book of Jonah, but the mythos of nature as he presents it seems drawn from the Book of Job; the seaman's life in Mapple's vision is less beneficently and divinely ordained than horrific. Ishmael specifically describes the whale pursued by Ahab as "a Job's whale" (p. 183), and, Job-like, both he and Ahab define the whale not as instrument of a beneficent and merciful God but as a tormenting expression of "all evil," "all the subtle demonisms of life and thought" (p. 181). And it is of course the Book of Job, a darkly ambiguous theodicy, that provides the extract with which *Moby-Dick* begins as well as the epilogue with which it ends.[148]

Far more telling in significance than the chapel painting is the canvas Ishmael encounters in the Spouter-Inn, the building that serves as a kind of secular portal to *Moby-Dick*. As is the case with the general canvas of *Moby-Dick*, dark chaos rules so mightily in this painting as to blot all light.

The iconographic significance of the painting in the Spouter-Inn has long been recognized;[149] this canvas and Ishmael's encounter with it stand as a redaction of *Moby-Dick*'s profound purposes as well as its tactics of presentation. Melville's multiple perspectives on the whale, his delvings into mythology, cetology, paleontology, and a spate of other disciplines,

148. For an assessment of the significance of the Book of Job in *Moby-Dick* and a reading of Ishmael's vision as Jobian, see Nathalia Wright, "Moby Dick: Jonah's or Job's Whale?" *American Literature* 37 (May 1965): 190-195. It should be noted here that the Book of Job, with *Paradise Lost*, is the most often cited work of literature in eighteenth-century discourse on the sublime; see, for example, Burke's *Enquiry*, pp. 63, 65-66, 67, and Robert Lowth, *Lectures on the Sacred Poetry of the Hewbrews*, trans. G. Gregory (London, 1787), II, 428, 424.

149. The most incisive reading of the painting's significance is Howard P. Vincent's "Ishmael, Writer and Art Critic," in *Themes and Directions in American Literature*, ed. Ray B. Browne and Donald Pizer (Lafeyette, Indiana: Purdue University Press, 1969), pp. 69-79. See also Edward H. Rosenberry, *Melville and the Comic Spirit* (Cambridge: Harvard University Press, 1955), pp. 135-136.

find their synecdochic analogs in Ishmael's "diligent study" of the obscure painting, his "series of systematic visits to it," and "careful inquiry of the neighbors" in regard to the meaning of the painting, while the many tactics employed in Melville's attempts to define Moby Dick are imaged in the great array of mangled whaling implements and weapons that are hung on the wall opposite the painting. The picture is a perfect emblem of the book, and the manner in which Ishmael engages it is metonymous with the over-reaching design of Melville's argument.

The painting is

> ... so thoroughly besmoked, and every way defaced, that in the unequal crosslights in which you viewed it, it was only by diligent study and a series of systematic visits to it, and careful inquiry of the neighbors, that you could in any way arrive at an understanding of its purpose. Such unaccountable masses of shades and shadows, that at first you almost thought some ambitious young artist, in the time of the New England hags, had endeavored to delineate chaos bewitched. But by dint of much and earnest contemplation, and oft repeated ponderings, and especially by throwing open a little window towards the back of the entry, you at last come to the conclusion that such an idea, however wild, might not be altogether unwarranted. (p. 10)

As Ishmael struggles to ascertain what thing in nature the picture might objectify, he fixes his gaze on a mass in its center:

> But what most puzzled and confounded you was a long, limber, portentous black mass of something hovering in the centre of the picture over three blue, dim, perpendicular lines floating in a nameless yeast. A boggy, soggy, squitchy picture truly, enough to drive a nervous man distracted. Yet was there a sort of indefinite, half-attained, unimaginable sublimity about it that fairly froze you to it, till you involuntarily took an oath with yourself to find out what that marvellous painting meant. Ever and anon a bright, but, alas, deceptive idea would dart you through. — It's the Black Sea in a midnight gale. — It's the unnatural combat of the four primal elements. — It's the breaking-up of the ice-bound stream of Time. But at last all these fancies yielded to that one portentous something in the picture's midst. *That* once found out, and all the rest were plain. But stop; does it not bear a faint resemblance to a gigantic fish? even the great leviathan himself?

Finally discovered to depict a whale in the stupendous act of impaling itself on the broken masts of a typhoon-ravaged ship, this amazing fiction can only be appreciated in all its originality if it is recalled that Melville created it more than half a century before the advent of non-objective art. The search for its antecedent will foster the realization that, in creating a fit pictorial correlative for his whale and whale-hunt, Melville thrust beyond the frontiers of painterly conventions in his day.

Some light would seem to be shed on the origins of the painting through Ishmael's remark that it might have been "the endeavor of some ambitious young artist in the time of the New England hags." But this clue is probably another deceptive corsslight, for such a groping, impressionistic critique as Ishmael's could not conceivably be evoked by the sharply delineated forms, merely decorative use of color, baldness of subject matter, and ineptly static rendering of movement characteristic of primitive American art. As Roger B. Stein has pointed out,[150] aside from landwardly perceived harbor scenes that served as pilots' maps or tributes to marine commerce, true seascape painting was almost unknown in America prior to the late decades of the eighteenth century. The sea was in fact almost never a prominent feature in pre-Revolutionary American art; when it did appear it was nearly always merely glimpsed in the distance through background windows in indoor portraits of eminent persons. There were, to be sure, isolated instances of horrifically sublime American sea paintings, but even Copley's *Watson and the Shark* (1778), the most striking example, is neo-classical in the sense that the artist's compositional emphases are on control, order, and the strivings of human community.[151]

Ishmael's painting, it must be stressed, is of a ship-wreck, and, as T.S.R. Boase has elaborately demonstrated,[152] this subject did not achieve any pictorial vogue in Europe or America until the break-down of neo-classical aesthetic principles in the plastic arts during the early decades of the nineteenth century. Such an unrestrained and sensational subject as disaster at sea could hardly be accepted as long as the hegemony of Reynoldsian principle endured, but by 1818 a writer in the *Quarterly Review* could remark of shipwrecks that "The subterraneous scenes of Ann Radcliffe, and all the imaginary horrors of our melo-dramas and our tragedies, shrink to nothing before the real horrors of this dreadful catastrophe."[153] This writer's enthusiasm marks the full ascendancy of the Burkean horrific sublime and the demise of the species of neo-classical sublime that had been largely contained, for a full century, within the confines of rationalistic deism. Yet in America the acceptance of this new mode of seascape was delayed for at least two and perhaps as many as four decades. Even the most Salvatorean seascapes of Durand, Allston, and Cole — romantics who had all been exposed to European painting — fall short of the horrific and remain within the

150. *Seascape and the American Imagination*, pp. 1-36 and passim. Stein's essay accompanies a superb collection of plates.

151. Stein notes that "The formal configuration of the painting has important political overtones: [Copley's] political contemporaries had supported the Lockean order announced in the Declaration of Independence and the Constitution, but they deplored the sublime excesses of Sam Adams, Tom Paine, and above all the French Revolution; Copley shared with his artistic contemporaries the belief that art — including seascape art — aspired toward the depiction of human order and control" (p. 20).

152. "Shipwrecks in English Romantic Painting," *Journal of the Warburg and Courtauld Institute* 22 (1959): 337-344.

153. Vol. XVIII, 1818, p. 168; as cited by Boase, p. 332.

bounds of the moral sublime. It was only with the generation of painters who came of age in the later decades of the nineteenth century — Albert Pinkham Ryder, Winslow Homer, Frederick Church, and Thomas Moran — that Americans produces seascapes in any way analogous to the horrific sublime of the Spouter-Inn painting. When they did so it was under the unmistakable influence of a British master of Melville's generation, J.M.W. Turner. In the middle decades of the century only Turner's seascapes had captured the "indefinite, half-attained, unimaginable sublimity" sufficient to evoke the sort of wildly speculative response voiced by Ishmael in regard to the Spouter-Inn painting, and a variety of evidence internal and external to *Moby-Dick* suggests that Turner's seascapes may lie behind that painting.

Recording his encounter with the painting, Ishmael employs a phrase that ties the canvas to Turner's seascapes through that champion of Turner's art, John Ruskin. What "most puzzled and confounded" Ishmael in the painting was

> a long, limber, portentous black mass of something hovering in the centre of the painting over three blue, dim, perpendicular lines floating in a nameless yeast. (pp. 10-11)

"Nameless yeast" is a curious figure, even in *Moby-Dick*, a book notable for its coinages. It is a figure more likely borrowed than invented. Melville read deeply in Shakespeare during the composition of *Moby-Dick*, and possible sources might be the "yesty waves" that "confound and swallow navigation up" in *Macbeth* IV.i.53, or the "yest and froth" of the *Winter's Tale* III.iii,94. An even more probably source is Ruskin's discussion of stormy seascapes in *Modern Painters*, a passage to which Melville was exposed as early as 1848.[154] In Part II, Section V, Chapter II, "Of Water, as Painted by Turner," Ruskin devotes several pages to the "Effects of sea after prolonged storm," a subject which would be of paramount interest to Melville, who was already known in the late 'forties for his seascape descriptions. Ruskin's vision is strikingly apposite to that presented in the Spouter-Inn painting. I have italicized the most pertinent sections:

---

154. Lemuel Shaw borrowed Vol. II of the Smith, Elder edition of *Modern Painters* (London, 1846-1860) from the Boston Athenaeum while Melville was visiting his household in July, 1848; Shaw often borrowed books for his son-in-law's use. See Sealts, *Checklist*, entry no. 430. Melville was very likely aware of and possibly owned the Wiley and Putnam edition of *Modern Painters* (New York, 1847); Wiley and Putnam had published Melville's first novel, and they appended to their edition of Ruskin's book nine closely printed pages of reviews of *Typee* drawn from the British and American press. Duyckinck, in whose library Melville did much of his important reading, surely had one or more editions of *Modern Painters*, for the *Literary World* published favorable reviews of nearly all his works.

Few people, comparatively, have ever seen the effect on the sea of a powerful gale continued without intermission for three or four days and nights, and to those who have not, I believe *it must be unimaginable*, not from the mere force or size or surge, but from the *complete annihilation of the limit between sea and air. The water from its prolonged agitation is beaten*, not into mere creaming foam, but *into masses of accumulated yeast*.[155]

Ruskin placed an asterisk at "masses of accumulated yeast" and appended a long note on the validity of the figure, citing Shakespeare's "yesty waves" as well as a passage of seastorm description in Fenimore Cooper that he praises for its verisimilitude; for Melville, who read Shakespeare with extraordinary subtlety and who found the rendering of marine storms a talent "peculiarly Cooper's,"[156] Ruskin's note would underscore the value of a figure that he would recall and employ in describing the Turneresque seascape in the Spouter-Inn. Ruskin invites his reader to conveive of the surges of "yeast"

... in their utmost pitch of power, velocity, vastness and madness, listing themselves in precipices and peaks, furrowed with their whirl of ascent, through all this chaos; and you will understand that there is indeed *no distinction left between sea and air; that no object, nor any landmark or natural evidence of position is left; that the heaven is all spray, and the ocean all cloud,* and that *you can see no farther in any direction than you could see through a cataract.*

The magnificence of this passage is tempered only by the fact that Ruskin describes in it neither an imagined nor an experienced scene but Turner's painting, *Snowstorm: Steamboat off a Harbour's Mouth* (1842) [Pl. VIII]. In this canvas a barely discernible steamship seems to hover amid a chaos of swirling mist, foam, and spray. The innumerable waves, lashed by the wind, have a frenzied, seething life to them, and seem indeed to be masses of "accumulated yeast." Like the Spouter-Inn painting, it is a vision of "chaos bewitched," a dark vortex of kinetic power in which are obliterated with the horizon virtually all distinctions of form and mass.

In fashioning his own dark seascape, Melville may have been inspired by Turner's *Snowstorm* itself, as well as by Ruskin's description of it, for it is probable that he saw the controversial painting while in London in 1849.[157] Evidence suggests that by 1850-1851, the period in which *Moby-Dick* was composed, he had come to associate Turner's manner of

155. This and all subsequent quotations from *Modern Painters* are drawn from the Wiley and Putnam edition (New York, 1847), pp. 374-376.

156. See Melville's review of *The Sea Lions* in the *Literary World,* 5 (April 28, 1849), p. 370.

157. Melville visited the National, Dulwich, Hampton Court, and Greenwich galleries while in England in 1849; see the *Journal of a Visit to London and the Continent by Herman Melville, 1849-1850,* ed. Eleanor Melville Metcalf (Cambrdige: Harvard University Press, 1948). *Snowstorm* was in the National Gallery at the time, but whether it was still on public exhibition is not known.

impressionistic sublimity with the subject of whaling. On the title page of his copy of Thomas Beale's *Natural History of the Sperm Whale* — a source of primary importance for *Moby-Dick* — he accurately noted that "Turner's pictures of whales were suggested by this book."[158] He was referring to the four oils of whales and whaling scenes composed by Turner in 1845-1846 that were inspired by the painter's reading of Beale's *Natural History* (two of these paintings have the phrase "*Vide* Beale's *Voyage*" appended to their titles). Illustrating Beale are several cuts by W. J. Linton, one of which serves as a frontispiece; from this plate Turner borrowed the format of *The Whale Ship*[159] [Pl. IX]. The same plate is praised by Ishmael, a most demanding critic of whaling pictures, in chapter fifty-six of *Moby-Dick*; Beale's "frontispiece," he remarks, "... though no doubt calculated to excite the civil scepticism of some parlor men, is admirably life-like in its general effect" (p. 266). Melville's note on Turner's debt to Beale was written on the title page of his copy of the *Natural History* directly facing the Linton frontispiece, suggesting that he may have had *The Whale Ship* particularly in mind when making his marginal comment. The most obscure of Turner's paintings of whaling scenes, *The Whale Ship* presents, in the middle distance, a storm-tossed whaler whose lines are all but lost in the mists and low-flying clouds. The horizon is all but obliterated. In the foreground is a breaching sperm

158. Melville's copy of Beale's *Natural History* (London: Van Voorst, 1839) is at the Harvard College Library. His marginal note on Turner is reprinted in Vincent, *The Trying-Out of "Moby-Dick,"* p. 216. Melville's extensive use of Beale in *Moby-Dick* is chronicled by Vincent.

159. Now at the Metropolitan Museum of Art (a preliminary sketch is at the Fogg Museum, Harvard University). The location of the painting while Melville was in London in 1849 is uncertain. C.F. Bell's *List of the Works Contributed to Public Exhibition by J.M.w. Turner, R.A.* (London: George Bell and Sons, 1901), p. 152, reports that *The Whale Ship* passed into private hands in 1851 and that it was sold to the Metropolitan in 1896. In his *Catalogue of the Paintings in the Metropolitan Museum of Art* (New York: Metropolitan Museum of Art, 1912), p. 173, Bryson Burroughs argued that the painting was purchased by Dr. Munro of Novar, a Turner patron, at the Royal Academy Exhibtion in 1846. Munro's collection was to a limited extent available to the public. In any case, Burroughs' catalogue is not entirely reliable, as his note that *The Whale Ship* had not been engraved prior to 1912 suggests; a fine cut of the painting appeared in the *Turner Gallery* in 1879. Boase reproduces the painting as well as the Linton engraving, and he notes that "Without Linton's cut it would be difficult to work out the actual scene in the turbulence of the waters in Turner's *The Whale Ship*" (p. 344); Melville must have known the painting very well in order to recognize its antecedent in the Linton plate. I have found no reference to the painting or to the subtitle that mentions Beale prior to the publication of the *Turner Gallery*, and it would seem higly unlikely that Melville's note in his copy of Beale could be dated later than 1850-1851 for the simple reason that he would have no cause to return to and annotate a book he had thoroughly mined during the composition of *Moby-Dick*.

Plate VIII. J.M.W. Turner, *Snowstorm: Steamboat Off a Harbour's Mouth* (1842). The Tate Gallery.

Plate IX. J.M.W. Turner, *The Whaleship* (1845-46). The Metropolitan Museum of Art, New York. Wolfe Fund.

whale in the line of the ship's bow. Turner's ship, to be sure, is in no immediate peril, but the arc described by the whale's up-thrusting form impends over its hull and masts. As it is evident that Melville had Ruskin and Turner in mind when he composed "The Spouter-Inn," *The Whale Ship* may well have been the antecedent and inspiration of the "unimaginable sublimity" of Melville's "boggy, soggy, squitchy" composition.

The possibly direct influence of Turner's paintings on Melville's chapter is but one aspect of extensive confluences in the works of the two artists, confluences that point up important aspects of Melville's aesthetics. Affinities between the two, all but wholly ignored in American scholarship,[160] were immediately evident to early British reviewers of Melville's work. *White-Jacket* prompted one such reviewer to remark, in 1850, that "Mr. Melville stands as far apart from any past or present marine painter in pen and ink as Turner does from Vandervelt."[161] Another, acerbic as he was keen, noted of the catastrophic conclusion of *Moby-Dick* that "... in its whirl of waters and fancies, it resembles one of Turner's later nebulous transgressions in gamboge."[162] Turner's "transgressions" were the controversial seascapes — including the whaling scenes — and landscapes of the 'thirties and 'forties in which the painter, choosing as subject scenes of enormous natural power, turned away from the distribution of masses as organizing principle for his paintings and took up a vortex of light or dark in its stead. Avoiding the propensity of natural masses, whether they be mountains, vegetation, rocks, or even waves, to effect an impression of stasis, Turner seized upon the vortex as the means of achieving acutely kinetic effects. In such seascapes as *Stafa, Fingal's Cave* (1832), *A Rough Sea* (1830-1832), *Rockets and Blue Lights* (1840), and the famous *Slavers Throwing Overboard the Dead and Dying – Typhoon Coming On* (1840), the vortex form becomes the means of capturing and organizing tempestuous marine scenes without abating their essential chaos. These works create in the viewer an impulsion toward the center of their vortices while at the same time effecting the impression of great natural force radiating and whirling outward through the vortices. A similar achievement is found in Turner's landscapes of the period. In the famous *Snowstorm: Hannibal Crossing the Alps* (1822),

160. Chauncey Brewster Tinker remarked the shared interest in Beale's book in 1938, but he made no connection with the Spouter-Inn painting; see *Painter and Poet: Studies in the Literary Relations of Painter and Poet* (Cambrdige: Harvard University Press, 1938), p. 119. In the Northwestern-Newberry edition of *Moby-Dick* (p. 749), Mansfield and Vincent note the possibility that Melville may have seen at least two of Turner's whaling oils, but they, too, omit notice of the Spouter-Inn painting.
161. Henry F. Chorley's review in the *Athenaeum* (London), Feb. 2, 1850; cited by Leyda, *The Melville Log*, I, 365.
162. W.H. Ainsworth's review in the *New Monthly Magazine* (London), 98 (July 1853): 308.

Snowstorm, Avalanche, and Inundation (1837), *Shade and Darkness – The Evening of the Deluge* (1843), and most strikingly, *Rain, Steam, and Speed – The Great Western Railway* (1844), the vortex both organizes and evokes the energy and movement of the scenes presented. Turner's subject in these paintings is of course the sublime of nature. If, as Burke had demonstrated, all sublimity finds its source in "some modification of Power,"[163] and the expression of power is movement, the challenge to the painter of the sublime of nature is to break through the frontiers of an essentially static art so as to create kinetic effects. This Turner accomplished through the vortex, and with the adoption of the vortex as primary form of composition he abandoned the delineation of masses in favor of the intensely kinetic possibilities of refracted light.

The vortex also held special interest for Melville. A seascapist in words, he evinces throughout *Moby-Dick* a painterly interest in the problems of mass, form, and movement in presenting marine scenes. To his mind the vortex was at once the kinetic image of power and the image of the essential multiplicity nature, and his sense of the deceptive appearance of all natural surfaces led to the repeated use of the vortex image. As was the case with Turner, who tagged his paintings with lines from his grimly fatalistic poem, the *Fallacies of Hope*, Melville's vision was both transcendental and pessimistic; for him the vortex imaged the penetration of surface appearances and evoked the horror of vacuity that reaches almost obsessive intensity in *Moby-Dick*. The vortical depths through which the Platonist falls to his death in "The Mast-Head" appear again in the seething white vortex that is the agency of the *Pequod*'s final destruction.

If Melville had read British critical journals of his day he would have been aware of yet another confluence of his and Turner's art. The color white was traditionally condemned by painters and critics as unpicturesque, and for their use of the hue Turner and his followers were attacked as the "White Painters."[164] As Turner explored the sublime of nature through the 'thirties and 'forties he turned ineluctably away from mass and form to light and, ultimately, to white light itself as superlatively sublime. Melville, anatomizing his symbolic whale, followed the same progression. Through such chapters as "Cetology," "Monstrous Pictures of Whales," "Less Erroneous Pictures of Whales," "Of Whales in Paint, in Teeth, & c.," "The Blanket," and "Measurement of the Whale's Skeleton," Melville posited the view that the appearances of all natural forms are deceptive and that essential nature is unknowable; the whale, Ishmael tellingly remarks, "must remain unpainted to the last" (p. 265).

163. *Enquiry*, p. 64.
164. A.J. Finberg, *Life of J.M.W. Turner, R.A.* (London: Oxford University Press, 1961), p. 185.

If form is not an adequate basis for defining *Moby-Dick*, neither is color. Chapter forty-two, Ishmael's famous "whitelead chapter on whiteness" (p. 192), presents colors as "but subtile deceits, not actually inherent in substances, but only laid on from without";

> ... the great principle of light, for ever remains white or colorless in itself, and if operating without medium upon matter, would touch all objects, even tulips and roses, with its own blank tinge — pondering all this, the palsied universe lies before us a leper.[165]

The sinister dimensions of white light, to Melville's mind, balance and neutralize all the benign cultural associations of the color.

Melville arrived at his leprous vision of the world of white light through Newton's theory of color. Turner had also followed the implications of Newton's theory, and, as his paintings suggest, he came to the same paradoxical conception of color that so troubled Melville. He took up Goethe's theory of color, which had been written partly as a polemic against Newton, and devoted two paintings, *Light and Color: The Morning After the Deluge* (1843) and *Shade and Darkness: The Evening of the Deluge* (1843), to the German poet's conception of "plus" and "minus" colors.[166] Both are vortex paintings. In *Light and Color* the plus colors — reds and yellows, Goethe's colors of happiness and warmth — radiate outward, effecting an impression of exploding light. In *Shade and Darkness* light refracts in blues, greens, and purples — Goethe's negative colors — and draws the eye through a dark, chaotic tunnel toward an eerie, green-tinted vacuity. While Goethe hailed light as the benign first principle of God's universe, and saw in the opposition of light and dark the eternal conflict of divine order and chaos, Turner's canvases seem to expose the paradox latent in the poet's theory. The same principle of light is the basis of both vortices, yet their effects are opposed, reflecting, respectively, salvation and annihilation. The meaning of light would seem to depend on its refraction; white, unrefracted light may become paradoxically, a kind of darkness. As John Gage observes, just as Turner felt "the sun was God, so his dark pessimism expressed itself increasingly in terms of light, and light in terms of the colour he had spent a lifetime in learning to control." Even *Light and Color*, the "plus" vision of the story from Genesis, is suffused with sublime ambiguity. The painting's caption, drawn from the *Fallacies of Hope*, read,

---

165. For a discussion of the important aesthetic implications of this chapter see below, pp. 233-246.

166. See John Gage, *Colour in Turner* (London: Studio Vista, 1969), pp. 173-188. Turner knew Goethe's *Farbenlehre* (1817) through *Goethe's Theory of Colours* (London: Murray, 1840), a translation by his friend, Sir Charles Eastlake.

167. Gage, p. 187.

The ark stood form on Ararat: th' returning sun
Exhaled earth's humid bubbles, and emulsions of light
Reflected her lost forms, each in prismatic guise
Hope's harbinger, ephemeral as the summer fly
Which rises, flits, expands and dies.[168]

Earth's "lost forms" depend for their rebirth on the bubbles radiating colored light in the painting, bubbles "ephemeral as the summer fly" and presumably as deceptive as the forms themselves.

Melville's enthusiasm for Turner's work grew rather than abated after the publication of *Moby-Dick* in 1851, the year of Turner's death. In London during the spring of 1857 he visited the Turner Gallery at the National, noting in his journal with evident pleasure the "Sunset scenes" of Turner, *Burial of Wilkie*, *The Shipwreck* and *The Fighting Temeraire*.[169] To the last of these works Melville devoted a fine lyric — "The Temeraire" — and in the fourth stanza of his poem he alludes to yet another Turner canvas, the magnificent *Angel Standing in the Sun*. We can expect that this painting had special appeal for Melville, for it is the very image of the paradox the writer had found in "The Whiteness of the Whale." Emerging from a vortex of blazing light, Turner's angel seems at once ecstatic and agonized. A host of twisted and cowering figures flee in the foreground beneath the bright angel whose sword heralds exile and darkness. As Harry Levin has observed of *Moby-Dick*, "Whiteness, by virtue of a culminating paradox, is blackness in perversely baffling disguise";[170] Turner had discovered precisely the same profound ambiguity at the heart of the sublime.

Most of Melville's American contemporaries knew of Turner's work only through Ruskin — the *Turner Gallery*, a massive collection engravings, was not available until 1879 — and the privileged few who viewed the paintings first-hand tended to be perplexed or inclined to esteem the genius of Ruskin over that of Turner.[171] Thomas Cole betrayed the neo-classical bias that lingered longer in American art criticism than it did in Britain when he judged Turner's art against the standard of "truth to

168. The caption and painting are discussed by Gage, pp. 186-187, to whose argument I am indebted. Gage points out that Turner replaced the rainbow of the Covenant with the radiant bubbles that, being "'Hope's harbinger,' are like the rainbow, but they are also the emblems of fallacious hope"; cf. Ishmael's comment that "rainbows do not visit the clear air; they only irradiate vapor" (p. 372).

169. Leyda, *The Melville Log*, II, 576.

170. *The Power of Blackness* (New York: Alfred Knopf, 1970), p. 222.

171. For comment on Turner's reputation in America during Melville's times, see Roger B. Stein, *John Ruskin and Aesthetic Thought in America, 1840-1900* (Cambridge: Harvard University Press, 1967). Turner's works, especially the sublime compositions of the 'thirties and 'forties, were almost unknown among non-artists in America.

nature."[172] He praised the sublimity and chiaroscuro effects of Turner's work, possibly because of what he saw as a likeness to the idealized landscapes of Claude and Poussin, but he could not accept Turner's subordination of mass and form to light and color; some of the British painter's canvases, he remarked, are "destitute of all appearance of solidity: all appears transparent and soft, and reminds one of jellies and confections." Suggesting the tenacity with which Lockean rationalism endured in the full tide of American romaticism, Cole's attack is based on the view that, while nature may have her darkness, "above all she possesses *solidity.*"[173] Implicit in Cole's view is the principle that the artist should paint nature as it is rationally or abstractedly known, not as it appears to the senses. In regard to this classical verity Melville was, no less than Turner, a heretic. The rationalistic cetological chapters of *Moby-Dick* — fully a quarter of the book — culminate in Ishmael's statement that all human science is "but a passing fable," and the entire book rests on the conviction that

> Only in the heart of quickest perils; only when within the eddyings of his angry flukes; only on the profound unbounded sea, can the fully invested whale be truly and livingly found out. (p. 451)

Acceding to Cole's aesthetic values, Oliver Wendell Holmes qualified his estimate of Turner as the best living landscapist by lamenting that the painter had "doubtless been led away from the truth of nature" and that he had followed — note the echo of Reynolds' Seventh Discourse — "too ardently the seductive light of his imagination."[174] Such a perspective on Turner may now seem wide of the mark, but what Cole and Holmes found objectionable in the painters's work was not an absence of verisimilitude but the sense in which they evinced the last stage of the ascendancy of subjectivity over neo-classical aesthetic values. Truth of sensation and neo-classical "truth to nature" had never been adequately reconciled by eighteenth-century aestheticians, for a cult of private sensation in the arts rather than art that elucidates the general truth of nature seems to have been the inevitable consequence of the conviction that knowledge is wholly rooted in sensation. But the tendency of romantic artists toward solipsistic subjectivity was held in check by associationist psychology and the notion of a community of taste. These constraints were, however, less easily applied to the art of the sublime

172. Ruskin had of course defended Turner against the same standard; Cole had in mind the general nature of Reynolds.

173. Cole's reflections are found in Noble, *The Life and Works of Thomas Cole*, p. 81; they are excerpted and discussed by Stein, pp. 23-26.

174. "The Allston Exhibition," *North American Review* 50 (April 1840): 379; Holmes's views are insightfully analyzed by Stein, *John Ruskin and Aesthetic Thought in America*, pp. 19-23.

than to the art of the beautiful or picturesque, for, as early as Burke's *Enquiry* and perhaps as early as the aesthetic tracts of Dennis and Addison, immediacy, intensity, and the irrational were considered requisites of the sublime. It is precisely this effect of immediacy and intensity of sensational experience that Turner achieved in such a painting as *Snowstorm: Steamboat off a Harbour's Mouth*, and which brought him the ridicule of the critics. Of *Snowstorm* he said that he had only "... wished to show what such a scene was like,"[175] but his public wanted "truth to nature," not nature or sensation itself. The piece was described as a "frantic puzzle" in which nature's solidity was obliterated: "Where the steamboat is — Where the harbour begins, or where it ends — Which are the signals ... are matters past finding out." *Snowstorm* was finally damned as a "mass of soapsuds and whitewash,"[176] as Melville's masterpiece, linked to Turner's work, would be dismissed as a "whirl of waters and fancies."

Possibly at the behest of Melville, his Berkshire friend and neighbor, Hawthorne visited the Turner Gallery while abroad in 1857. He confessed he was "wholly unable to understand more than a very few" of Turner's paintings, and he preferred the more conventional, ideal landscapes that depicted the "better truth etherealized out of the prosaic truth of nature." Nevertheless, he found the later and more controversial works "tantalizing," and his impressions of them read like a parody of Ishmael's search for the meaning of the Spouter-Inn painting:

> At a certain distance, you discern what appears to be grand and beautiful picture, which you shall admire and enjoy infinitely if you can get within the range of distinct vision. You come nearer, and find only blotches of color, and dabs of the brush, meaning nothing when you look closely, and meaning a mystery at the point where the painter intended to station you.[177]

Ishmael has the same difficulties with the "unaccountable shades and shadows" of the Spouter-Inn painting, and his quest for a proper perspective is Melville's romance-anatomy in minature. Each chapter of the endlessly rich *Moby-Dick* is a new perspective on the sublime mystery that ultimately eludes both Ahab's harpoon and Ishmael's defining pen. That mystery is the meaning of the sublime of nature, a mystery which is, like Melville's "boggy, soggy, squitchy picture ... enough to drive a nervous man distracted." We know such a man in Ahab, for whom "all

175. Finberg, *Life of J.M.W. Turner*, p. 390.
176. Ibid.
177. *The English Notebooks of Nathaniel Hawthorne*, ed. Randall Stewart (New York: Russell and Russell, Inc., 1941), pp. 614-615. Hawthorne preferred Claude to Turner, believing that the former "catches the 'light that never was on sea nor land,' without quite taking you away from nature for it"; the quotation is from Wordsworth's "Elegaic Stanzas," a lyric which suggests the poet's — and, by extension, Hawthorne's — hostility to the horrific sublime.

visible objects" — color, form, and ultimately matter itself — "are but as pasteboard masks" (p. 161). For Ishmael no less than for Ahab, the noumenal world beyond the mask of appearance is not morally but horrifically sublime. As Melville's narrator confesses in the first chapter of the book,

> Not ignoring what is good, I am quick to perceive a horror, and could still be social with it — would they let me — since it is but well to be on friendly terms with all the inmates of the place one lodges in. By reason of these things, then the whaling voyage was welcome; the great flood-gates of the wonder-world swung open, and in the wild conceits that swayed me to my purpose, two and two there floated into my inmost soul, endless processions of the whale, and, mid most of them all, one grand hooded phantom, like a snow hill in the air. (p. 6)

Unequaled in his capacity to transmute into art the subtlest concerns of his culture, Melville could not have done better than choose the manner of Turner for an icon of Ishmael's grand hooded phantom

The White Whale as Quintessential Sublime

Perhaps no aspect of *Moby-Dick* has occasioned more critical contention than the fact that, while Ishmael swims through libraries and has to do with whales with his living hands in preparing to anatomize the whale, the grand hooded phantom he evisions at the start of his book remains hooded and phantasmic at its close. The most basic source of the obscurity of the book is of course what one critic has called its "shrouded idiom";[178] *Moby-Dick* abounds in such aspecific terms as "nameless," "inscrutable," "measureless," "ungraspable," "resistless," "unfathomable," "illimitable," "impenetrable," "unknown," and "unimaginable." From Conrad's allegation of a fundamental meretriciousness in *Moby-Dick* through recent scholarly discussions of Ishmaelian masks, moods, and multiple languages,[179] twentieth-century commentators have been troubled by this rhetoric of inscrutability and the apparent obfuscation it effects. While it is undeniably true that, as James Guetti has argued,

---

178. C.C. Walcutt, *Man's Changing Mask: Modes and Methods of Characterization in Fiction* (Minneapolis: University of Minnesota Press, 1966), p. 108.

179. Conrad's claim that *Moby-Dick* has "not a single sincere line in the three vols. of it" is reprinted in "Moby-Dick" as Doubloon: Essays and Extracts, 1851-1970, ed. Hershel Parker and Harrison Hayford (New York: W.W. Norton & Company, 1970), pp. 122-123. In *Ishmael's White World*, Brodtkorb relates the obscuring shifts of mood, voice, idiom and point of view in *Moby-Dick* to the subjectivity he sees as Melville's primary theme. In *Nil: Episodes in the Literary Conquest of Void During the Nineteenth Century* (New York: Oxford University Press, 1966), Robert Martin Adams notes that much of Ishmael's language is "hopelessly, and no doubt deliberately, irrelevant to the fact[s] which it pretends to demonstrate" (p. 144), while Walcutt speaks of Ishmael's "double and triple talk" (*Man's Changing Mask*, p. 108).

much of Ishmael's language "functions to display its insufficiency,"[180] it by no means follows that his language disguises a vacuity of meaning or purpose at the heart of Melville's book. For in taking up the sublime Melville engaged a subject that by its very definition transcends all but a negative relation to earthly things and that therefore defies containment in language itself. The object of Ishmael's anatomy is not the whale as species or a particular whale so much as it is the White Whale, the quintessentially sublime "Leviathan."

As an anatomy of essential nature, a quest in definition, *Moby-Dick* seems, by turns, to be feigned or aborted. If, through apposition to Ahab, Ishmael may be seen as a huntsman armed with word and idea, then it must be confessed that he expends the bulk of his anatomizing by restlessly exchanging weapons that he brandishes at his Leviathan and sets aside as inadequate to the task of definition. His apparent determination that his prey shall elude his defining pen is evinced on every level of the book, from the "conscious insufficiency"[181] of his language to the massive collage of discrete perspectives — no one of which contains the whale — that supplies the structural logic of the book. "To make any thing very terible, obscurity seems in general to be necessary," wrote Burke, for a "clear idea ... is another name for a little idea."[182] To invoke Burke's rather bald statement of psychological fact may suggest a certain justice in the view of Melville as an obscurantist. But, as Ahab would say, a little lower layer is in order, a layer of the phenomenology of the sublime that Burke never successfully articulated. Unwilling or unable to transcend his sensationist bias, Burke muddled his analysis of the sublime with discussion of notched poles and the like in an attempt to suggest the point at which a vast object or vast sequence of images begins to evoke the sense of infinity. Melville had, of necessity, to attend to this point — or its environs — through the course of his romance; *Ne plus ultra* of natural sublimity, Moby Dick must remain vast, not relatively large; he must be essentially shapeless or protean, as definite shape is definite extension. In "Loomings" we should be immediately alerted to the fact that Melville quests less after a living beast than the sublime idea of the infinite it effects. There Ishmael envisions not a living whale but a "grand hooded phantom" who is "mid most" in an "endless procession" (p. 6).

The sublime of nature had been, since its inception in the late seventeenth century, apprehended as a transcendental aesthetic. While Dennis, Addison, Hutcheson, and Baillie as well as the associationist

180. *The Limits of Metaphor: A Study of Melville, Conrad, and Faulkner* (Ithaca, N.Y.: Cornell University Press, 1967), p. 41.
181. Adams, *Nil*, p. 147.
182. *Enquiry*, pp. 58, 83.

aestheticians of the later eighteenth century had successfully elaborated upon the way in which the sublime of nature pressed beyond the limits of the imaginative faculty and thus effected a sense of spiritual transport, their Lockean presuppositions precluded any ultimately satisfactory analytic of the transcendental dimension of the sublime. Confronted by the infinite they could, of course, turn to God, to the sense in which His dread powers seemed immanent in the sublime, but their aesthetic tracts fall short of metaphysics, and they write less as philosophers than materialistic psychologists.[183] Burke was the first to break free of the easy convention of the religious sublime so dominant in the arts of the eighteenth century, but, in respect to the problem of transcendence in the sublime, his sensationism was an even more inadequate perspective than the associationism against which he reacted: "When we go but one step beyond the immediately sensible qualities of things," he wrote, "we go out of our depth."[184] A thoroughly penetrating analytic of the transcendental aspect of the sublime had to await a mind conversant with the British tradition of psycho-dynamic aesthetics yet one that had also embraced idealism. It had to await Kant.

As E. F. Carritt has demonstrated,[185] Kant read extensively in British aesthetics prior to the completion of his analytic of the sublime in *Die Kritik der Urtheilskraft* (1790). He seems to have been influenced by Lord Kames's *Elements of Criticism* (translated in 1764), by Hutcheson's *Enquiry into the Original of our Ideas of Beauty* (translated in 1762), and

183. Wasserman notes that under the aegis of associationism correspondence between mind and matter "had become a phase of psychology, not ontology" ("Nature Moralized," p. 68). Everywhere apparent in late eighteenth-century psychological aesthetics, the limited utility of associationism in regard to the sublime is suggested in the following passage by the associationist Reid: "What we call the sublime in description, or in speech of any kind, is a proper expression of the admiration and enthusiasm which the subject produces in the mind of the speaker ... The true sublime cannot be produced solely by art in the composition; it must take its rise from grandeur in the subject, and a corresponding emotion raised in the mind of the speaker" (*Essays on the Intellectual Powers of Man* [Edinburgh: T. & T. Clark, 1785], p. 730); the analysis is psychologically circular because as an associationist Reid cannot accurately postulate "grandeur," a term which refers to an emotive state, as a quality of matter. It may be worth noting that the concept of the sublime has gone out of aesthetic currency in the twentieth century precisely because the demise of idealism and final ascendance of materialism now preclude faith in transcendental experience.

184. *Enquiry*, pp. 129-130. Burke seldom connects divinity with the idea of the infinite, which to his mind seems to have been an absolute without any necessary religious implication. But so radical was his sensationism that he could not even accept the limited efficacies of Locke's intuitive faculty; he connects the sublime with ignorance rather than with a kind of knowledge as had Addison and those that followed him.

185. "The Sources and Effects in England of Kant's Philosophy of Beauty," *The Monist* 35 (1925): 315-328.

especially by Addison's *Spectator* papers (translated in 1745) and Burke's *Enquiry* (translated in 1762). He came to share Addison's view that "Our Imagination loves to be filled with an object or to grasp at anything that is too big for its capacity,"[186] and he may have been spurred on to his transcendental conception of the sublime through Addison's barely articulated sense of the transcendent "Soul"; Addison thought that the "Defect of the Imagination," its incapacity to apprehend infinitudes that the Reason may grasp, "may not be in the Soul itself, but as it acts in Conjunction with the Body."[187] As Burke had done in the *Enquiry*, Kant explained the sublime as the exact opposite of the beautiful, which achieves its effect through the complete harmony between an object and our faculties of knowledge. A sublime object, he argued,

> ... may appear ... in point of form to contravene the ends of our power of judgment, to be ill-adapted to our faculty of presentation, and to be, as it were, *an outrage on the imagination*, and yet it is judged all the more sublime on that account.[188]

Apparently so as to bracket under one aesthetic head two currents of English speculation on the sublime, Kant postulated two sub-categories of the sublime, the "Dynamic" and the "Mathematical." The dynamic sublime seems to be an adumbration of Burke's sublime of terror; it is evoked not by an object but by power, power so vast it effects a sense of the infinite. The mathematical sublime, possibly developed from Burke's reflections on uniformity, repetition, and sensory deprivation as sources of the sublime,[189] arises from formlessness, vast size, or the endless iteration of features that are uniform. Whether Kant referred to the mathematical or the dynamic sublime he always related the aesthetic to the faculty of reason that, reaching beyond the mind's capacity to form images, apprehended a transcendental or supra-natural reality of the infinite. As Monk has commented, Kant's

> Beauty is concerned with limited objects, with forms; the sublime is to be found in objects that are limitless, that have no form, through they are always accompanied with a "super-added" thought of totality. The beautiful, therefore, implies an effort of the *understanding*, the faculty that determines objects by specific conception; the sublime implies an effort of the *reason*, the faculty that seeks an unconditional totality. Hence delight in the beautiful is associated with a representation of quality; in the sublime, with a representation of quantity.[190]

186. *The Spectator*, ed. Donald F. Bond (Oxford: The Clarendon Press, 1965), III, 540.

187. Ibid., p. 577.

188. *Kant's Critique of Aesthetic Judgment*, translated by James Creed Meredith (Oxford: Oxford University Press, 1911), p. 91. Subsequent citations refer to this edition.

189. Something like a primitive version of Kant's mathematical sublime seems to be at work in Burke's idea of "The Artificial INFINITE" (*Enquiry*, pp. 139-143).

190. *The Sublime*, p. 6.

It should be evident that this line of reasoning would lead to the conclusion that there can be, strictly speaking, no sublime of nature, for no object of nature is either limitless or formless. This had long been a problem in discourse on the sublime. It doubtless caused the abiding semantic ambiguity of the term — whether sublimity is a state of mind or a quality of matter. Burke had himself engaged the problem in arguing that

> There are scarce any things which can become the objects of our senses that are really and in their own nature infinite. But the eye not being able to perceive the bounds of many things, they seem to be infinite, and they produce the same effects as if they were really so. We are deceived in the like manner, if the parts of some large object are so continued to an indefinite number, that the imagination meets no check which may hinder its extending them at pleasure.[191]

Kant's idealist suppositions enabled him to deal with the problem by ranging beyond the psychological dynamics that confined British discourse on the sublime; sublimity was for him neither a state of mind nor a quality of matter. "We express ourselves on the whole inaccurately," he argued, "if we term any Object of Nature sublime."[192] For, "The sublime is that, the mere capacity of thinking which evidences a faculty of mind transcending every standard of sense."[193] Yet Kant does not dismiss the sublime of nature as a pseudo-problem. In fact, in his effort to retain the sublime of nature as aesthetic he mars his discourse with a curious and telling contradiction. "That is sublime," he writes, "in comparison with which all else is small ... Nothing, therefore, which can be an object of the senses is to be termed sublime when treated on this (quantified) footing."[194] If the

> ... aesthetic judgement is to be *pure (unmixed with any teleological judgement ...)*, ... we must not point to the sublime in works of art ... where a human end determines the form as well as the magnitude, *nor yet in things of Nature, that in their very concept impart a definite end*, e.g. animals of a recognized natural order, *but in rude Nature merely as involving magnitude.*[195]

Kant's stricture that purposive relation to a recognized natural order precludes the sublime would seem entirely to exclude animate nature from the purview of his discourse; for what beast — especially in an age still dominated by deistic faith in natural order — might be said to have no purposive relation to a natural order? Yet he insists that "Nature ... is sublime in such of its phenomena as in their intuition convey the idea of their infinity."[196]

191. *Enquiry*, p. 73.
192. *Critique of Aesthetic Judgment*, p. 91.
193. Ibid., p. 98.
194. Ibid., p. 97.
195. Ibid., p. 100.
196. ibid., p. 103.

Whether or not Melville knew of Kant's analytic of the sublime — there seem good reasons to believe he did[197] — he was acutely aware of the problems that led to Kant's contradiction. What has seemed to be a flaw of obscurantism in *MobyDick* is in fact the best index of Melville's awareness, for, even as Ishmael presents the appearance of a zoological anatomy of the whale as species, Moby Dick remains abstractly, quint-essentially sublime, an ageless, formless, dimensionless cipher of Kant's "rude Nature" involving unimaginable "magnitude." Cetacea may, in the course of the book, be apprehended as a natural order, as a flayed corpse, as a skeleton, as a raw industrial resource, as a fossil, and even as a meal, but no matter how precise the sensational apprehension of his kind may be, Moby Dick transcends relation to his species. Being that which in comparison all things are small, he transcends any but negative definition. Ishmael is always self-consciously aware of the formidable task of defining his undefinable symbol, as this comic but serious passage suggests:

> How then, with me, writing of this Leviathan? Unconsciously my chirography expands into placard capitals. Give me a condor's quill!! Give me Vesuvius' crater for an inkstand! Friends, hold my arms! For in the mere act of penning my thoughts of this Leviathan, they weary me, and make me faint with their outreaching comprehensiveness of sweep, as if to include the whole circle of the sciences, and all the generations of whales, and men, and mastodons, past, present, and to come, with all the revolving panoramas of empire on earth, and throughout the whole universe, not excluding its suburbs. (p. 379)

As no image can circumscribe Moby Dick's significance, he is never sensationally apprehended. He is the

> ... mightiest animated mass that has survived the flood; most monstrous and m ost mountainous! That Himmalehan [sic], salt-sea Mastodon, clothed in such porten-tousness of unconscious power, that his very panics are more to be dreaded than his most fearless and malicious assaults. (p. 62)

This language is indeed self-consciously insufficient, turning as it does to abstract superlatives and monstrous images that are nonetheless inade-quate to the thing Ishmael strives to image. And it is unremittingly insufficient, even as the White Whale finally breaches into sight very late in the book:

> A mighty joyousness — a mighty mildness of repose in swiftness, invested the gliding whale. *Not* the white bull Jupiter swimming away with ravished Europa clinging to his graceful horns; his lovely, leering eyes sideways intent upon the maid; with smooth bewitching fleetness, rippling straight for the nuptial bower in Crete; *not* Jove, *not* that great majesty Supreme, did surpass the glorified White Whale as he so divinely swam. (p. 539; italics added)

197. See above, p. 71.

This depiction — or, more properly, non-depiction — drives away from representation. With each repetition of the negative particle the pictorial analog of the whale is subverted as inadequate. Through this and like passages Moby Dick comes to seem Kant's aesthetic paradox, transcendence incarnate, a living infinite.

Of course, the whales sought by the *Pequod*, a ship trimmed between Kant and Locke, are also things of oil and blubber. The Kantian sublime after which Melville quests was in many ways inimical to the American critical currents — especially those of New York — dominant during his age. In a review that Charvat cites as indicative of the "essence of American critical thinking in the first third of the century,"[198] A. H. Everett, editor of the *North American Review*, remarked the "wild and ethereal air" of Kant's system:

> It fills the mind with lofty and glorious imaginations, transports us from the cold and formal realities of the world around us into empyreal regions ... It gratifies our longing after a nobler and loftier destiny than that which we can here aspire to, by bringing our minds into nearer contact ... with the sublime spirit whose energy pervades and governs the universe.

"But," Everett wrote in characteristic qualification,

> when we come to a close survey of the doctrines of the idealists, we find that, as they are animated by the spirit of poetry, so they share the faults to which it naturally leads. They are too apt, ... to accommodate the "shows of things to the desires of the mind," rather than to the reality of sober fact ...[199]

It was toward sober fact, toward "Mechanism," as Lockean philosphy was called, that Knickerbocker literary circles were inclined in the 'forties and 'fifties, and they were consistently hostile to the heresies of Concord idealists. *Moby-Dick* has its full measure of apparently sober fact. The anatomical chapters of the book, what Vincent has called its "cetological center,"[200] loom so large and elaborate that many readers have concluded that, however trimmed between two metaphysics the *Pequod* may be, the book leans heavily toward Locke, toward naturalism, and toward tar and blubber as opposed to metaphysic. Yet, if these chapters are read critically and if their scientific appearance is recognized for the deception that it is, the Lockean cetological center will be seen as the chief device with which Melville refines the transcendental sublimity of Moby Dick. These chapters do not, as Zoellner contends, supplant Ahab's transcendental vision of the whale with an Ishmaelian naturalistic vision.[201]

198. *The Origins of American Critical Thought*, p. 85.
199. As cited by Charvat, p. 85.
200. *The Trying-Out of "Moby-Dick,"* pp. 121-368.
201. *Salt-Sea Mastodon*, pp. 146-165. Zoellner's thesis is an extreme extension of the idea, as commonplace as it is essentially sound, that in J.A. Ward's terms, the cetological chapters "balance the extraordinary with the ordinary" ("The Function of the Cetological Chapters in *Moby-Dick*," *American Literature* 28 [January 1967]: 170).

Rather, they actually subvert Moby Dick's relation to any natural order of being by denying that cetacea are susceptible of scientific definition. And, what is more important, they adumbrate agelessness, formlessness, colorlessness, and a spate of other negatives of less thematic significance as the salient features of Moby Dick. From the cetological center Moby Dick emerges as the Kantian sublime and the noumenon of animate nature.

"Cetology," the first of Ishmael's pseudo-scientific digressions, establishes the burlesque of scientific method that dominates most of the cetological chapters that follow. Fully aware, as J. A. Ward has put it, that "To treat his subject in purely heroic terms would probably have been disastrous,"[202] Melville generously laces his book with passages of sustained mockery. These relieve the otherwise unbearable tensions that arise from Ishmael's rhetoric of superlatives and inscrutability. But Ishmael's jocularity, his "forced high spirits,"[203] are not fostered at the expense of the grandeur of the White Whale, for they arise from a cynicism that is largely self-directed. Ishmael constantly doubts his own capacity to manage his subject. To engage whales is a "ponderous task," he confesses,

> To grope down into the bottom of the sea after them; to have one's hands among the unspeakable foundations, ribs, and very pelvis of the world; this is a fearful thing. What am I that I should essay to hook the nose of this leviathan! The awful tauntings in Job might well appal me. "Will he (the leviathan) make a covenant with thee? Behold the hope of him is vain!" But I have swam through libraries and sailed through oceans; I have had to do with whales with these visible hands; I am in earnest; and I will try. There are some preliminaries to settle.[204] (p. 131)

Those preliminaries are never settled. Ishmael's definition of the whale as "*a spouting fish with a horizontal tail*" (p. 132) is patently inaccurate. Finding that whales may take infinitely various forms, Ishmael remarks of Cetology, "The classification of the constituents of a chaos, nothing less is here essayed" (p. 129). Assigning whales to folio, octavo, and

202. "The Function of the Cetological Chapters," p. 176.
203. Ronald Mason, *The Spirit Above the Dust: A Study of Herman Melville* (London: John Lehman, 1951), p. 112. For further comment on the function of the comic in *Moby-Dick*, see Rosenberry, *Melville and the Comic Spirit*, pp. 93-138; Chase, *Herman Melville*, pp. 43-102; and Matthiessen, *American Renaissance*, p. 431. In a book so invested with superlative sublimity as *Moby-Dick*, Melville was ever confronted with the frontier of the ridiculous; the ease with which he could cross and recross that frontier may have in part redeemed the book from the melodramatic excess of such a work as Mathews' *Behemoth*.
204. Ahab, Peleg informs Ishmael, "has been in colleges" (p. 79). Established in the epistemological reflections of "Loomings," the division of knowledge into the categories of abstract and experiential is reiterated in Melville's portraits of Ishmael and Ahab as well.

duodecimo volumes according to the absurdly chosen principle of size, the "classification" collapses into Shandean farce as Ishmael is lost in "unshored, harborless immensities" (p. 129). What remains, of course, is precisely that measure of chaos, of indefiniteness, that permits extravagant exploitation of the whale as cosmic symbol.

When Kant in his analytic of the sublime included the infinite of "time past"[205] with the infinite of space as sources of the sublime he merely acceded to a long standing tradition of British discourse on the sublime. Agelessness, always associated with the sublime, became an especially prominent resource of the aesthetic with the Celtic Revival in the late eighteenth century, and the taste for the sublime of agelessness was brought to America by British aestheticians, particularly by Hugh Blair, whose rhetoric had much to say on the sublimities of Ossianic verse. American artists were hard pressed to find native materials that might effect this form of sublimity, and it might be fairly said that it was not artists but the historian Prescott who, in his chronicles of Aztec and Inca civilization, most successfully captured it. In any case, artists of Melville's generation found in the primordial aspect of raw nature at least a viable substitute for the sublimity ancient human civilization of Europe. Mathews' *Behemoth* and *Moby-Dick* stand as the exemplary essays in the American sublime of time past, although it is vestigially at work in Cooper also.

Throughout *Moby-Dick* the sublime attribute of agelessness is ascribed to whales and to Moby Dick in particular. Melville devotes two entire chapters — "The Honor and Glory of Whaling" and "Jonah Historically Regarded" — to the ancientness of the whalehunt and of its prey, which, says Ishmael, "have been spouting all over the sea" for "six thousand years — and no one knows how many millions of ages before" (p. 367). "The more I dive into this matter of whaling," he remarks,

and push my researches up to the very spring-head of it, so much the more am I impressed with its great honorableness and antiquity; and especially when I find so many great demi-gods and heroes, prophets of all sorts, who one way or other have shed distinction upon it, I am transported with the reflection that I myself belong, though but subordinately, to so emblazoned a fraternity. (p. 360)

Among this estimable fraternity Ishmael numbers Perseus, St. George, Hercules, Jonah, and Vishnoo,[206] suggesting that the whalehunt antedates history itself, being sourced in the primordial well-springs of myth:

205. *Critique of Aesthetic Judgment*, p. 102. Garard, Hume, Kames, hartley, and Blair, among others, had discussed the sublime of time past.
206. Such a catalogue could hardly be said to "de-mythologize" the whale, which is, according to Zoellner (p. 154), the function of Ishmael's cetological chapters.

Who can show a pedigree like Leviathan? Ahab's harpoon had shed older blood than the Pharaohs'. Methusalah seems a schoolboy. I look round to shake hands with Shem. I am horror-struck at this antemosaic, unsourced existence of the unspeakable terrors of the whale, which, having been before all time, must needs exist after all humane ages are over. (p. 380)

Interest in the excavated remains of pre-historic beasts extended far beyond the scientific community in Melville's day, and Melville, sharing that interest, exploits paleontologically discoveries to foster the "pre-adamite" (p. 453) awesomeness of the whale.[207] Pretending to have stood among "mighty Leviathan skeletons, skulls, tusks, jaws, ribs, and vertebrae," Ishmael sees their affinities with the annihilated antichronical Leviathans":

I am, by a flood, borne back to that wondrous period, ere time itself can be said to have begun; for time began with man. Here Saturn's grey chaos rolls over me, and I obtain dim, shuddering glimpses into those Polar eternities. (p. 454)

Presented as "foundering down upon us from the head-waters of the Eternities" (p. 455), the whale, according to Ishmael, will neither diminish nor perish:

In Noah's flood he despised Noah's Art; and if ever the world is to be again flooded ..., then the eternal whale will still survive, and rearing upon the topmost crest of the equatorial flood, spout his frothed defiance to the skies. (p. 459)

Whales, and particularly the grand hooded phantom of whales, are literally timeless. Remarking the rumored ubiquity of Moby Dick, Ishmael adduces the immortality of the White Whale, "for immortality is but ubiquity in time" (p. 179).

The ubiquity of Moby Dick is a thematically telling fiction, for it suggests the beast's infinitely protean quality. As Slotkin has observed, Ishmael's cetological chapters, most of which are expended on the subject of the whale's form, present no definite view of him;

They view him from every conceivable viewpoint, portray him in every conceivable shape, denying none and accepting none. By the time the whale is slighted, his character has been established as protean and many-levelled.[208]

Some of the whale's protean levels extend beyond animate nature itself,

207. Vincent, The Trying-Out of "Moby-Dick," pp. 346-352, offers an extensive list of sources, "none of them certain, but several possible," for Melville's paleontological relfections in "The Fossil Whale." One certain source of the Zeuglodon, a fossil whale discussed in the chapter, is an article on the subject by Richard Owen which Melville plagiarized; see my note on "Owen's and Melville's Fossil Whale," American Transcendental Quarterly 26 (Spring 1975): 24. On Melville's considerable geological knowledge, see Elizabeth Foster, "Melville and Geology," American Literature 17 (March 1945): 50-56, and "Another Note on Melville and Geology," American Literature 22 (January 1951): 479-487.
208. Regeneration Through Violence, p. 546.

as one of Ishmael's comic yet serious digressions suggests. After describing images of whales in cliffs and strewn boulders, he turns to the sky:

> Nor when expandingly liften by your subject, can you fail to trace out great whales in the starry heavens, and to boats in pursuit of them; as when long filled with thoughts of war the Eastern nations saw armies locked in battle among the clouds. Thus at the North have I chased Leviathan round and round the Pole with the revolutions of the bright points that first defined him to me ... With a frigate's achors for my bridle bitts and fasces of harpoons for spurs, would I mount that whale and leap the topmost skies, to see whether the fabled heavens with all their countless tents really lie encamped beyond my mortal sight! (p. 233)

The object of Ishmael's hunt is for the most part less than cosmic, however; most of the cetological chapters seek to define a particular limited aspect of the whale's form. Yet even these chapters — there are nearly a score of them — together subvert any clear definition of the shape of the whale.

In the three-chapter sequence comprised of "Monstrous Pictures of Whales," "Less Erroneous Pictures of Whales," and "Of Whales in Paint, in Teeth, &c," Ishmael resumes his role of art critic; he damns as "all wrong" virtually every picture of the whale that has come to his attention, and excoriates those who have taken a "sort of license ..., not only in most popular pictures of the whale, but in many scientific presentations of him" (p. 261). He tours "the old Galleries" (p. 262), ridiculing Guido's and Hogarth's pictures of Perseus and the sea monster, as well as pictures of whales on bookbindings, in primers, and in illustrated bibles.[209] Portraits of whales in natural history texts as well as chronicles of sea voyages similarly come under his derisive eye; the cut of a whale in Goldsmith's *History of Animated Nature* seems to Ishmael an "amputated sow" (p. 263) and Frederick Cuvier's picture of the beast is "not a Sperm Whale, but a squash" (p. 264). Through attack on "scientific presentations" of the whale Ishmael implies that "veritable gospel cetology" (p. xxxix) — the truth of the whale — will forever elude the reductionist methods of scientific definition:

> Most of the scientific drawings have been taken from the stranded fish; and these are about as correct as a drawing of a wrecked ship, with broken back, would correctly represent the noble animal itself in all its undashed pride of hull and spars ... The living whale, in his full majesty and significance, is only to be seen at sea in unfathomable waters; and afloat the vast bulk of him is out of sight ... and out of that element it is a thing eternally impossible for mortal man to hoist him bodily into the air, so as to preserve all his mighty swells and undulations. (p. 265)

A whale out of water is no whale, as is demonstrated by the example of a young suckling whale that, hoisted out of its element to a ship's deck,

---

209. All of the pictures mentioned by Ishmael in the three chapters are reproduced by Sumner W.D. Scott, "The Whale in *Moby-Dick*" (Ph.D. dissertation, University of Chicago, 1950).

assumes such an "outlandish, eel-like, limbered, varying shape" that "his precise expression the devil himself could not catch" (p. 265). Yet, with the relish of a learned connoisseur, Ishmael extends his critique of whaling art to illustrations of books on the whalehunt. These he finds no less chimerical and monstrous, although he finds several by the French painter Garnery tolerable and extends a singular compliment to Linton, the artist who illustrated Beale's *Natural History*. "All Beale's drawings of this whale are good, except the middle figure in the picture of three whales in various attitudes .... His frontispiece, boats attacking Sperm Whales ... is admirably correct and life-like in it s general effect" (p. 266); this had been the inspiration, we recall, of Turner's *The Whale Ship*. Ishmael does not, in his apparently learned digression, seek a satisfactory picture of the whale with the expectation of success, for it is his intention to demonstrate that the form of the whale shall forever elude definition. "You must needs conclude," he remarks,

> that the great Leviathan is that one creature in the world which must remain unpainted to the last. True, one portrait may hit the mark much nearer than another, but none can hit it with any very considerable degree of exactness. So there is no earthly way of finding out precisely what the whale really looks like. And the only mode in which you can derive even a tolerable idea of his living contour, is by going whaling yourself; but by so doing, you run no small risk of being eternally stove and sunk by him. (p. 266)

Like his language, Ishmael's tactics, his methods of definition, are also self-consciously insufficient.

Any true vision of nature, Melville insists, must accommodate the sublime Leviathan, "For," in Ishmael's words, "unless you own the whale, you are but a provincial and sentimentalist in Truth" (p. 336). As he would have the reader own the whale, Ishmael essays to paint, "as well as one can without canvas, something like the true form of the whale as he appears to the eye of the whaleman" (p. 261). But, avoiding anything like a portrait of the whale as an integrated, unified mass, he devotes short chapters to the anatomy of discrete and limited parts of the creature's physiology. Far from succumbing himself to the trap of reductionism, Melville exploits it; the whale's significance, we are given to believe, transcends the sum total of its parts. These parts themselves never emerge in sharp pictorial detail and the chapters in which they are minutely scrutinized never cohere into a composite portrait of the whale. Unity, that obsessive ideal of romanticism, eludes articulation in *Moby-Dick*. As for British and American romantics, it is a mystery for Melville, but a mystery of a decidedly dark and portentous cast.

In accordance with Ishmael's Yankee common sense, the physiological anatomy of the whale begins with the skin. About this, "The Blanket" of the whale, Ishmael has had "controversies" with "experienced whalemen afloat, and learned naturalists ashore" (p. 303), for in anatomizing the whale, a thing of controversy, we may not pass beyond the skin before contention arises. Ishmael is confronted from the start of his chapter with the question, "What and where is the skin of the whale?" (p. 304) Whether it is the thick layer of blubber investing the body or whether it is the "infinitely thin, transparent substance, somewhat resembling the thinnest shreds of isinglass," that covers the blubber, Ishmael cannot decide; but, he argues,

> That same infinitely thin ... substance, which, I admit, invests the entire body of the whale, is not so much to be regarded as the skin of the creature, as the *skin of the skin*. (p. 304; italics added)

Here the bemused Ishmael happens upon the layered pasteboard of matter that had been for Ahab — to borrow Kant's phrase — an "outrage upon the imagination." But while Ahab strikes out at the layered mask of matter, Ishmael probes it with his mind. He becomes prepossessed of the "numberless straight marks in this array, something like those in the finest Italian line engravings," with which the transparent surface of the whale is "all over obliquely crossed and re-crossed" (p. 305). But these marks, he continues,

> do not seem to be impressed upon the isinglass substance above mentioned, but seem to be seen through it, as if they were engraved upon the body itself. Nor is this all. In some instances, to the quick, observant eye, those linear marks, as in a veritable engraving, but afford the ground for far other delineations. These are hieroglyphical. (p. 305)

Ishmael is struck with the resemblance of these markings to those on "the famous hieroglyphic palisades on the banks of the Upper Mississippi"; "Like those mystic rocks, too," he concludes, "the mystic-marked whale remains undecipherable" (p. 305).

Defining the mystery Ishmael seeks as ultimately impenetrable, "The Blanket" is a striking index of Melville's knowledge and comprehension of the sublime. Behind the reference to the "finest Italian line engravings" that resemble the hieroglyphical maze of marks on the whale may well be the engravings of Giovanni Battista Piranesi, the eighteenth-century Italian artist. Possibly stimulated by De Quincey's *Confessions of an English Opium-Eater*, which he "read enthusiastically"[210] just prior to the writing of *Moby-Dick*, Melville took a special interest in *The Prisons*, Piranesi's collection of maddeningly intricate line drawings.[211] With Coleridge as

210. See Sealts, *Checklist*, entry no. 180. On the multiple allusions to De Quincey's *Confessions* in *Moby-Dick* see Mansfield's and Vincent's notes in the Northwestern-Newberry edition as well as Frederick S. Rockwell, "De Quincey and the Ending of *Moby-Dick*," *Nineteenth-Century Fiction* 9 (Spring 1954): 161-168.

211. See Furrow, "The Terrible Made Visible," pp. 249-251, for a brief discussion of Melville and Piranesi. Furrow cites references to Piranesi in *Clarel* as well as possible allusions to *The Prisons* in *Pierre*, but she omits the likely reference to the artist's work in "The Blanket" chapter of *Moby-Dick*.

well, De Quincey had found in these drawings the perfect correlative to the infntely complex architectural nightmares of his opium dreams. As he saw in them horrifically "endless growth and self-reproduction"[212] of geometric forms generated by the inner self, so melville came to see them as a nightmarish inner landscape of the soul. In *Clarel* he would write of Piranesi's "Interiors measurelessly strange":

> Stairs upon stairs which dim ascend
> In series from plunged bastiles drear —
> Pit under pit; long tier
> Of shadowed galleries which impend
> Over cloisters, cloisters without end.

The "thing implied," he continued, "is one" with mankind, who "see / Paul's 'mystery of iniquity.'"[213] Piranesi's drawings are the greatest pictorial manifestation of what Kant called the mathematical sublime, the power of formless immensities or endlessly iterated features to effect the idea of infinity. And it is only fitting that his etchings should come to Melville's mind in "The Blanket," for the mathematical sublime is precisely what Ishmael finds in the "numberless" lines that "crossed and re-crossed" the hieroglyphical body of the whale. The imagery of the chapter itself suggests that Melville had read quite recently either Kant's analytic of the mathematical sublime or Lord Kames's discussion of it in the *Elements of Criticism*. He may well have read both.[214] In the *Critique of Aesthetic Judgement* Kant had restricted the mathematical sublime to nature alone, yet, in contradiction, the only examples he gives of it are the dome of St. Peter's and the pyramids. As Carritt has demonstrated, Kant's peculiar turn of mind stemmed from the fact that he had simply borrowed his examples from Lord Kames, who had cited the same structures as examples of the same variety of the sublime.[215] These

212. *The Confessions of an English Opium-Eater* (London: J.M. Dent, 1949), p. 238.

213. *The Works of Herman Melville* (London: Constable, 1924), XIV, 316-317.

214. The pertinent section if Kames is in volume I, chapter 5, of the *Elements of Criticism* (Boston: Samuel Etheridge, 1768), p. 212; any of a dozen British and American editions of Kames would be readily available to Melville, for the *Elements of Criticism* had been a standard text in American academies since the early decades of the century. Its omission from Duyckinck's well stocked library would be unthinkable. Although most of Kant's works had been translated and published in American editions prior to 1850-1851, a complete translation of the tract on aesthetics was not available; however, *Prose Writers of Germany*, a collection of translations edited by the aesthetician and Germanophile F.H. Hedge, included among excerpts from the *Critique of Aesthetic Judgement* the section on the mathematical sublime, translated by J.E. Cabot. A popular collection — Carey and Hart of Philadelphia issued it in 1847 and again in 1849 — it was very likely a source of Melville's knowledge of Kant and other German idealists.

215. "The Sources and Effects in England of Kant's Philosophy of Beauty," p. 320.

structures tellingly recur in close proximity in "The Blanket," and they are the chapter's only architectural images. The hieroglyphics on the whale call the pyramids to Ishmael's mind, and, in the second of two references to St. Peter's in the chapter, Ishmael remarks,

> ... how hopeless to teach these fine things! Of erections, how few are domed like St. Peter's! of creatures how few vast as the whale! (p. 306)

In "The Sphinx" Ishmael continues his cetological anatomy, celebrating the beheading of a sperm whale as "a scientific anatomical feat, upon which experienced whale surgeons very much pride themselves" (p. 308). Yet even as he restricts his attention to one aspect of the whale's anatomy, he demonstrates the arbitrariness of any division of parts in an essentially formless beast. "Consider," he asks his reader,

> that the whale has nothing that can properly be called a neck; on the contrary, where his head and body seem to join, there, in that very place, is the thickest part of him. (p. 308)

Ahab addresses the "'vast and venerable head'," asking for the secrets that it, having "'dived the deepest'" and witnessed the horrors of the sea's "insensate maw" (pp. 309-310), has been party to. The question is appropriately held in suspense through the timely interlarding of two digressive chapters on different subjects. When the subject of the whale's head and the question of its knowledge again are broached, the *Pequod* is in the "very poor plight" of being badly trimmed between a Kantian sperm whale's head and a Lockean right whale's head; from a question of knowledge Melville appropriately turns to prior questions of epistemology. The epistemological controversy imaged in the two whale heads has been discussed above, and here we need only underscore Ishmael's choice for further anatomizing of the Kantian rather than the Lockean head. Melville's business is, in the physical and metaphysical sense, with superlatives; likened to the debasing image of a large shoe, the Lockean head is quickly cast off from Ishmael's attention as he focuses on the Kantian head of the sperm whale. "The most imposing physiognomical view to be had of the Sperm Whale," he remarks, "is that of the full front of his head. This aspect is sublime" (p. 344). Fully six consecutive chapters are devoted to this aspect, each of them advancing Ishmael's adumbration of formlessness, enormous size, and impenetrable mystery as the attributes of the whale.

Placing the sperm whale's head before his reader, Ishmael would have him, as "a sensible physiologist," form "some unexaggerated, intelligent estimate of whatever battering-ram power may be lodged there." This is a vital point," for "you must either satisfactorily settle this matter with yourself, or for ever remain an infidel" as to the "appalling" capacity of a whale to destroy a ship (p. 334). Noting that the whale has no nose and that the eyes and ears of the creature are on the sides of its head, "nearly one third of his entire length from the front," Ishmael develops the battering ram of the sperm whale's head as something like the abstract idea of mass itself. "Without a single organ of tender prominence of any sort whatever," the "front of the Sperm Whale's head is a dead, blind wall" (p. 335). Noting that he does "not think that any sensation lurks in it," Ishmael speculates that the ram is comprised of "mystical lung-celled honeycombs" that are filled with air; "If this be so, fancy the irresistibleness of that might, to which the most impalpable and destructive of all elements contributes" (pp. 335-336). This "dead, impregnable, uninjurable wall" — precisely the wall through which Ahab would strike — swims at the fore of "a mass of tremendous life, only to be adequately estimated as piled wood is — by the cord; and all obedient to one volition, as the smallest insect" (p. 336).

Ishmael devotes an entire chapter to the case of the whale, which he likens to the greatest cask in the world, "The Great Heidelburgh Tun." The tapping of this cask, the drawing from it of spermaceti, is elaborately described in the famous chapter that follows, "Cistern and Buckets." Here the drowned Narcissus of "Loomings" surfaces in the company of Plato. Bailing oil from the whale's case, Tashtego slips and plunges into it, only to be saved from a "delicious death" by Queequeg's "running delivery" of him through a hole hacked in the head. The obstetrical joke catches up the several strands of Melville's critique of idealism and the problem of self and external reality at its core. Had "Tashtego perished in that thead, it had been a very precious perishing ... How many, think ye, have likewise fallen into Plato's honey head, and sweetly perished there?" (p. 343)

In the next chapter on the head of the whale, Melville employs a favorite topographical metaphor in imaging the whale's brow as "The Prairie." After a characteristic confession of insufficiency — "I try all things; I achieve what I can" — he attempts to apply "two semi-sciences," physiognomy and phrenology,[216] to the whale's forehead, although he is aware that

> Such an enterprise would seem almost as hopeful as for Lavater to have scrutinized the wrinkles on the Rock of Gibraltar, or for Gall to have mounted a ladder and manipulated the Dome of the Pantheon. (p. 343)

216. Physiognomy is appropriately tagged a "semi-science," for it attempts to read the features of the face as transcendental ciphers of spirit; Johann Kaspar Lavater wrote a text on the subject that Melville bought in London in 1849 (Sealts, *Checklist*, entry no. 322) and that was of special interest among European and American idealist circles. Melville probably knew that Emerson repeatedly mentioned Lavater in his works. See Tyrus Hillway, "Melville's Use of Two Pseudo-Sciences," *Modern Language Notes* 64 (March 1949): 145-150.

Taking a tour of the whale's battering-ram in a "jolly-boat," Ishmael develops a superbly comic digression into an anatomy in miniature of the sublime. he moves from the grandeur of the curved brow of the bull to the majesty of the elephant's brow; "Human or animal, the mystical brow is as that great golden seal affixed by the German emperors to their decrees. It signifies 'God: done this day by my hand'." Through the inevitable topographical conceit, Ishmael defines the whale's brow as supremely sublime. In man the brow is usually "but a mere strip of alpine land lying along the snow line," for few are the foreheads that

> ... like Shakespeare's of Melancthon's rise so high, and descend so low, that the eyes themselves seem clear, eternal, tideless mountain lakes; and all above them in the forehead's wrinkles, you seem to track the antlered thoughts descending there to drink ... But in the great Sperm Whale, this high and mighty god-like dignity inherent in the brow is so immensely amplified, that gazing on it, in that full front view, *you feel the Deity and the dread powers more forcibly than in beholding any other object in living nature*. (pp. 344-345; italics added)

Nearly every aesthetician who discoursed of the sublime remarked the capacity of a mass that is featureless or formless to effect the idea of infinity, and it is precisely this effect that Ishmael is remarking in the whale's brow; for in it, he reports,

> you see no one point precisely; not one distinct feature is revealed; *no nose, eyes, ears, or mouth; no face; he has none,* proper; nothing but that one broad firmament of a forehead, pleated with riddles; dumbly lowering with the doom of boats and ships, and men. (p. 345; italics added)

The "horizontal, semi-crescentic depression" in the forehead's middle is seen by Ishmael as "Lavater's mark of genius":

> But how? Genius in a Sperm Whale? Has the Sperm Whale ever written a book, spoken a speech? No, his great genius is declared in his doing nothing in particular to prove it. It is moreover declared in his pyramidical silence. (p. 345)

Seeing that silence as finally and eternally impenetrable, Ishmael defines the shapeless mass of the whale's brow as an ultimate enigma. If the "profounder and more subtle meanings" in the "simplest peasant's face" cannot be read, he concludes, "how may unlettered Ishmael hope to read the awful Chaldee of the Sperm Whale's brow?" (p. 345)

Having repeatedly confessed his incapacities, Ishmael nevertheless drives toward the logical conclusion of anatomical dissection of the whale. In "The Nut" he bores through the skull of the whale in search of the seat of its intelligence. The chapter opens in mystification, for, "If the Sperm Whale be physiognomically a Sphinx, to the phrenologist his brain seems that geometrical circle which it is impossible to square" (p. 346). So thoroughly secreted behind endless layers of mass is the whale's brain that some whalemen known to Ishmael have flatly denied its existence. "Phrenologically the head of this Leviathan, in the creature's living intact state, is an entire delusion," for the brain of the beast is extraordinarily remote from the surface of its ram-like brow. And, Ishmael continues, "As for his true brain, you can then see no indications of it, nor feel any. The whale, like all things that are mighty, wears a false brow to the common world" (p. 346). When Ishmael finally exposes the whale's brain he reaches a trying pass in his anatomy, for, having in "The Nut" and elsewhere attributed great intellective powers to the whale, he must somehow cope with the apparent paradox of the diminutive size of the brain relative to the creature's total mass. He does so by insisting that the phrenologist must, in dealing with the whale, push his "investigations from the cerebellum through the spinal canal." The whale's vertebrae seem to bear a striking resemblance to "a strung necklace of dwarfed skulls" (p. 347), suggesting that the intellect of the whale rests not in the brain merely but in the entire spinal cavity from cranium to tail.[217] This argumentative tactic of the endlessly resourceful Ishmael effectively fuses two types of sublimity, Kant's mathematical sublime, which finds its source in form and extension, and dynamic sublime, which is the sublime of power. The whale's brain — its intellective organ — is but the extension of its tail, the source of its power.

Ishmael's anatomy of the whale appropriately culminates in the chapter on "The Tail," wherein he adumbrates something like an aesthetic of power. All of the tail's "flexions," whether wielded "in sport, or in earnest, or in anger," are "invariably marked by exceeding grace. Therein no fairy's arm can transcend it" (p. 374). Combining as it does horrific power and incomparable grace, the tail of the whale is the perfect embodiment of the moral ambiguity that Melville insists lies at the heart of the sublime of nature. As the hieroglyphical markings of the whale's brow remain forever encoded, so the gestures of the whale's tail are "mystic" and seem akin "to Free-Mason signs and symbols" (p. 376). Having reached the end of his anatomy, Ishmael once again insists that the absolute meaning of the whale forever eludes the reductionist approach to its form:

> Dissect him how I may, then, I but go skin deep; I know him not, and never will. But if I know not even the tail of this whale, how understand his head? much more, how comprehend his face, when face he has none? (p. 376)

With devilishly clever parody of Exodus 33:23, Ishmael subverts the complacencies of the religious sublime by hinting at a malignant link between the enigma of the whale and that of God:

217. Melville has here hit upon a physiological fact; a variety of neurological responses take place not in the cerebellum but in the spinal cavity. His suggestion, made in "The Chart" and elsewhere, that the whale is capable of a kind of calculation, is also accurate; the whale's brain is exceeded only by the human brain in its mass of white matter, the substance in which abstraction occurs.

> Thou shalt see my back parts, my tail, he seems to say, but my face shall not be
> seen. But I cannot completely make out his back parts; and hint what he will about
> his face, I say again he has no face. (p. 377)

Ostensibly a quest for what Ishmael calls the "true form" of the whale,
the cetological chapters of *Moby-Dick* actually establish the whale as
protean, and subvert any clear definition of its form. They are perhaps
the finest index of Melville's creative control, for in them he refined and
heightened the sublimity of the whale while apparently employing
materials and methodologies that, as they effect definition, by their very
nature are inimical to the sublime. The range of difficulties he faced may
be suggested by citing but one — that of fostering the appearance of an
exhaustive empirical anatomy of the whale in which the essential tool of
empiricism, precise measurement, is necessarily excluded. Knowing full
well that clearly defined extension implies clearly defined form, and that
clear extension or form in the whale would preclude its effecting the idea
of infinity, Melville had to exclude measurement from his cetological
chapters; thus from "The Blanket" through "The Tail" in place of
measurement he provides stupendous and therefore unimaginable analogies of size. The issue of the size of the whale is finally confronted in "A
Bower in the Arsacides," "Measurement of the Whale's Skeleton," and
"The Fossil Whale," a three-chapter sequence that is placed rather late in
the novel after Ishmael's cetological anatomizing has been largely
suspended for some sixteen chapters. Recalling his visit to the skeleton of
a stranded whale in the Arsacides, Ishmael avails himself of the opportu-
nity to set before the reader the whale "in his ultimatum; that is to say, in
his unconditional skeleton" (p. 445). Here precise measurement would
seem to be ineluctable, but Ishmael manages to turn "A Bower in the
Arsacides" and the two chapters that follow into a masterpiece of
obfuscation. The whale skeleton forms a sylvan bower, the first of a
catalogue of topographical analogues that indefinitely expand the whale's
size rather than define it. It becomes the Cretan labyrinth as Ishmael, like
Theseus, employs a ball of twine to find his way among the skeleton's
"many winding, shaded collonades and arbors" (p. 447). Ishmael admits
to have taken measurements during his tour, but before yielding them up
he launches into several temporizing digressions the last of which
suggests that even measurement, the most precise mode of apprehending
the external world, is subjective. The question of external reality always
becomes a question of self; the whale's measurements were, Ishmael
jokingly insists, tattooed on his arm,

> ... as in my wild wanderings at that period, there was no other secure way of
> preserving such valuable statistics. But as I was crowded for space, and wished the
> other parts of my body to remain a blank page for a poem I was then composing, ...
> I did not trouble myself with the odd inches; nor, indeed, should inches at all enter
> into a congenial admeasurement of the whale. (p. 449)

In "Measurement of the Whale's Skeleton" Ishmael finally offers his figures, but not before he has countered their definitive effect through another catalogue of expansive analogies and metaphors. The whale's carcass would "outweigh the combined population of a whole village of one thousand one hundred inhabitants"; brains, "like yoked cattle, should be put to this leviathan, to make him at all budge to any landsman's imagination"; the ribs of the whale resemble "the hull of a great ship new-laid upon the stocks"; piled vertically, the vertebrae would rival Pompey's Pillar or a Gothic spire (pp. 450-451). The skeleton he finally confesses to have been less than a hundred feet long, but without pause, he dismisses the figure as an utter deception. It is "vain and foolish" to mistake the "utter blank" that is the whale's skeleton as index of the reality of the beast, for the bones convey "half of the true notion of the living magnitude" of the whale (pp. 450-451). As a dissected whale is no whale, a dead whale is no whale:

> No. Only the heart of quickest perils; only when within the eddyings of his angry flukes; only on the profound unbounded sea, can the fully invested whale be truly and livingly found out. (p. 451)

Or, as Ahab put it, nature is mere pasteboard without its sublime dynamism, without "the living act, the undoubted deed" (p. 161).

Broadly regarded, the cetological chapters of *Moby-Dick* have two general aesthetic effects, both of which had been discussed in eighteenth-century aesthetic discourse as conducive of the sublime. First, by fostering a conception of the whale as a formless, protean unity from which no discrete feature may be isolated, they connect the whale to that "unity as boundless or endless allness"[218] that Coleridge defined as the ultimate sublime. The same sort of sublimity Kant had discussed as obtainable in an object "even devoid of form," so far

> ... as it immediately involves, or else by its presence provokes, a representation of limitlessness, yet with a super-added thought of its totality.[219]

Kant's super-added thought of totality functions importantly in the second aesthetic effect of the cetological chapters, for without it the endlessly multiplied cetological perspectives generated by Ishmael would effect a merely picturesque complexity as opposed to sublimity. As Coleridge had remarked,

> Where the parts by their harmony produce an effect of a whole, but where there is no seen form of a whole producing or explaining the parts of it, where the parts only are seen and distinguished, ... the picturesque [is effected].[220]

218. From a letter reprinted in the Shawcross edition of *Biographia Literaria*, II, 309.
219. *Critique of Aesthetic Judgment*, p. 90.
220. *Biographia Literaria*, II, 309.

Had Ishmael not consistently disparaged his anatomy of parts as an inadequate means of defining the whole, the super-added thought of the whale's totality would be lost; the Lockean whale-head, to borrow Melville's conceit, would overbalance the Kantian. The anatomy of parts is ingeniously constructed to achieve what Coleridge called "majesty," an effect that arises where "the impression of the whole, i.e., the sense of unity, predominates so as to abstract the mind from the parts,"[221] but as those parts all foster, through expansive, analogical imagery, a sense of vastness, they are in a special sense uniform; as the aesthetician Baillie had written in 1747, "... when the Object is uniform by seeing *Part*, the least glimpse gives a full and compleat Idea of the *Whole*, and thus at once may be distinctly conveyed the vastest Sensation."[222] Just as Ishmael's gargantuan metaphors for the whale suggest that in his wholeness the creature is ultimately unimaginable, the epic effort of the anatomical chapters suggests what Kant described as the sublime straining of the imagination "to receive in a single intuition a measure for magnitudes which it takes an appreciable time to apprehend."[223]

While Melville expends nearly thirty chapters on formlessness, ageless-ness, and limitlessness of power as sublime qualities of the whale, he devotes but one chapter — "The Whiteness of the Whale" — to the subject of its colorlessness. Rightly assessed by Harry Levin as "one of the farthest ranging chapters in our literature,"[224] this extraordinary complex of myth, anthropology, iconography, physics, epistemology, and aesthetic does more to define Moby Dick as the quintessential sublime than all of the cetological chapters together. In accordance with its thematic importance, "The Whiteness of the Whale" is located very early in the book so that the epistemological and aesthetic ambiguities it establishes may invest the symbolic whale many chapters before it is seen.[225] And the portentous statement with which Ishmael opens the

221. Ibid.

222. John Baillie, *An Essay on the Sublime* (Los Angeles: Augustan Reprint Society, 1953), p. 18. Baillie's essay represents an important stage in the development of the sublime toward the subjectivism of Kant; see Monk, *The Sublime*, pp. 72-77.

223. *Critique of Aesthetic Judgement*, p. 108. Addison may have had something similar in mind when he remarked the pleasures that arise from contemplation of expansive horizons; "The Mind of Man naturally hates every thing that looks like Restraint upon it, and is apt to fancy it self under a sort of Confinement, when the Sight is pent up in a narrow Compass," he wrote in *Spectator*, No. 412 (*The Spectator*, III, 540-541). Cf. Burke's remarks on "Difficulty" as a source of the sublime (*Enquiry*, p. 77).

224. *The Power of Blackness*, p. 28.

225. Mansfield and Vincent (*Moby-Dick*, p. 710) present compelling evidence tha t the chapter was composed fairly late in the composition of the book; this, coupled with its placement in the first quarter of *Moby-Dick*, supports the likelihood that Melville discovered the potential aesthetic implications of his books as he composed it.

chapter defines the analytic of whiteness as a crux of the book:

> It was the whiteness of the whale that above all things appalled me. But how can I hope to explain myself here; and yet, in some dim, random way, explain myself I must, else all these chapters might be naught. (p. 185)

That not even that extraordinary rarity, the albino whale, could be called "white" in any strict sense itself suggests that behind Melville's initial choice of the hue lay his awareness of its symbolic potentialities. Possibly taking his inspiration from published accounts of Mocha Dick,[226] a mottled whale, he chose what Ishmael calls "the colorless all-color" (p. 193) as that in which the ambiguity of chromatic phenomena is most intense.[227] but neither his choice of the color nor his exploitation of its epistemological and aesthetic ambiguities was made, as most students of *Moby-Dick* have thought, *in sui generis*. In "The Whiteness of the Whale" we are confronted not with a paucity but with a superabundance of sources.

Since Locke, developing the implications of Newton's *Opticks*, relegated color to the category of illusory, secondary attributes of matter, the sublime had come to be associated in paintings, literature, and aesthetic discourse with dramatic chiaroscuro, with darkness, or with colorless light. The form to which Melville was first exposed to Locke's idea of color is most suggestive. Lindley Murray's *English Reader*,[228] the textbook he owned and used at the Albany Academy, included an imaginary dialogue by Lyttelton in which Locke and the French sceptic Bayle discuss the implications of chromatic phenomena. From Locke's theory Bayle concludes that color is not, as Locke would have it, the means by which God beautifies the earth for man's pleasure but the means by which He fosters an insidious deception. That Melville was taken by this heretical idea is suggested by the fact that he sought out and purchased a complete edition of Bayle's *Dictionary* in 1849 and that he subsequently

226. See Mansfield's and Vincent's notes, *Moby-Dick*, pp. 691-695. Notices of encounters with Mocha Dick appeared in the *Knickerbocker Magazine* in May, 1839, July, 1846, and March, 1849; an encounter with the notorious whale in 1840, rumors of which Melville may have heard while aboard the *Acushnet*, was reported in the Detroit *Free Press* on April 3, 1892.

227. Melville seems always to have been interested in the symbolic potential of whiteness, as the digression on the White Shark in *Mardi* (pp. 39-42) and the use of the color in *White-Jacket* suggest. For a catalogue of Melville's use of whiteness that is, unfortunately, of little interpretive value, see George Raymond Creeger, "The Symbolism of Whiteness in Melville's Prose Fiction," *Jahrbuch für Amerikanstudien* 5 (1960): 147-163 as well as the more general study of Max Frank, *Die Farb und Lichtsymbolik im Prosawerk Herman Melvilles* (Heidelberg: Carl Winter, 1967).

228. Sealts, *Checklist*, entry no. 380; see John T. Frederick, "Melville's Early Acquaintance with Bayle," *American Literature* 39 (January 1968): 545-547.

garnered from it much material that he put to fictive use.[229] Melville could hardly have avoided many repeated encounters with the idea of color as a secondary attribute of matter, for among the aesthetic tracts he is known to have read nearly all contain discussions of the matter. Addison, Akenside, Burke, Hartley, Hume, Alison, Goethe, and Ruskin all confront Locke's chromatic ideas and any one of them could provide sufficient information to serve as a catalyst for Melville's analysis of whiteness. Doubtless Melville's readings beyond aesthetic discourse also played some part in the composition of "The Whiteness of the Whale." He was probably exposed to popularizations of Newton's and Locke's ideas that were common in the periodicals of his day.[230] Having read deeply in English romantic verse, he was surely aware of the disruptive effects that Newton's analysis of the rainbow had had on romantic faith in nature; the delusive rainbow of "The Piazza" and the rainbows of *Moby-Dick* that "only irradiate vapor" and "never visit the clear air" (p. 372) demonstrate his interest in the problem. In Eckermann's *Conversations of Goethe*, to which there are repeated references in *Moby-Dick*, he came across the efforts of an idealist to counter Newton's mechanistic conception of light and color with a transcendental theory, and he well may have read in Sir Charles Eastlake's translation of Goethe's *Farbenlehre*.[231] He must have known the "Digression Concerning Blackness" in *Pseudodoxia Epidemica*, one of his favorite books, as well as the chapter entitled "Of that which is Signified by the Colours White and Blue" in Rabelais, a translation of whose works he borrowed from Duyckinck in 1848.[232] Poe had worked toward the same sort of horrific sublime in *The Narrative of Arthur Gordon Pym* (1838) as Melville took up in *Moby-Dick*,

229. Sealts, *Checklist*, entry no. 51; see Bell, "Pierre Bayle and *Moby-Dick*," pp. 626-648; while she points to Bayle as the likely source of Melville's idea of color, Bell omits notice of another important connection; in the *Historical and Critical Dictionary* (London: J.J. and P. Knapton, 1734-1738), IV, 654, Bayle asks, rhetorically, if God deceives men in respect to colors, "what hinders but he may deceive them with respect to extension?"

230. Mansfield and Vincent (*Moby-Dick*, pp. 704-705) cite an article entitled "The Doctrine of Colours" that appeared in the *American Magazine of Useful and Entertaining Knowledge* (Vol. 2 [May 1836]: 375) under the editorship of Hawthorne; it offers a respectable summation of Newton's idea of color.

231. On references to Goethe's theory of color in the *Conversations* see Mansfield and Vincent, *Moby-Dick*, p. 705.

232. Melville borrowed three volumes of Browne's *Works* from Duyckinck in 1848 and bought a one-volume folio edition in 1849 (Sealts, *Checklist* entry nos. 89, 90). On his reading in Rabelais (Sealts, *Checklist*, no. 417) in relation to the chapter on whiteness, see W.H. Wells "Moby-Dick and Rabelais," *Modern Language Notes* 38 (February 1923): 123.

and it would seem at least likely that Melville knew of the ghastly use of whiteness Poe had made in his concluding chapter.[233]

Considering how thoroughly Ishmael's wide-ranging hunt for the source of the power of whiteness has been explicated, it is remarkable that no student of Melville has noticed that the bulk of "The Whiteness of the Whale" is expended not in hunting but in exposing the poor heft and inadequate temper of the conventional weaponry of perceptual theories. "Dim" Ishmael's speculations may be, but "random" they are not; for the chapter presents in sequence associationism, sensationism, and intuitive idealism, the three epistemological theories available in Melville's day. As Ishmael takes up each theory, he tests its capacity to explain the power of whiteness.

The first half of "The Whiteness of the Whale" tests an associationist perspective on the power of whiteness. Ishmael begins by developing a gargantuan catalogue of the benign associations of the color: whiteness "refiningly enhances beauty," as in marbles, japonicas, and pearls; "various nations have ... recognized a certain royal pre-eminence in this hue"; the royal standards of Pegu, of Siam, of the Austrian Empire, were white; it gives "the white man ideal mastership over every dusky tribe"; it is "significant of gladness"; it is the "emblem" of the "innocence of brides," the "benignity of age," the "deepest pledge of honor"; in the "higher mysteries of the most august religions" it is the "symbol of the divine spotlessness and power"; from the Latin word for white "all Christian priests derive the name of one part of their sacred cassock"; the throne of God is white and "the Holy One that sitteth there white like wool" (pp. 185-186). These are but a fraction of the exempla of Melville's catalogue, which is fostered at once to suggest the richness of associations that have accreted to whiteness and to demonstrate the insufficiency of the associationist epistemology. In a period of nearly four hundred fifty words, scores of benign associations of whiteness are preceded by an initial, qualifying "though," a term that potently establishes an aura of anticipation sustained through a maze of subordinate clauses and qualifying phrases. All the cumbrous machinery of association finally collapses as the conclusion of the period breaches with a climactic "yet":

... yet for all these accumulated associations, with whatever is sweet, and honorable, and sublime, there yet lurkes an elusive something in the innermost idea of this hue, which strikes more of panic to the soul than that redness with affrights in blood. (p. 186)

It is this elusive quality in the innermost idea of whiteness, argues

233. For an incisive and detailed discussion of the aesthetic of the sublime in Poe see Kent. P. Ljungquist, "Poe and the Sublime: His Two Short Sea Tales in the Context of an Aesthetic Tradition," *Criticism* 17 (Spring 1975): 131-151.

Ishmael, that "causes the thought of whiteness, *when divorced from more kindly associations,* and *coupled with any object terrible in itself, to heighten that terror to the furthest bounds"* (p. 186; italics added). Here Ishmael effectively dismisses associationist epistemology — especially in its aesthetic phase — as inadequate to the task of accounting for the power of whiteness; abstracted from objects or phenomena in themselves regarded as good, whiteness is portentous and horrific. The qualifying clause, "coupled with any object terrible in itself," confines the range of subsequent examples of white phenomena to the sublime; Ishmael immediately instances the white polar bear and the white shark, beasts that effect sublime horror in themselves and not through cultural association.

Although Melville need not have had Burke specifically in mind at this point in "The Whiteness of the Whale," it may be illuminating to regard his notion of whiteness as a catalyst of heightened terror as an addendum, of sorts, to Burke's *Enquiry.* Sections xiv through xviii in Part Four of Burke's treatise are devoted to "Locke's opinion concerning darkness," to the idea that "Darkness [is] terrible in its own nature," to the question of "Why darkness is terrible," to "The effects of Blackness," and to the moderation of the effects of blackness. Countering Locke's idea that blackness and darkness are frightening through the accretion of negative associations, Burke argues that they are terrifying in and of themselves. Immediately after confining the range of his argument to objects terrible in themselves, Ishmael shifts from an associationist view of his problem to something like Burkean sensationism. "Bethink thee of the albatross," he remarks,

> whence come those clouds of spiritual wonderment and pale dread, in which that white phantom sails in all imaginations? *Not Coleridge first threw that spell; but God's great, unflattering laureate, Nature.* (p. 187; italics added)

Here Ishmael dismisses one epistemology and takes up another, following an important current of late eighteenth-century aesthetics away from the tempered experiential world of association toward immediacy of sensory impact. While to the associationist aestheticians a complex of cultural associations forged by human laureates interceded between a percipient and the raw data of experience, Burke helped to foster new and romantic worlds for art by legitimizing immediate and intense sensation as aesthetic experience. The moral dimension of that experience was for Burke non-reflective and as instantaneous as an instinctive pity or fear. Like Burke, Melville moves toward the conviction that the creations of "God's great, unflattering laureate, Nature" are truly in and of themselves benign or horrific. Melville's subject is of course not Burke's blackness but whiteness, but Ishmael's view that whiteness is nature's "crowning attribute of the terrible" (p. 189), is at the very least consistent with the epistemology behind Burke's aesthetic.[234]

Sensing that the distinction between Coleridge's and nature's albatross has not adequately carried his aesthetic argument, Ishmael appends to he lines I have italicized above the longest footnote in Melville's fiction. "In a matter like this," Ishmael says later in his chapter, "subtlety appeals to subtlety, and without imagination no man can follow another to these halls" (p. 190). As Melville expended no little imagination in finding order in these halls — epistemological labyrinths might be a better figure — it is only fit that we follow him. The chief function of the note on the albatross is to support the contention that the power of whiteness exists independent of cultural association. Ishmael recalls his first encounter with an albatross:

> It was during a prolonged gale, in waters hard upon the Antarctic seas. From my forenoon watch below, I ascended to the overclouded deck; and there, dashed upon the main hatches, I saw a regal, feathery thing of unspotted whiteness, and with a hooked, Roman bill sublime ... Though bodily unharmed, it uttered cries, as some king's ghost in supernatural distress. Through its inexpressible, strange eyes, methought I peeped to secrets which took hold of God. As Abraham before the angels, I bowed myself; the white thing was so white, its wings so wide, and those forever exiled waters, I had lost the miserable warping memories of traditions and of towns.

Awakening from a trance-like state, Ishmael asks a sailor to identify the bird:

> A goney, he replied. Goney! I never had heard that name before; is it conceivable that this glorious thing is utterly unknown to men ashore! never! But some time after, I learned that goney was some seaman's name for albatross. So that by no possibility could Coleridge's wild Rhyme have had aught to do with those mystical impressions that were mine, when I saw that bird upon our deck. For neither had I then read the Rhyme, nor knew the bird to be an albatross. (pp. 187-188)

Not yet content that he has sufficiently grounded his argument, Ishmael provides yet another catalogue of examples, this time composed of white things that are either neutral or terrifying in terms of their emotive impact. He cites the white Steed of the prairies that evokes "trembling reverence and awe" (p. 188); the albino human who, though "as well made as other men," is "more strangely hideous than the ugliest abortion" (p. 189); the White Squall of the South Seas and the White Hoods of Ghent; the "king of terrors" who, when "personified by the evangelist," rides a "pallid horse" (p. 189). "Therefore, in his other moods," he concludes, "symbolize whatever grand or gracious thing he will by whiteness, no man can deny that in its profoundest idealized

234. Glenn ("Melville and the Sublime in *Moby-Dick*," pp. 165-182) points to Melville's significant debt to Burke's *Enquiry*: see also Richard S. Moore, "Burke, Melville, and the 'Power of Blackness' in *Moby-Dick*," *American Transcendental Quarterly* 29 (February 1976): 30-33.

significance it calls up a peculiar apparition to the soul" (pp. 189-190). Again he insists that the power of whiteness may be abstracted from objects invested by the color and that it is in some undefinable way independent of psychological association. "Why," he asks, does the man "of *untutored ideality*" find the bare mention of "Whitsuntide" sufficient to evoke "dreary, speechless processions of slow-pacing pilgrims, down cast and hooded?"

> Or, to the *unread, unsophisticated* Protestant of the Middle American States, why does the passing mention of a White Friar or a White Nun, evoke such an eyeless statue in the soul? (p. 190; emphasis added)

Turning to the city of Lima, he argues that the "remembrance of her cathedral-toppling earthquakes," the "stampedoes of her frantic seas," and her wrecked buildings, "wrenched cope-stones," and crumbled crosses are not together sufficient cause for the dreadful atmosphere of the place; for

> ... it is not these things alone which make tearless Lima, the strangest, saddest city thou can'st see. For Lima has taken the white veil; and there is a higher horror in this whiteness of her woe.[235] (p.191)

And he cites similar phenomena, among them the sailor

> beholding the scenery of the Antarctic seas; where at times, by some infernal trick of legerdemain in the powers of frost and air, he, shivering and half shipwrecked, instead of rainbows speaking hope and solace to his misery, views what seems a boundless church-yard grinning upon him with its lean ice monuments and splintered crosses.[236] (p. 192)

Momentarily in despair that the power of whiteness has eluded his grasp, Ishmael suspends his catalogue:

> But thou sayest, methinks this white-lead chapter about whiteness is but a white flag hung out from a craven soul; thou surrenderest to a hypo, Ishmael. (p. 192)

White-lead is the primary ingredient of white paint. Hunting out a power that is ultimately ineffable, Ishmael is reduced to fostering white images that do not explain the power of whiteness but merely exemplify its horrific portentousness. He offers, however, one last example of the sort of phenomenon he is attempting to explain, and in this example he moves from a sensationalist epistemology to idealistic intuitionism.

235. Doubtless Melville had in mind when writing this passage that the earthquake that devastated Lima in 1746 had a profoundly unsettling effect on deistic faith in the order and benignity of nature.

236. These lines were probably inspired by Caspar David Friedrich's famous painting, *The Polar Sea* (1824), which Melville may have seen abroad in 1849, or by a number of American paintings that were themselves inspired by Friedrich's painting. "Hope," the name affixed to the wreck in the painting, is a tribute to Turner, who had written a long philosophical poem on *The Fallacies of Hope* and who was much admired by Friedrich.

Tell me, why this strong young colt, foaled in some peace-valley of Vermont, far removed from all beasts of prey — why is it that upon the sunniest day, if you but shake a fresh buffalo robe behind him, so that he cannot even see it, but only smells its wild animal muskiness — why will he start, snort, and with bursting eyes paw the ground in phrensies of affright? There is no remembrance in him of any gorings of wild creatures in his green northern home, so that the strange muskiness he smells cannot recall to him anything associated with the experience of former perils; for what knows he, this New England colt, of the black bisons of distant Oregon?

No: but here thou beholdest even in a dumb brute, the instinct of the knowledge of the demonism of the world. (p. 192)

Burke, who believed that "When we go but one step beyond the immediately sensible qualities of things, we go out of our depth,"[237] could brook no "demonism" in the world, and for him terror had nothing whatever to do with the "knowledge" of which Ishmael writes. "Thus, then," Ishmael continues,

the muffled rollings of a milky sea; the bleak rustlings of the festooned frosts of mountains; the desolate shiftings of the windrowed snows of prairies; all these, to Ishmael, are as the shaking of that buffalo robe to the frightened colt! (p. 193)

In his immediate, instinctive panic when confronted by such phenomena Ishmael intuits super-sensible, noumenal reality. Though neither knows

where lie the nameless things of which the mystic sign gives forth such hints; yet with me, as with the colt, somewhere those things must exist.

This is clearly the conviction of a transcendentalist who finds a terrifying malignity behind the appearances of the phenomenal world.

Ishmael's transition from sensationism to idealism may strike a twentieth-century reader as a sorely trying pass, but, regardless of the philosophical difficulties that attend it, it is consistent with the currents of American aesthetic and epistemological thought in Melville's day. Perhaps because they were always inescapably confronted with the paucity of civilization in the American wilds, American thinkers had always been devoted to Locke and to sensation as the ultimate test of truth, and, Burke's assault on Lockean associationism notwithstanding, their enthusiasm for Burke's Enquiry attests to an abiding concern for the immediacy of sense data. As has been discussed, with the rise of romantic idealism in American many thinkers attempted the no doubt impossible reconciliation of sensationalism and idealistic intuitionism, or, as Ishmael would have it, Locke and Kant. We recall that Emerson had opened Nature, his idealist aesthetic manifesto, with a dismissal of cultural associations and a call for a radically immediate immersion in nature. Although there is no doubt an impassable difference of metaphysic between sensationism and idealism, there is a special sense in which

237. Enquiry, pp. 129-130.

Emerson and other transcendental thinkers in America arrived at an idealist position via an extreme extension of Lockean ideas. "Standing on the bare ground," in naked and immediate relation to Nature, Emerson first "becomes" sensation itself and then becomes "nothing"; his head "bathed by the blithe air and uplifted into infinite space," he finds that "all mean egotism vanishes":

> I become a transparent eyeball; I am nothing; I see all; the currents of the Universal Being circulate through me; I am part or parcel of God. The name of the nearest friend sounds then foreign and accidental: to be brothers, to be acquaintances, master or servant, is then a trifle and a disturbance.[238]

There is no *structural* difference in this paradigm of the experience of the sublime and Ishmael's encounter with the albatross through which he loses "the miserable warping memories of traditions and of towns" (p. 187). But there is a profoundly important *moral* difference, for "The Whiteness of the Whale" and the book in which it is the aesthetic crux stand as Melville's virulent assault on the complacent assumption that the noumenon, the "Universal Being" of the transcendentalists, is in any sense benignant.

It is significant that the seeds of Melville's revolt against the moral sublime through an analysis of chromatic phenomena were sown at the very beginnings of discourse on the sublime. In *Spectator* No. 413 Addison interrupted his celebration of the grace of God in natural beauty with a troubling digression. "Things would make but a poor Appearance to the Eye, if we saw them only in their proper Figures and Motions," he remarked:

> And what Reason can we assign for their exciting in us many of those Ideas which are different from any thing that exists in the Objects themselves, (for such are Light and Colours) were it not to add Supernumerary Ornaments to the Universe, and make it more agreeable to the Imagination? We are every where entertained with pleasing Shows and Apparitions, we discover imaginary Glories in the Heavens, and in the Earth, and see some of this Visionary Beauty poured out upon the whole Creation; but what a rough unsightly Sketch of Nature should we be entertained with, did all her Colouring vanish? In short, our Souls are at present delightfully lost and bewildered in a pleasing Delusion, and we walk about like the Enchanted Hero of a Romance, who sees beautiful Castles, Woods and Meadows; and at the same time hears the warbling of Birds, and the purling of Streams; but upon the finishing of some secret Spell, the fantastik Scene breaks up, and the disconsolate Knight finds himself on a barren Heath, or in a solitary Desert. It is not improbable that something like this may be the State of the Soul after its first Separation, in respect of the Images it will receive from Matter.[239]

In Addison's transformation of the knight's woods and meadows into a barren wilderness we find an aesthetic and epistemological version of

238. *Works*, I, 10.
239. *The Spectator*, III, 546-547.

Adam's Fall from grace, a Fall that would be repeated often among romantic artists. We find it surfacing, for example, in Emerson: "We have learned," he wrote in "Experience,"

> that we do not see directly, but mediately, and that we have no means of correcting these colored and distorting lenses which we are, or of computing the amount of their errors. Perhaps these subject-lenses have a creative power; perhaps there are no objects.[240]

And, as if in parody of both Addison and Emerson, we find the Fall recounted in the conclusion of "The Whiteness of the Whale": "Is it by its indefiniteness," asks Ishmael, that whiteness

> shadows forth the heartless voids and immensities of the universe, and thus stabs us from behind with the thought of annihilation, when beholding the white depths of the milky way? Or is it, that as in essence whiteness is not so much a color as the visible absence of color, and at the same time the concrete of all colors; is it for these reasons that there is such a dumb blankness, full of meaning, in a wide landscape of snows — a colorless, all-color of atheism from which we shrink? And when we consider the natural philosophers, that all other earthly hues, every stately or lovely emblazoning — the sweet tinges of sunset skies and woods; yea, and the gilded velvets of butterflies, and the butterfly cheeks of young girls; all these are but subtile deceits, not actually inherent in substances, but only laid on from without; so that all deified Nature absolutely paints like the harlot, whose allurements cover nothing but the charnel-house within; and when we proceed further, and consider that the mystical cosmetic which produces every one of her hues, the geat principle of light, for ever remains white or colorless in itself, and if operating without medium upon matter, would touch all objects, even tulips and roses, with its own blank tinge — pondering all this, the palsied universe lies before us a leper; and like wilful travellers in Lapland, who refuse to wear colored and coloring glasses upon their eyes, so the wretched infidel gazes himself blind at the monumental white shroud that wraps all the prospect around him. And of all these things the Albino whale was the symbol. Wonder ye then at the fiery hunt? (p. 194)

There could no more profound alienation from nature than is established here. To own the White Whale is to own the charnel house of noumenal nature. Faith is a function of the deception that is all natural beauty, and it is the infidel and not the faithful who faces the essential truth of nature.

Vortex: Nature's Center

Together with the cetological chapters that flay off the endless layers of appearance with which the whale is invested, Melville's chapter on the whiteness of the whale defines Leviathan as essential, trans-phenomenal nature. The quintessence of sublimity, Moby Dick is the magnificent anwer to the question Melville had broached in *Mardi*: "I may have come to the Penultimate," Babbalanja said, "but where ... is the Ultimate?"[241] This Ultimate — the terms Ideal or Absolute would serve

240. *Works*, III, 75-76.
241. *Mardi*, p. 390.

as well[242] — is of course no chimera unique to Melville, for it is the Absolute of idealist philosophy from Plato to Kant. But *Moby-Dick* is not and was not meant to be a treatise in metaphysics. Even in the most abstract phases of his book Melville is never far from pressing human concerns, from the mundane exigencies of human survival. Finally all metaphysical questions in the book are subsumed into one fundamentally moral question: In the light — or darkness — of nature's Absolute, what manner of moral relation may nature be said to bear to man? Or, to borrow the metaphoric terms to which Melville repeatedly returns, what manner of light may be distilled from the Absolute? This is not a question that might be pursued with philosophic disinterest. Metaphysical only in its preliminary phase, it is finally a moral and, it is fair to say, an aesthetic question.

The empiricism of Ishmael's "natural philosophers," Newton and Locke, provides only the framework of "The Whiteness of the Whale." The science of chromatics and the bifurcated world of primary matter and secondary appearance it implies merely provide the occasion for Melville's moral reflections; Ishmael is more the moralist than the natural philospher or metaphysician when he utters the climactic statement of "The Whiteness of the Whale": "Though in many of its aspects this visible world seems formed in love, the invisible spheres were formed in fright" (p. 193). It is only fitting that Ishmael should arrive at this nightmarish vision through reflection on chromatic phenomena, for the problem of color and light had been for a century and a half and would continue to be grounds of strife and contention between what may be loosely called the mechanistic and the idealist aesthetic visions of nature. The horrific collapse of vibrantly alive, richly colored natural prospects into the sort of deathly, leprous, and colorless landscape remarked by Ishmael was of course a characteristic mode by which the romantic imagination had lamented the estrangement of man from nature; we have in Addison's disenchanted knight and ghastly, barren heath the antecedents of the pale, loitering knight, withered sedge, and cold hillside of Keats's "La Belle Dam Sans Merci," of the bitter landscape in Coleridge's dejection ode, of the chromatically bizarre, rotting sea in the *Rime of the Ancient Mariner*, of the blighted landscapes in Wordsworth, and the like. Behind the stupendous and thoroughly fruitless effort that is Goethe's *Farben-lehre* — a work of special interest for the New England Transcen-

---

242. As R.V. Osbourn has remarked about the identity of Moby Dick as Absolute, Ideal, Ultimate, or Reality, "a fixed philosophical term with limited, tight meaning is not necessary or welcome" ("The White Whale and the Absolute," *Essays in Criticism* 6 [April 1956]: 162).

dentalists[243] — we find the same romantic despair that Newton's *Opticks* had somehow divested nature's colors of moral meaning. In the late eighteenth century, even the tracts of the Lockean associationists bespeak a sense of loss in the face of chromatic science, for few of their essays in aesthetics are without a groping attempt to fix the meaning of colors through appeal to association.[244]

Probably following Goethe's lead, the American Transcendentalists attempted to restore a measure of the meaning of colors through the idea of the identity of Spirit and light. The works of Thoreau and Emerson abound in vestiges of the idea, any number of which might serve as a revealing gloss to Melville's chapter on whiteness. In his journal Thoreau wrote that in the white-out of a blizzard he could discover "where we are and the infinite extent of our relations."[245] Emerson, who believed that "Nature always wears the colors of the spirit," stands in direct opposition to Melville in his complacent judgment that "There is no object so foul that intense light will not make beautiful." Like Melville he finds the zenith of sublimity in pure, unrefracted light, when "... the universe becomes transparent, and the light of higher laws than its own shines through it";[246] but he finds in the transparent universe an ecstatic confirmation of the union of mind and matter, not the horrific estrangement discovered by Melville.

It is tempting to attribute Melville's apparent assault on the transcendentally optimistic reading of the moral significance of light, his discovery of the "blackness of darkness" in light itself, to the radical subjectivism that surfaces several times in *Moby-Dick*. After all, white light no less than the Leviathan's tail may call to mind either Dante's hell or the archangels; it all depends, Ishmael says in "The Tail," upon what mood you are in. But to rest Melville's case on the idea of moral

243. See Pochmann, *German Culture in America*, pp. 442, 168, 228. Emerson, Bronson Alcott, and Margaret Fuller seem to have been especially interested in the book.

244. Hartley, Blair, Kames, Stewart, and Alison all reflected rather unsuccessfully on the aesthetic of color. For a particularly telling example of the problems they confronted, see Richard Payne Knight, *An Analytical Inquiry into the Principles of Taste* (London: G. Mercier & Company, 1805), Part I, Chapter V, "Of Sight," especially pp. 82-87. Attempting to refute Burke's sensationalist approach to the power of color, Knight argues that the power of colors rises not from "any organic pleasure" of sight but from "mental sympathies acting through the medium of the imagination." But he is troubled by the fact that the "cadaverous paleness of death or disease" is a "degree of whiteness" that we should "deem pure" in a "piece of marble or alabaster ... or the fairest damsel of the frigid zone."

245. Entry for March 29, 1853; *Writings*, XI, 64.

246. *Works*, I, 11, 15, 34.

relativism is to miss the full power of the aesthetic argument in *Moby-Dick*.

"The Whiteness of the Whale" may be capped with Melville's moral judgment that in its ultimate "invisible spheres" nature is "formed in fright," but most of the chapter is expended not on the horror but on the ambiguity of the "colorless all-color." The unstable compound of terror and awe that had always comprised the sublime is a subject to which Melville turns repeatedly in *Moby-Dick*, and in the chapter on whiteness he intensifies the moral and emotive tension of the aesthetic to its utmost limit. Whiteness had been associated at least since Plato with the Ultimate or Absolute, consciousness of which is the crux of the experience of sublimity, but as Edward Stone has demonstrated, "... increasingly white appears in the literature of western man as the color of terror (at God's creation) and despair (of His providence)."[247] That increasing terror and despair is an index of the sense of moral estrangement from nature. Following the centripetal impulsion to which his imagination was always given, Melville turned to the analysis of whiteness as a crux of aesthetic and moral faith. As the richness of his catalogue of the iconology of whiteness attests, he was deeply aware of the alternately divine and demoniacal associations that had accreted to the color.[248] In Carlyle he had before him the conspicuous example of a transcendentalist alive to both the horrific and the moral poles of the sort of sublimity he was exploring in *Moby-Dick*, and his treatment of Carlyle's resolution of the problem underscores his radical opposition not to idealism as a metaphysic but to the possibility of any humanly meaningful moral relation to the universe. Like Addison's and Keats's knights who are left endlessly sojourning in a lifeless, mechanistic landscape, Carlyle's Teufelsdroeck spent "dim years" in "a state of crisis" and in "mad Pilgrimmings":

> To me the Universe was all void of life, of Purpose, of Volition, even of Hostility: it was one huge, dead, immeasurable Steam-engine, rolling on, in its dead indifference, to grind me limb from limb ... Why was the Living banished thither

247. *Voices of Despair: Four Motifs in American Literature* (Athens, Ohio: Ohio University Press, 1966), p. 81. In his second chapter, "The Devil is White" (pp. 79-136), Stone provides a massive catalogue of writers in whose works whiteness is associated at once with terror and the Absolute; the group includes, among others, Schopenhauer, Carlyle, Zola, Poe, Pater, Twain, Harte, Crane, Dickinson, Norris, Frost, Mann, Wright, Aiken, and Penn Warren.

248. He may have taken his initial lead from the spate of references under "White" and "Whiteness" in Chambers' *Cyclopaedia*; for a list of other sources, some confirmed, some conjectural, see Mansfield's and Vincent's notes, *Moby-Dick*, pp. 704-717. On the psychological and mythic aspects of whiteness see Baird, *Ishmael*, pp. 256-277.

companionless, conscious? Why, if there is no Devil; nay, unless the Devil is your God?[249]

Convinced like Emerson that evil is a disease of the eye, Teufelsdroeck regenerates nature through regeneration of a positive vision, his "Everlasting Yea"; regarded through new eyes, "The Universe is not dead and demoniacal, a charnel-house with spectres; but godlike and my Father's!"[250] Melville refrains from or fails to achieve Carlyle's leap of faith; at the close of the chapter on whiteness the world remains the charnel-house from which Teufelsdroeck had recoiled. But *Moby-Dick* does not conclude with a dread vision of a dead, mechanistic universe, for Melville's vision is not that of the pessimistic naturalists that followed in his wake.[251] As in the bulk of the chapter on whiteness, most of Melville's aesthetic argument consists of a carefully managed counterbalancing of the benign with the malignant implications of sublimity.

A subtle but vitally important distinction rests on the implication of the tension of moral contraries Melville perceives in the sublime. To believe, as does Brodtkorb, that whiteness in *Moby-Dick* stands for the "nothingness with which all existence is secretly sickened,"[252] impels us to the conclusion that nature had become for Melville a mere pasteboard mechanism with nothing beyond. Yet such a conclusion is clearly at odds with Ishmael's adamant insistence that whiteness is a "mystic sign" that "gives forth hints" of "nameless things" and that "somewhere those things must exist" (p. 193). As Miller has remarked with great justice , Melville's ideas remained "to the end, implacably, defiantly, unrepentantly, transcendental."[253] To be sure, Melville's transvaluation of values,

249. *Sartor Resartus: The Life and Opinions of Herr Teufelsdrockh*, vol. I in *The Works of Thomas Carlyle* (London: Chapman and Hall, 1896; reprinted New York: AMS Press, 1969), pp. 128, 133. All subsequent quotations from Carlyle are taken from this edition, henceforth referred to as *"Works."* Melville seems to have been prepossessed with Carlyle's vision of the "dead indifference" of the universe; the phrase appears in "The Berg," a late lyric on the sublime of nature. On Melville's extensive debt to Carlyle see Mansfield's and Vincent's notes in *Moby-Dick*.

250. *Works*, I, 150.

251. There can be no doubt, as Newton Arvin has put it, that *Moby-Dick* "draws close at one pole to the bias of naturalism" (*Herman Melville*, p. 169), but no student of his work has convincingly portrayed him as a naturalist. In *The Fine Hammered Steel of Herman Melville* (Urbana: University of Illinois Press, 1952), Milton R. Stern has presented the most sustained attempt to define Melville's vision as naturalistic, but his omission of any significant treatment of *Moby-Dick* is as necessary to his argument as it is fatal to it. Zoellner (*The Salt-Sea Mastodon*, pp. 146-165 and passim) claims that Ishmael first "de-mythologizes" Ahab's transcendental whale, then defines it naturalistically, and finally "re-mythologizes" it; the structure of his argument, it is fair to say, is more complicated than his subject.

252. *Ishmael's White World*, p. 119.

253. "Melville and Transcendentalism," *Nature's Nation*, p. 196.

his location of the blackness of darkness in light itself and his sustained assault on idealist optimism, stands unmitigated to the end. But so, too, does the tension of moral contraries in the sublime, and in this phase Melville's argument is more profound than the darkest naturalistic pessimism. For through it Melville does not merely discover evil where his age found good but, what is infinitely more unsettling, he demonstrates that the noumenal Absolute is ultimately beyond any moral apprehension whatsoever. The transvaluation of values that Melville effects in the chapter on whiteness and in the endless associations of natural beauty and horror that run throughout his book are superseded by the profoundly darker argument that the Absolute finally transcends valuation altogether. Thus the aesthetic argument of *Moby-Dick* finds its analogue in the dark rhetorical questions of Job, questions drawn from a passage that Burke had presented as the supreme example in our literature of the sublime of power: "Canst thou draw out Leviathan with an hook? Will he make a covenant with thee?"[254] To these questions *Moby-Dick* stands as, to borrow Carlyle's phrase, an "everlasting no."[255]

Burke had included among his excerpts from Job a third question pertaining to Leviathan: "Shall not one be cast down even at the sight of him?"[256] It is in the inviolability of the Absolute broached by this question that we come to the grounds on which the aesthetic argument of *Moby-Dick* forms the perfect complement of its tragic dimension. Abetted by his readings in Sophocles and Shakespeare, Melville built into his book a fabric of metaphors having to do with sight and blindness that carries the symbolical and psychological penalties of knowledge of the Absolute. Ishmael establishes his identity as a "water-gazer" in the first chapter of the book, and before the *Pequod* has left her moorings the portentous quality of what he will experience as a seer is established. In "The Ship" he explains to Peleg that he is signing on to a whaling crew in order to see the world; Peleg instructs him to look over the bulwarks to the open sea:

> The prospect was unlimited, but exceedingly monotonous and forbidding; not the slightest variety that I could see.
> "Well, what's the report?" said Peleg, "... what did ye see?"
> "Not much," I replied — "nothing but water; considerable horizon though, and there's a squall coming up, I think." (p. 72)

Adumbrated over and over in Ishmael's rhetoric of inscrutability, the "forbidding" aspect of the sublime culminates in the Leviathan. The only way to see the whale in "living contour" is, Ishmael tells us, "by going a

---

254. Job 41: 1, 4; as misquoted by Burke, *Enquiry*, p. 66.
255. *Works*, I, 128.
256. Job 41: 9; as quoted by Burke, *Enquiry*, p. 66.

whaling yourself"; "Wherefore, it seems to me you had best not be too fastidious in your curiosity touching this Leviathan" (p. 266). Ishmael's warning, half humorous here, becomes more serious in his remarks on the whale's spout:

> I have heard it said, and I do not much doubt it, that if the jet is fairly spouted into your eyes, it will blind you. The wisest thing the investigator can do then, it seems to me, is to let this deadly spout alone. (p. 371)

Ishmael repeatedly defines the loss of sight as the price that must be paid for knowledge of the Absolute. Ahab's quadrant is equipped with "colored glasses" that shield the eye from the "unrelieved radiance" of the sun, from "the insufferable splendors of God's throne" (p. 493). Like Ishmael's "wilful travellers in Lapland, who refuse to wear colored and coloring glasses upon their eyes," and like the "wretched infidel" who "gazes himself blind" (p. 194) in a whitened landscape, Ahab spurns the coloring lenses of the quadrant and stares into the blinding sun:

> "Where is Moby Dick? This instant thou must be eyeing him. These eyes of mine look into the very eye that is even now beholding him; aye, and into the eye that is even now equally beholding the objects on the unknown, thither side of thee, thou sun!" (p. 494)

He casts the quadrant into the sea:

> "Curse thee, thou vain toy; and cursed be all the tings that cast man's eyes aloft to that heaven, whose live vividness but scorches him, as these old eyes are even now scorched with thy light, O sun! Level by nature to this earth's horizon are the glances of man's eyes; not shot from the crown of his head, as if God had meant him to gaze on his firmament." (p. 494)

With Ahab's hunt firmly established as a type of hubris, it is fitting that Captain Boomer is rendered "blind as a bat — both eyes out" (p. 436) in his disastrous encounter with Moby Dick. Ahab is himself temporally blinded on the first day of the chase after Moby Dick, and, in the final combat with the whale, "I grow blind" (p. 563) is his anguished cry.[257]

Ahab's blindness is of course metaphorical as well as literal; it stands in part as spiritual blindness, the penalty he pays for his Promethean revolt. Forever exiled from the "goblet's rim" of earth's colored loveliness, he leaves a "white and turbid wake" (p. 165) of death wherever he sails, and life itself seems to vacate itself before the prow of the ship. Blind to color, "gnawed within and scorched without" (p. 184), Ahab appears as a man "cut away from the stake, when the fire has overrunningly wasted all the

---

257. Rust ("Vision in *Moby-Dick*," pp. 73-75) has suggested the remarkable complexity of sight and blindness metaphors in *Moby-Dick*, noting that the fiery glance of Fedallah, a fire-worshipper, overawes Ahab, whose "despot eye" mesmerizes the crew. Starbuck, recognizing that Stubb has been "blinded" by Ahab, exhorts: "'Madman! look through my eyes if thou hast none of thine own" (p. 497).

limbs without consuming them" (p. 120). His very soul is blighted by the white thing he hunts:

> Therefore, the tormented spirit that glared out of bodily eyes, when what semed Ahab rushed from his room, was for the time being, a ray of living light, to be sure, but without an object to color, and therefore a blankness in itself. (p. 200)

The "all-color" whiteness is, as the painter Turner had discovered, the vortex into which all distinctions of light are consumed. The center of the chromatic spectrum that blinds Ahab and blanches his soul, it is nevertheless only one form of that ultimate center of nature, the annihilating vortex toward which the *Pequod* relentlessly drives.

While Ahab's ship must make a three-year's journey to the other side of the globe before it takes its final dive into the seething white vortex of the Absolute, the *Pequod* is symbolically caugt up in the centripetal tug of the vortex before it lifts anchor in Nantucket. In a psychological and mythological sense, Ahab's fated death through assimilation or absorption into the Absolute is suggested in "Loomings," Ishmael's first chapter. Narcissus, we recall, had been defined by Ishmael as the primogenitor of all water-gazers, all those who are drawn toward knowledge of the Absolute. Like Narcissus, who "could not grasp the tormenting ... image" of the "ungraspable phantom of life" and "plunged into it and was drowned" (p. 3), Ahab is monomaniacally possessed of that phantom and is drawn to his death within it.

Melville creates the sense of an imminent but unimaginable catastrophe through the initial foreshadowing of the *Pequod*'s final destruction in "Loomings" as well as the repeated foreshadowings established in multiple planes throughout *Moby-Dick*. The most obvious and direct — and therefore least profound — of these is "The Affidavit," Ishmael's catalogue of recorded assaults on ships by whales; this is intended to dispell the "profound ignorance" of a reader who might otherwise "scout at Moby Dick as a monstrous fable" (pp. 202-203). Far more important are the subtler foreshadowings that enrich the symbolic implications of the *Pequod*'s ultimate catastrophe. Among these are the young Platonist's fatal plunge into Cartesian vortices, the encounter with the grasping, radiating arms and formless white horror of the giant squid, the superstition that the sight of the squid dooms a seaman to a watery death, the remark of the *Samuel Enderby*'s captain that Moby Dick "doesn't bite so much as he swallows" (p. 438), and the spate of references to the "sharkishness" and universal cannibalism of the natural world. *Moby-Dick* is so saturated with references to the all-devouring shark as to suggest that an annihilating, insatiable maw more than a regenerative force lies at nature's center. The imagery of death even taints "The Grand Armada," the only joyful celebration of biologistic sublimity in the later chapters of the book. There, deep at the center of a herd of circling

whales, Queequeg points to an infant whale whose umbilical cord has
been fatally and symbolically intertwined with the hemp harpoon line;
even at this center of generation, the line of life is a line of death.[258]

The connection between Moby Dick as Absolute, as nature's center, is
brilliantly fostered in mad Pip's reflections on the doubloon, another
passage that foreshadows the *Pequod*'s doom. As Moby Dick is nature's
inviolable center, so the doubloon, "the white whale's talisman" (p. 427),
is the center of Pip's world, the ship:

> "Here's the ship's navel, this doubloon here, and they are all on fire to unscrew it.
> But, unscrew your navel, and what's the consequence? Then again, if it stays here,
> that is ugly, too, for when aught's nailed to the mast it's a sign that things grow
> desperate. Ha, ha! Old Ahab! the White Whale; he'll nail ye!" (p. 132)

Pip's rude joke broaches what the cultural anthropologist Mircea Eliade
has called the myth of the "Sacred Center,"[259] a myth richly at work in
Moby Dick. We search in vain for the specific sources through which
Melville became acquainted with this myth, for, as Eliade has convincingly demonstrated, it is archetypal and omnipresent in world religion
and literature. The quest for the Sacred Center is vestigially present in the
earliest of Melville's works, and, as Martin Leonard Pops has shown,[260]
it is an abiding concern of the fiction and poetry of his later years. He was
certainly not alone in his interest in the Sacred Center — it is abundantly
evinced in the works of Emerson, Thoreau, and even Poe — for the quest
for the nexus between the phenomenal and noumenal worlds, or, as
Carlyle put it, for the juncture between the natural and the supernatural,
is a defining characteristic of romantic platonism. The Sacred Center is,
as Eliade defines it, nature's "zone of absolute reality,"[261] and it is only
fitting that the final catastrophe of *Moby-Dick* should occur in such a
zone; as the quintessence of natural sublimity, as the animated mass of
incomparable power and magnitude that for Kant could unveil the
Absolute, Moby Dick is himself a living nexus between phenomena and
noumena, and it is to the depths of the Sacred Center that he drags Ahab.

Among Eliade's architectonic symbols of the Center, the "*axis mundi*"
or "meeting point of heaven, earth, and hell"[262] is particularly relevant to

258. The "armada" itself forms a vortex; the whales swim in "revolving circles,"
and those "in the more central circles" form "contracting orbits" (p. 385). The image
of death intertwined with life is more richly developed in the whale-skeleton that is
laced with vines in "A Bower in the Arscides": "Life folded Death; Death tellised Life;
the grim god wived with youthful Life, and begat him curly-headed glories" (p. 447).

259. *The Myth of the Eternal Return*, trans. Willard R. Trask (New York: Pantheon
Books, 1954), pp. 12-18 and passim.

260. *The Melville Archetype* (Kent, Ohio: Kent State University Press, 1970),
especially pp. 1-132.

261. *The Myth of the Eternal Return*, p. 18.

262. Ibid., p. 12.

the conclusion of *Moby-Dick*. Melville was early alive to the power of the axis symbol, for in "Hawthorne and His Mosses," written during the completion and revision of *Moby-Dick*, he remarked the capacity of genius to probe the "very axis of reality."[263] The doubloon, Pip's navel of the world, is minted at equatorial Quito, in a "country planted in the middle of the world"; the sun imaged on the coin is, Ishmael pointedly remarks, at the "equinoctial point" (p. 428). The White Whale, for whom the doubloon is talismanic, is finally engaged on the equatorial south Pacific, seas that are for Ishmael sacred, primordial, and central. The Pacific, he says in his equisite apostrophe to that sea, "rolls the midmost waters of the world" as Moby Dick swims midmost the endless processions of animate nature. The Indian Ocean and the Atlantic are "but its arms," and its waves "wash the moles of the new-built Californian towns, but yesterday planted by the recentest race of men, and lave the faded but still gorgeous skirts of Asiatic lands, older than Abraham." Fusing time to come with time past, this "mysterious, divine Pacific zones the world's whole bulk about; makes one bay to it; seems the tide-beating heart of earth." The sacred geophysical center, it is also the eternal center of time:

> There is, one knows not what sweet mystery about this sea, whose gently awful stirrings seem to speak to some hidden soul beneath; like those fabled undulations of the Ephesian sod over the buried Evangelist St. John. And meet it is, that over these sea-pastures, wide-rolling watery prairies and Potter's Fields of all four continents, the waves should rise and fall, and ebb and flow unceasingly; for here, millions of mixed shades and shadows, drowned dreams, somnambulisms, reveries all that we call lives and souls, lie dreaming, dreaming still; tossing like slumberers in their beds; the ever-rolling waves but made so by their restlessness. (p. 478)

As the *Pequod* emerges into this great south Sea, the "long supplication" (p. 478) of Ishmael's youth is answered; his three-year's voyage has brought him from the mere suburbs of reality, from the illusory, picturesque of the New England hills, to the sublime center of nature.

With the first breaching of Moby Dick in the South Seas comes a great surge of centripetal impulsion in Melville's book. It is as though the *Pequod* is caught up like the whales in "The Grand Armada" in the "contracting orbits" of nature's vortex; like those whales, who plunge into chaos by "violently making for one centre" (p. 389), the *Pequod* dashes ineluctably for the place of its doom and, whirling, plunges into the Absolute:

> And now, concentric circles seized the lone boat itself, and all its crew, and each floating oard, and every lance-pole, and spinning, animate and inanimate, all round in one vortex, carried the smallest chip of the Pequod out of sight. (p. 566)

263. *Moby-Dick*, ed. Harrison Hayford and Hershel Parker (New York: W.W. Norton & Company, 1967), p. 541.

The mast of the *Pequod* itself pierces the Sacred Center, becomes itself the axis mundi that links heaven, earth and hell. The "captive form" of the sky hawk, "the bird of heaven," becomes folded in the flag of Ahab and goes down with his ship,

> which, like Satan, would not sink to hell till she had dragged a living part of heaven along with her, and helmeted herself with it. (p. 566)

Melville ends his quest in sublimity far from American landscape aesthetics and his point of departure in the pleasant valley of the Saco. but the distance is in a special sense only apparent. As the *Pequod*'s "vengeful errand" concluded,

> small fowls flew screaming over the yet yawning gulf; a sullen white surf beat against its steep sides; then all collapsed, and the great shroud of the sea rolled on as it rolled five thousand years ago. (p. 566)

Melville's sea rolls "as it rolled five thousand years ago," at the time, according to Biblical chronology, of the Flood. It was after the waters had subsided that God is said to have set the rainbow in the skies as an emblem of the everlasting covenant with man and every living creature on earth. In the first half of the nineteenth century Americans had come to see the rainbow of Genesis arched above the American wilderness, signifying the renewal of the divine covenant. Melville, for whom the Flood had never subsided, could find in nature no such pact between man and god.

Ishmael's epilogue begins with an epigraph from Job; like the book of Job, a theodicy that collapses into unresolved ambiguity, *Moby-Dick* concludes in a vision of nature as impenetrable mystery:

> *So, floating on the margin of the ensuing scene, and in full sight of it, when the half-spent suction of the sunk ship reached me, I was then, but slowly, drawn towards the closing vortex. When I reached it, it had subsided to a creamy pool. Round and round, then, and ever contracting towards the button-like black bubble at the axis of that slowly wheeling circle, like another Ixion I did revolve.* (p. 567)

It is fruitless to attempt to mitigate the mystery of Ishmael's lone survival through appeal to any of the several forms of redemptive vision he is often alleged to have achieved. Ishmael may come to recognize the fundamentally alien dimension of Emerson's "NOT-ME," but his salvation cannot in any acceptable sense have stemmed from a resulting recognition of the vital importance of the brotherhood of man; before the profoundly metaphysical tragedy of *Moby-Dick* man's social exigencies pale. Nor can the transcendental vision of the benign unity of self and universe that others allege Ishmael achieves do justice to the book's conclusion. The very fact that an horrific vision of nature can and has been cogently inferred from the book suggests that Melville provided no firm basis for interpreting Ishmael's vision to be benignantly redemptive.

Ultimately neither an exclusively dark nor a bright reading seems adequate to the book whose resolution transcends moral apprehension. At nature's center a coffin is a life-raft, wheeling whiteness resolves itself in a black axis, and all contraries, all humanly perceived distinctions, moral and intellectual, are obliterated. The universal cannibalism of Nature may be for Ishmael momently suspended, but, it cannot be too adamantly insisted, *Moby-Dick* ends in a metaphor not of redemption or renewal but of exile:

> Buoyed up by that coffin, for almost one whole day and night, I floated on a soft and dirge-like main. The unharming sharks, they glided by as if with padlocks on their mouths; the savage sea-hawks sailed with sheathed beaks. On the second day, a sail drew near, nearer, and picked me up at last. It was the devious-cruising Rachel, that in her retracing search after her missing children, only found another orphan. (p. 566)

CHAPTER III

THE DESCENT TO THE FORECASTLE: AFTER *MOBY-DICK*

Few students of Melville's work have denied the presence of a disjunction in his career subsequent to the publication of *Moby-Dick* in 1851. T he writer who had been, as D. H. Lawrence put it, "mad to look over our horizons ... anywhere out of *our* world,"[1] turned within in *Pierre*. After *Moby-Dick* the limitless horizons of Melville's imagination are radically circumscribed; the view from the masthead is displaced by interior landscapes, and the treatment of outward nature undergoes a gradual diminution until, in *The Confidence-Man*, the sense of place is utterly obliterated. Of this retreat from nature "The Piazza" is paradigmatic. Dressing himself in the clothing of his former sea-going days and dressing his language in a seaman's idiom, the narrator of "The Piazza" retraces Melville's quest in and ultimate retreat from the sublime of nature. The ascerbic irony of the sketch is precisely the mode in which nearly all of Melville's work after *Moby-Dick* is written. And "The Piazza" also presents many of the important thematic concerns of the prose of the later phase: the illusory quality of natural beauty; the opposition of the aesthetic and the moral life; the estrangement from nature; the estrangement and isolation of man from man; and the tragic inviolability of the moral and metaphysical Absolute.

The inward turning of Melville's creative imagination in the later phase of his career accompanied an inward turning in his private life. The reclusive tendencies remarked by his acquaintances during the last stages of the composition of *Moby-Dick*[2] increased through the eighteen-fifties and sixties, culminating in the nearly total isolation of his life as a customs clerk in Manhattan. For present purposes, his sudden disaffiliation with Duyckinck and the "Young America" group is of special interest, for it illuminates the change of manner and theme in Melville's fiction after *Moby-Dick*. In February, 1852, Melville wrote a pointedly curt note to the "Editors of *Literary World*"[3] requesting cancellation of his subscription to the journal. The break with the *Literary World* may have

---

1. Studies in Classic American Literature, p. 134.
2. See Mansfield, "Glimpses of Herman Melville's Life in Pittsfield," pp. 47-48.
3. *Letters,* p. 149.

been triggered by Duyckinck's rather negative review of *Moby-Dick*,[4] but the poor notice was more likely the occasion than the cause of the rift. A most dramatic unfolding of Melville's ideas had occurred during the completion of *Moby-Dick*, an unfolding that precluded further service by Melville to the cause of the literary nationalists. Like its creator, the book Duyckinck had seen in manuscript as "something quite new in literature" had also unfolded, and the vision of nature it finally offered was clearly inimical to the patriotic and romantic naturalism upon which the Duyckinck circle hoped to found an American literature. Melville would eventually restore at least cordial relations with Duyckinck, but in *Pierre* he devoted book XVII, "Young America in Literature," to a scathing assault on the nationalists. Justifying his chapter with a boast of independence that is unmistakably directed toward Duyckinck — "I write precisely as I please" — he lampooned his former friend as the "inoffensive, non-committal" editor of the "Captain Kidd Monthly"[5] and satirized the literature of "Young America," including his own early writings, as mere puerility.

Melville did not, it must be insisted, write *Pierre* precisely as he pleased. As it was initially conceived, *Pierre* was to be a romance in the manner of Bulwer, or Thackeray, or the popular sentimental novel. In his famous letter to Sophia Hawthorne on January 8, 1852, he compared the new book, then still in progress, with *Moby-Dick*: "I shall not again send you a bowl of salt water," he wrote; "The next chalice I shall commend, will be a rural bowl of milk."[6] Like *Moby-Dick*, *Pierre* was initially intended to capture the popular readership that eluded Melville's grasp since the success of *Typee* and *Omoo*. The book, he wrote to Richard Bentley, his English publisher, would be

---

4. While Duyckinck thought the book a "remarkable sea-dish," he objected to "intense Captain Ahab as too long drawn out," and he liked even less the "piratical running down of creeds and opinions"; "We do not like to see what, under my view," he wrote, "must be to the world the most sacred associations of life violated and defaced" (from the issue of November 22, 1851, as excerpted by Leyda,*The Melville Log*, I, 437). Hawthorne, in a letter to Duyckinck, objected that the notice was unfair: "It hardly seemed to me that the review of [*Moby-Dick*], in the Literary World, did justice to its best points" (Leyda, *The Melville Log*, I, 431).

5. *Pierre: or, The Ambiguities*, ed. Harrison Hayford, Hershel Parker, and G. Thomas Tanselle (Evanston and Chicago: Northwestern University Press and The Newberry Library, 1971), pp. 244, 246, 253. All subsequent quotations from *Pierre* are drawn from this edition.

6. *Letters*, p. 146; Davis and Gilman note that "The phrase might have been appropriate to an early stage of the story. Applied to the full novel it could only be ironic" (*Letters*, p. 146n).

very much more calculated for popularity than anything you have yet published of mine — being a regular romance, with a mysterious plot to it, & stirring passions at work, and withall, representing a new & elevated aspect of American life ...[7]

But, again like *Moby-Dick*, *Pierre* became in final form a creation strikingly at odds with the sort of popular book Melville had hoped to write. Unless the opening chapters that treat of Pierre's idyllic youth underwent extensive revision at some late date in the book's composition, the rural bowl of milk that *Pierre* was to be was curdled in the bitterest irony from the very start. A brackish tincture from Melville's late tragic venture in the sublime is immediately evident in the dedication of the new book "TO GREYLOCK'S MOST EXCELLENT MAJESTY":

> In old times authors were proud of the privilege of dedicating their works to Majesty. A right noble custom, which we of Berkshire must revive. For whether we will or no, Majesty is all around us here in Berkshire, sitting as in a grand Congress of Vienna of majestical hill-tops, and eternally challenging our homage.
>
> But since the majestic mountain, Greylock — my own more immediate sovereign lord and king — hath now, for innumerable ages, been the one grand dedicatee of the earliest rays of all the Berkshire mornings, I know not how his Imperial Purple Majesty (royal-born: Prophyrogenitus) will receive the dedication of my own poor solitary ray.
>
> Nevertheless, forasmuch as I, dwelling with my loyal neighbors, the Maples and the Beeches, in the amphitheater over which his central majesty presides, have received his most bounteous and unstinted fertilizations, it is but meet, that I here devoutly kneel, and render up my gratitude, whether, thereto, The Most Excellent Purple Majesty of Greylock benignantly incline his hoary crown or no.

Here begins Melville's penchant for private irony and veiled autobiographical allegory that is so marked in the fiction of the mid-'fifties, and that culminates in "The Piazza," the last of the short fiction Melville wrote. Only Hawthorne and a few others among Melville's Berkshire acquaintances would recognize in the dedication a connection with *Moby-Dick*, the masterpiece that was composed in sight of Greylock. The inspirational relationship between that mountain and *Moby-Dick*, several times mentioned in Melville's letters, was remarked by Hawthorne in *The Wonder-Book* (1852),[8] but the most sensitive among the reading public no doubt failed to see the link between the ironic ambivalence of the dedication of *Pierre* and the aesthetic resolution of *Moby-Dick*. As though to point up that link and so justify the peculiar disjunction in his career, Melville returned to the "amphitheatre" of Greylock's slopes in "The Piazza," wherein he allegorized the quest in the sublime that is

---

7. *Letters*, p. 150.

8. See *Letters*, pp. 132-135. Hawthorne wrote that "On the hither side of Pittsfield sits Herman Melville, shaping out the gigantic conception of his 'White Whale,' while the gigantic shape of Graylock [sic] looms upon him from his study-window" ("*A Wonder Book*" and "*Tangle-Wood Tales*," Centenary Edition [Columbus: Ohio State University Press, 1972], p. 169).

Moby-Dick as well as the disillusion that followed that quest and generated the bitterly ironic pastoral of *Pierre*. The "genius" of the sublime sperm whale is, Ishmael decides in *Moby-Dick*, "declared in his pyramidical silence" (p. 345); Greylock, the odd muse of *Pierre*, imposes through the same indifferent silence, and "Silence," says the narrator of *Pierre*, "is at once the most harmless and the most awful thing in all nature ... Silence is the only Voice of our God" (p. 204). The mountain quest in "The Piazza" concludes in the same sense of estrangement, though it is expressed in a different metaphor; Truth "comes in with darkness," says the narrator of the sketch, for "No light shows from the mountain."[9]

As *Moby-Dick* moves from the confines of the city and of civilization to the savage heart of wildness, its structural dynamic is expansion; *Pierre*, which begins in a natural idyll and concludes in an urban dungeon, is structured through the steady circumscription of space. Yet, although *Pierre* reverses the direction of *Moby-Dcik*, the two books are intimately related on an aesthetic plane. Borrowing his lead from Northrop Frye, Pops has assigned *Moby-Dick* and *Pierre* to sequential mythic categories:

> *Moby-Dick* represents "The Mythos of Summer: Romance," a tale of marvellous adventures, a "romance-anatomy" ... *Pierre* represents "The Mythos of Autumn: Tragedy," Melville's attempt at an American tragedy.[10]

The association of *Pierre* with the tragic mythos of autumn is certainly legitimate, for it is a critical commonplace that Pierre is an American Hamlet. Yet the first thirteen books of the novel, those that take place in Saddle Meadows (Greylock was alternately known as Saddleback), clearly belong to the mythos of spring, the phase of romance that takes place in a pastoral or Arcadian world. As Frye himself has noted, "*Pierre* opens with a sardonic parody of this phase, the hero still dominated by his mother but calling her his sister."[11] With this opening reversion to the earliest of Frye's mythoi in mind, it may be seen that Melville begins *Pierre* by reverting to a stage of experience that is in a special sense prior to that in which *Moby-Dick* had opened. Young Pierre might be an Ishmael before his exile at sea. In the first thirteen chapters of *Pierre* is an elaborate romance of a relationship to nature that is caught up and curtly dismissed as illusory in Ishmael's painting of the Saco valley. Melville's sardonic — one might say bitterly ironic — tone in the opening pastoral of *Pierre* suggests that he is pointing to the illusion of romantic naturalism as the root of the quest in nature that ultimately resolved itself into the tragedy of *Moby-Dick*. Like the language of the narrator of "The

9. *Piazza Tales*, p. 15.
10. *The Melville Archetype*, p. 251.
11. *The Anatomy of Criticism*, p. 200.

Piazza" prior to the disenchanting ascent of Greylock, the opening chapters of *Pierre* are saturated in the idiom and imagery of pastoral and romance.

As it could hardly refer to the incest, murder, and madness that the public found so offensive in *Pierre*, the "elevated aspect of American life" with which Melville had promised to deal in *Pierre* must surely be the peculiarly courtly and chivalric quality of the Saddle Meadows pastoral. Melville's dialogue is undeniably and self-consciously mannered, although the precise intentions behind the inflated and stately idiom in *Pierre* are still a matter of critical contention. While it is probably true, as William Braswell has most forcefully argued, that the "insipidly sentimental" exchanges between Pierre and others in the book do not comprise a "serious attempt at beautiful prose" but are merely "mock-romantic,"[12] the motives behind the book's style are doubtless complex. In spite of the break with the Duyckinck circle, Melville retained through the fifties a measure of nationalistic fervor, and the Saddle Meadows pastoral, with its elegance and formal refinement, seems to have been calculated in part as proof that an American arcadia might be as fine as the European. Certainly the spirit of the narrator's celebration of Pierre's noble lineage and the "matter of large estates, and long pedigrees" (p. 11) is boastful patriotism. having once committed himself to investing Pierre's family with feudal grandeur, Melville would quite naturally find himself committed to a stately idiom. And it must not be forgotten that Melville's mother, who was descended from the first partroon, a fact of which she was proud, loomed large in *Pierre*; the ambivalence behind the book's mannered style, the way it seems by turns mawkishly affected or serious, may be the ambivalence of Melville's attitude toward his mother. In any case, Pierre is driven from the American arcardia to the hellish city through the discovery of sin, egoism, and corruption in the heart of that arcadia; the pastoral world of Saddle Meadow, like that viewed from "The Piazza," is set up only to be destroyed.

Like "The Piazza," which is a redaction of Melville's career through the writing of *Pierre*, his romance of 1852 has a primary purpose the exposure of an impassable gulf between romance and truth. Everywhere apparent in *Pierre*, that gulf is exposed in the chapter on "Young America in Literature" through a vehicle that is especially relevant to the significance of aesthetics in Melville's career. In the absurdly pretentious prospectus for an illustrated edition of Pierre's works, the publishing firm of "Wonder and Wen" propose a title page in which "That world-famed

---

12. "The Early Love Scenes in Melville's *Pierre*," *American Literature* 22 (November 1950): 284.

production, 'The Tropical Summer: a Sonnet'" (p. 247) heads a patheti-
cally limited list of fragments by Pierre. If this list has autobiographical
reference — and there seems good reason to believe it does[13] — then the
derisively chosen title of Pierre's "world-famed production" must surely
point not only to the early South Sea romances that had become, by 1852,
somehing of an embarrassment for Melville, but also to the non-reflective
state of romantic and naive naturalism that is unrelentingly undermined
in the early chapters of *Pierre*. The question of natural beauty had
become for Melville thoroughly mired in ambiguity. Hence it is not
surprising to find, among Pierre's works, "Beauty: an Acrostic."[14] As for
Melville the collapse of faith in romantic naturalism attended the
transcendental quest in the sublime that is *Moby-Dick*, it is appropriate
that romance and transcendentalism are played against each other in the
retrospect of his literary career; among the invitiations received by Pierre
to lecture before lyceums Melville instances a letter addressed to the
"*Author of the 'Tropical Summer,'* &c." from the "'Urquhartian Club for
the Immediate Extension of the Limits of all Knowledge, both Human
and Divine'" (p. 251). In *Mardi* Melville's tropical romance had resolved
itself into an abstract allegory that concludes with the promise of a search
in a "realm of shades" and "over an endless sea" (p. 654). *Moby-Dick*
fulfills that promise in a quest that concludes at the sublime nexus
between nature and infinity, time and eternity, an Absolute that demolishes the possibilities of romance.

As *Moby-Dick* is a hunt in nature's Absolute, Pierre chronicles the
search for a moral Absolute. The sphere of the latter quest is, in Lewis
Mumford's words, "not the universe, but the ego."[15] Nevertheless, the
philosophical ideas that had prepossessed Melville n *Moby-Dick* recur in
Pierre. Exasperated by the reception of *Moby-Dick*, he gives bitter vent to
his frustrations in having expended enormous energies in that book
chiefly through the sustained attack on transcendental philosphy in

13. See Henry A. Murray's notes to his edition of *Pierre* (New York: Hendricks
House, Inc., 1952), pp. 480-482, as well as the "Historical Note" by Leon Howard and
Hershel Parker appended to the Northwestern-Newberry edition (pp. 365-407).
Beyond the many allusions to Duyckinck and his circle, references to Melville's early
work are also common. The following passage, to cite but one example, clearly looks
back to the success of *Typee* and *Omoo*: "In the inferior instances of an immediate
literary success, in very young writers, it will be almost invariably observable, that for
that instant success they were chiefly indebted to some rich and peculiar experience in
life, embodied in a book, which because, for that cause, containing original matter, the
author himself, forsooth, is to be considered original" (p. 259).

14. Other titles listed are "The Weather: A Thought," "Life: an Impromptu," "The
Late Reverend Mark Graceman: an Obituary," "Honor: a Stanza," "Edgar: an
Anagram," "The Pippin: a Paragraph" (p. 247).

15. *Herman Melville* (New York: Harcourt, Brace and Company, 1929), p. 145.

Pierre. Unlike Ahab, whose grandeur is somehow heightened by his final plunge into the vortex, Pierre is the fool of truth who, like the absurd "Urquhartians," would identify "Both Human and Divine" truth. As Ahab's climactic engagement with the Absolute has been imaged by a descent into the vortex, so Pierre's resolve to devote himself to a moral Absolute is signalized by his being "Sucked within the maelstrom" (p. 182). But, whereas Ahab seems at the close of Ishmael's saga more a Prometheus than a victim, Pierre's struggles are diminished in dignity by Melville's persistently sardonic voice:

> Pierre was not arguing Fixed Fate and Free Will, now; Fixed Fate and Free Will were arguing him, and Fixed Fate got the better in the debate. (p. 182)

Like the whale whose essence remains impenetrable no matter how many layers of its skin are flayed, the soul of man remains eternally elusive:

> far as any geologist has yet gone down into the world, it is found to consist of nothing but superinduced superfices. By vast pains we mine into the pyramid; by horrible gropings we come to the central room; with joy we espy the sarcophagus; but we lift the lid — and no body is there! — appallingly vacant as vast is the soul of man! (p. 285)

Having found in "The Whiteness of the Whale" an emptiness that may secretly blight all creation, Melville finds in *Pierre* the more horrific possibility that the human soul itself may be a void or a matrix of Cartesian vortices:

> Appalling is the soul of a man! Better might one be pushed off into the material spaces beyond the uttermost orbit of the sun, than once feel himself fairly afloat in himself! (p. 284)

Melville had been "fairly afloat in himself" as early as the composition later portions of *Mardi*, and Book XXI of *Pierre*, which is entitled "Pierre Immaturely attempts a Mature Work," must surely look back to that failed foray in metaphysics. The Book opens with Pierre "permanently lodged in three lofty adjoining chambers of the Apostles" (p. 282), a cabal of transcendentalists. Here he is "bent on producing some thoughtful thing of absolute Truth," and he disowns "even those fine fruits of a care-free fancy, which, written at Saddle Meadows in the sweet legendary time of Lucy and her love" (pp. 282-283), he had refrained from publishing. The point is clear: Pierre would leave romance behind for the sake of higher truth, a process metonymous with the design of *Moby-Dick* as well as *Mardi*. That the chapter on Pierre's work under the influence of transcendental ideas also refers to *Moby-Dick* is suggested in the narrator's remark that once in the "ultimate element" of absolute Truth "our own strong limbs support us, and we float over all bottomlesses with a jeering impunity" (p. 283); "I have written a wicked book, and feel spotless as a lamb,"[16] Melville wrote to Hawthorne after the completion of *Moby-Dick*. The note of private exultation in both letter and book was, however, short lived. Before the conclusion of the first section of Book XXI of *Pierre* the narrator claims that exile to the outermost orbit of the sun is preferable to the maelstrom of the self, and the second section of the same Book catalogues the symbolic consequences of Pierre's pursuit of the moral Absolute:

First: his mother was dead.
Second: all Saddle Meadows was become Glen Stanly's.
Third: Glen Stanly was believed to be the suitor of Lucy. (p. 285)

Mrs. Glendinning is the matriarch of the pastoral world of Pierre's youth, and her death signals his irreversible exile from that world. His exile is further sealed by his cousin's usurpation of control of Saddle Meadows, Pierre's "noble patrimony" (p. 287), and of Lucy Tartan, who, as the fair heroine of conventional romance, symbolized the spiritual innocence of Pierre's life at Saddle Meadows. The causes of Pierre's exile are brought into sharper focus in the third section of Book XXI through his encounter with the Grand Master of the Apostles, Plotinus Plinlimmon. Named for Plotinus, third-century Neoplatonist, and for the Welsh mountain in Gray's "The Bard," Plinlimmon would seem to be in part a portrait of Emerson.[17] His pamphlet on "Chronometricals and Horologicals," which Pierre receives when embarking for the city and loses shortly thereafter, sets in neat opposition chronometrical time, which

16. Dated November 17 (?), 1851; *Letters*, p. 142.
17. Mount Plinlimmon is mentioned in Scott's *The Betrothed* as well as Coleridge's *Table Talk*, and a character named Plinlimmon appears in Thackeray's *Pendennis* (see Murray's notes in the Hendricks House edition of *Pierre*, pp. 475-476), but the likelihood of Gray as Melville's source is suggested by the parallel between lines in "The Bard" and the dedication of *Pierre*. Gray wrote of "Modred, whose magic song / Made huge Plinlimmon bow his cloud-topt head" while Melville renders his gratitude to Greylock "whether, thereto ... Greylock benignantly incline his hoary crown or not." As Murray points out, "A connection ... between Greylock and Plotinus is suggested by the peculiar occurrence of '(royal born: Porphyrogenitus)' in Melville's dedication. The most famous pupil of Plotinus was named Porphyry because he was royal born" (p. 476). Although the connection between Plinlimmon and Emerson remains conjectural, some evidence is too suggestive to be dismissed. Plinlimmon disdains the works of others and the "sleazy works that went under his name" were "nothing more than his verbal things" that were "bunglingly methodized by his young disciples" (p. 290). Millthorpe, one of Plinlimmon's disciples, may be the shadow of Thoreau; as the passage on Mark Winsome and Egbert in *The Confidence-Man* attests, Melville was interested in the relationship of Emerson and Thoreau. In any case, Pierre's ambivalent attitude toward Plinlimmon, his attraction to him and his conviction of Plinlimmon's "non-Benevolence" (p. 290), his veneration of Plinlimmon's pamphlet that is nevertheless a "sleazy rag" (p. 209) is consistent with his ambivalent attitude toward Emerson (see *Letters*, pp. 77-80).

suggests absolute time and absolute morality, and horological time, which suggests local time and relative morality:

> "'In short, this Chronometrical and Horological conceit, in sum, seems to teach this: — That in things terrestrial (horological) a man must not be governed by ideas celestial (chronometrical). (p. 214)

Loss of this pamphlet signals Pierre's loss of its wisdom; through his commitment to Isabel, the act that symbolizes commitment to heavenly truth and morality, Pierre falls victim to the tragic gulf between other-worldly truth and the practical exigencies of survival. That fall leaves the "lad that once sung to the world of the Tropical Summer" imprisoned in an urban garret, "shivering ... day after day in his wrappers and cloaks" (p. 306), while composing a hopelessly fragmented metaphysical romance.

Book XXII concerns Pierre's disillusionment with the quest for transcendental values that led to his exile from Saddle Meadows and the world of romance with which the estate is associated. Its title is ironically understated: "The Flower-Curtain Lifted from before a Tropical Author, with Some Remarks on the Transcendental Flesh-Brush Philosophy." Pierre's deceptive "Flower-Curtain" is not so much lifted as stripped away:

> From the fair fields of his great-great-great grandfather's manor, Summer hath flown like a swallow-guest; the perfidious wight, Autumn, hath peeped in at the groves of the maple, and under pretense of clothing them in rich russet and gold, hath stript them at last of the slightest rag, and then ran away laughing; prophetic icicles depend from the arbors round about the old manorial mansion — now locked up and abandoned; and the little, round, marble table in the viny summer-house where, of July mornings, he had sat chatting and drinking negus with his gay mother, is now spread with a shivering napkin of frost ...: it is Winter. (p. 295)

What follows is less a body of "remarks" on the Spartan life-style of the transcendentalist Apostles than a bitter assault on Idealism in general. Melville's narrator himself attacks the Idealist tradition earlier in Book XIV. He argues that the "Talismanic Secret" through which one might "reconcile this world with [the] soul" has "never yet been found" and that "it seems as though it never can be":

> Certain philosphers have time and time again pretended to have found it; but if they do not in the end discover their own delusion, other people soon discover it for themselves, and so those philosophers and their vain philosophy are let glide away into practical oblivion. Plato, and Spinoza, and Goethe, and many more belong to this guild of self-impostors, with a preposterous rabble of Muggletonian Scots and Yankees, whose vile brogue still the more bestreaks the stripedness of their Greek or German Neoplatonical originals. That profound Silence, that only Voice of our God, which I before spoke of; from that divine thing without a name, those imposter philosophers pretend somehow to have got an answer; which is absurd, as though they should say they had got water out of stone; for how can a man get a Voice out of Silence? (p. 208)

Particular targets are discernible in the reference to the "rabble of Muggletonian Scots and Yankees," a likely allusion to Carlyle and Emerson. If the "vile brogue" refers to Carlyle's turgid style and homely metaphors, then the attack is all the more remarkable, for Melville had himself acquired Carlyle's mannerisms along with his transcendental ideas. Later in *Pierre* the narrator lampoons the Apostles, who go about "huskily muttering Kantian Categories through teeth and lips dry and dusty as any miller's, with the crumbs of Graham crackers" (p. 300). The Apostles, who "reject the coarse materialism of Hobbes" and "incline to the airy exaltations of the Berkelyan philosphy," are morally and intellectually bankrupt, as is suggested through a figure recovered from *Moby-Dick*:

> Often groping in vain in their pockets, they can not but give in to the Descartian vortices; while the abundance of leisure in their attics (physical and figurative), unites with the leisure in their stomachs, to fit them in an eminent degree for that undivided attention indispensble to the proper digesting of the sublimated Categories of Kant; especially as Kant (can't) is the one great palpable fact in their impalpable lives.[18] (p. 267)

Once the "Flower-Curtain" that blinds Pierre has been destroyed, he joins this strained and joyless satire. The narrator quotes fragments of an abortive metaphysical romance on which Pierre labors fitfully; "'I own myself a broth of the clod, a child of the Primeval Gloom,'" laments Pierre's hero:

> "Away, ye chattering apes of a sophomorean Spinoza and Plato, who once didst all but delude me that the night was day, and pain only a tickle. Explain this darkness, exorcise this devil, yet can not. Tell me not, thou inconceivable coxcomb of a Goethe, that the universe can not sphare thee and thy immortality, so long as — like a hired waiter — though makest thyself 'generaly useful.' Already the universe gets on without thee, and could still spare a million more of the same identical kidney. Corporations have no souls, and thy Pantheism, what was that? Thou wert but the pretensious, heartless part of a man." (p. 302)

The points of reference in such passages are moral and metaphysical; the

18. But note the telling qualification that follows: "These are the glorious paupers, from whom I learn the profoundest mysteries of things ... Yet let me here offer up three locks of my hair, to the memory of all such glorious paupers who have lived an died in this world. Surely, and truly I honor them — noble men often at bottom — and for that very reason I made bold to be gamesome about them; for where fundamental nobleness is, and fundamental honor is due, merriment is never accounted irreverent" (p. 267). Writing to Duyckinck on March 3, 1849, he had called the Idealists men "all cracked right across the brow" and of Emerson he had said "let us call him a fool." Yet, he added, if Emerson is a fool then "had I rather be a fool than a wise man. — I love all men who *dive*." The precise intentions behind this demurrer are ambiguous because immediately after it Melville writes that "I'm not talking of Mr. Emerson now — but of the whole corps of thought-divers" (*Letters*, p. 79); this may be in part a compliment to Duyckinck, whose name suggests "deep-diver."

aesthetics of nature would seem to have no part in Pierre's — and Melville's — reaction against Idealism. But aesthetics function importantly in *Pierre*. Through them Melville extends significant currents of the thematic argument of *Moby-Dick*.

Abiding concerns of *Moby-Dick* had been the disjunction between aesthetic vision and reality as well as the clash between moral issues and aestheticism. Both problems surface in *Pierre* through discussion of the *"povertiresque,"* the ugly neologism that appears in Book XX. "If the grown man of taste," writes the narrator,

> possess not only some eye to detect the picturesuqe in the natural landscape, so also, has he as keen a perception of what may not unfitly be here styled, the *povertiresque* in the social landscape. To such an one, not more picturesquely conspicuous is the dismantled thatch in a painted cottage of Gainsborough, than the time-tangled and want-thinned locks of a beggar, *povertiresquely* diversifying those snug little cabinet-pictures of the world, which, exquisitely varnished and framed, are hung up in the drawing-room minds of humane men of taste, and amiable philosophers of either the "Compensation," or "Optimist" school. They deny that any misery is in the world, except for the purpose of throwing the fine *povertiresque* element into its general picture. Go to! God hath deposited cash in the Bank subject to our gentlemanly order; he hath bounteously blessed the world with a summer carpet of green. Begone, Heraclitus! The lamentations of the rain are but to make us our rainbows! (pp. 276-277)

The vogue for the picturesque had fostered disinterested aesthetic pleasure in images of decay and poverty, and it is not surprising to find Melville, whose family had suffered a grievous decline in fortune, assaulting the amorality of picturesque aestheticism. While Mrs. Glendinning, who is one of the "curious Optimists" who enjoy the picturesqueness of poverty in others, relishes the *"povertiresque"* in the ruined farmer and former peer, Millthorpe, Pierre finds "something else than the pure *povertiresque* in poverty," some "inklings of what it might be, to be old, and poor, and worn, and rheumatic, with shivering death drawing nigh" (p. 277). The reference to the "time-tangled and want-thinned locks of a beggar" suggests that Melville's criticism extends to the Wordsworthian moral picturesque as well as to the popular forms of the picturesque. Here, as well as in the passage on the mountain gloom of Marianna's life in "The Piazza," Melville might well have been working under the influence of his readings in Ruskin. But, be this as it may, it is clearly his intention to associate the *"povertiresque"* with Emerson and Thoreau, the "philosophers of either the 'Compensation' or 'Optimist' School."

To attribute a form of the picturesque vision to Emerson would seem to be a trying pass, for his landscapes tend to be unstable, not sharply pictorial, and they are seldom valued for "effects" alone. But in connecting the *"povertiresque"* with the "Compensation" school, Melville points up the grave disjunction he saw between the Emersonian

188

vision and the reality of natural and social evil. His fundamental respect
for deep-divers notwithstanding, he was deeply troubled by what he saw
in Emerson and Goethe alike as an inhumane evasion of moral responsi-
bility. In connecting the picturesque with Thoreau, Melville was on more
solid ground. He seems to have had Thoreau in mind when writing
Pierre, as is suggested by a passage in Book XVII. In March, 1851, he and
Hawthorne had jokingly resolved to write a travesty of *A Week on the
Concord and Merrimack Rivers*,[19] a project that was never undertaken; in
Pierre we may well have the shadow of that travesty in the narrator's
allusion to an "illustrious lad," the "author of 'A Week at Coney
Island',", whose first public lecture occasions "a portentous riot"[20] (p.
252). Through Hawthorne, who was for a time intimate with Thoreau,
Melville may have learned of Thoreau's intense interest in the picturesque. As William D. Templeman has pointed out, no one beyond
personal friends preoccupied Thoreau in his journals so much as Gilpin.[21]
In the writings of the British aesthete Thoreau found the sort of
etymological word-play to which he himself was so often inclined and
Gilpin also offered analyses of water-color techniques and natural light
effects from which Thoreau could generate metaphors. Pictorialism is of
course a key element of Thoreau's prose, and the significance of the
picturesque in the refinement of his descriptive technique is suggested by
the references to Gilpin in *Walden, The Maine Woods,* and *Cape Cod*, as
well as the spate of references in the journals. Gorden V. Boudreau's
careful study of these references has revealed that Thoreau's interest in
Gilpin's aesthetic crested between 1852 and 1853;[22] after that period
Gilpin seldom appears in Thoreau's writings. An entry in the journal in
1854 indicates growing disaffection for Gilpin and suggests that he had
become aware of the amoral aestheticism of the picturesque that
prompted Melville's disparaging remarks in *Pierre*: "Gilpin talked as if
there was some food for the soul in mere physical light and shadow," he
writes, "as if, without the suggestion of a moral, they could give man

19. In his old age Melville related this information to Theodore F. Wolfe, who
reported it in his *Literary Shrines* (Philadelphia: J.B. Lippincott, 1895), pp. 190-191;
the passage from Wolfe is reprinted by Hershel Parker in his edition of *The
Confidence-Man* (W.W. Norton & Company, 1971), p. 261. The travesty was to have
been titled "A Week on a Work-Bench in a Barn."
20. Although Thoreau never occasioned a riot, Melville may be referring ironically
to the wretched reception of *A Week*. It is conceivable that "A Week at Cony Island"
is a sly allusion to Thoreau's stay in Staten Island, a fact of which Melville would have
been aware through Hawthorne. but the connection between the "illustrious lad" and
Thoreau must remain conjectural.
21. "Thoreau, Moralist of the Picturesque," *PMLA* 47 (September 1932): 864-889.
22. "H.D. Thoreau, William Gilpin, and the Metaphysical Ground of the Picturesque," *American Literature* 45 (November 1973): 357-369.

pleasure or pain!"[23] "We never see any beauty but as the garment of some virtue,"[24] he later wrote. From such a point of view Gilpin necessarily seemed superficial: "He goes not below the surface to account for the effect of form and color, etc.,"[25] Thoreau complained. As Boudreau has shown, Thoreau's rejection of the sort of aestheticism represented by Gilpin drove him back to nature, the true gallery where, as he put it in his journal, "The perception of beauty is a moral test."[26] For Melville the rejection of aestheticism brought, by contrast, no reaffirmation of nature. Pierre, whose *"choice fate"* was *"to have been born and bred in the country"* is availed of a "rare and original development" through Nature: "Never mind if she proved ambiguous in the end" (p. 13), the narrator remarks with portentous irony. The perception of natural beauty can be for Melville no "moral test" for it, no less than picturesque paintings, abounds in deceptive "effects":

> Say what some poets will, Nature is not so much her own eversweet interpreter, as the mere supplier of that cunning alphabet, whereby selecting and combing as he pleases, each man reads his own peculiar lesson according to his own peculiar mind and mood. (p. 342)

This passage is as ambiguous as its subject. The "alphabet," not the percipient, is "cunning." While he is cognizant of the subjectivity of all perception, Melville's narrator here alludes to the same "unknown but still reasoning thing"[27] that ahab intuits behind the mask of appearances.

If Melville assaults the picturesque convention in *Pierre*, he by no means abandons the literary pictorialism that the aesthetic had fostered. By associating idealized or Claudian landscape with Lucy, the fair heroine of romantic convention, and the horrific or Salvatorean landscape with the dark Isabel, he effects an aesthetic argument similar to that achieved in *Moby-Dick* through the opposition between pastoral and sublime seascapes. The topography associated with Lucy, as Furrow has pointed out,[28] consists of the primordial zones of paradise, the valley and the plain. Representing innocence, Lucy urges Pierre away from the sublime mountains that seem desolate to him while he is under her influence. Lucy's form is invested with the radiant haze that American

23. *Works*, XII, 103.
24. *Works*, XVIII, 368.
25. *Works*, XII, 57.
26. *Works*, X, 126.
27. *Moby-Dick*, p. 157.
28. "The Terrible Made Visible," p. 246. I am indebted here to Furrow's argument. I do not, however, accede to her implied view that Melville had Claude and Salvator specifically in mind while composing landscapes in *Pierre*; at least as early as the eighteen-forties the names of the two masters had entered the voacabulary of American critics who used them to suggest a general antinomy of the idea of moral sublime and horrific sublime.

painters of ideal landscapes acquired from Claude; the setting sun, streaming through a window,

> bathed the whole form in golden loveliness and light; that wonderful, and most vivid transparency of her clear Welsh complexion, now truly glowed like rosy snow. Her flowing, white, blue-ribboned dress, fleecily invested her ... All her aspect to him, was that moment touched with an indescribable gayety, bouyancy, fragility, and an unearthly evanescence. (p. 58)

Isabel, who is associated with Pierre's subconscious as well as his commitment to moral absolutism, is approached in Pierre's night journey through an horrific landscape of ruin:

> On both sides, in the remoter distance, and also far beyond the mild lake's further shore, rose the long, mysterious mountain masses; shaggy with pines and hemlocks, mystical with nameless, vapory exhalations, and in that dim air black with dread and gloom. At their base, profoundest forests lay entranced, and from their far owl-haunted depths of caves and rotted leaves, and unused and unregarded inland overgrowth of decaying wood, ... from out the infinite inhumanities of those profoundest forests, came a moaning, muttering, roaring, intermitted, changeful sound; rain-shakings of the palsied trees, slidings of rocks undermined, final crashing of long-riven boughs, and devilish gibberish of the forest-ghosts. (pp. 109-110)

Passage into this landscape, borrowed from Gothic romance, signifies Pierre's plunge into the labyrinthine motives behind his commitment to Isabel. The unconscious is appropriately correlated with a primordial, unregenerate topography.

In Book XXI Melville exploits topographical symbolism in a manner that strikingly anticipates the allegorical retrospect in "The Piazza." The identity of the Saddle Meadows environs and those of Melville's Pittsfield estate is unmistakable. Fronting the Glendinning manor on the north side is an immense mountain:

> It was the phantasmagoria of the Mount of the Titans, a singular height standing quite detached in a wide solitude not far from the grand range of dark blue hills encircling his ancestral manor.

Although Melville clearly has Greylock in mind, he insists that the Mount of the titans had had a different and a telling name in former times:

> A high-aspiring, but most moody, disappointed bard, chancing once to visit the Meadows and beholding that fine eminence, christened it by the name it ever after bore; completely extinguishing its former title — The Delectable Mountain — one long ago bestowed by an old Baptist farmer, an hereditary admirer of Bunyan. (p. 342)

With the mountain's former title — "extinguished" like the light on Greylock's summit in "The Piazza" — are lost the redemptive possibilities of earthly pilgrimage that are suggested by Bunyan's name. The redeemed natural world of Christianity is supplanted by a primordial and pagan world of titan-gods.

The mountain excursion that follows establishes precisely the same aesthetic argument fostered by the excursion in "The Piazza." The view from the northerly piazza of Pierre's manor presented,

> of a soft haze-canopied summer's noon, ... a long and beautiful, but not entirely inaccessible-looking purple precipice, some two thousand feet in air, and on each hand sideways sloping down to lofty terraces of pastures.
>
> Those hill-side pastures, be it said, were thickly sown with a small white amaranthine flower, which, being irreconcilably distasteful to the cattle, and wholly rejected by them, and yet, continually multiplying on every hand, did by no means contribute to the agricultural value of those elevated lands ... (p. 343)

The amaranth recalls the white blossoms cankered by white worms in "The Piazza" and suggests leprose whiteness behind all natural appearances in *Moby-Dick*. Distasteful to cattle and diminishing the "agricultural value" of the land, the amaranth effects the displacement of the pastoral vision by the sublime: "'The small white flower, it is our bane,'" complain Mary Glendinning's tenants:

> "The aspiring amaranth, every year it climbs and adds new terraces to its sway! The immortal amaranth, it will not die, but last year's flowers survive to this! The terraced pastures grow glittering white, and the warm June still show like banks of snow: — fit token of the sterileness the amaranth begets!"

The sterility caused by the blossoms is also the blight attending loss of belief.

As in "The Piazza," altered perspective brings about the exposure of illusion:

> Now, on a somewhat nearer approach, the precipice did not belie its purple promise from the manorial piazza; — that sweet imposing purple promise, which seemed fully to vindicate the Bunyanish old title originally bestowed; — but showed the profuse aerial foliage of a hanging forest. Nevertheless, coming still more nigh, long and frequent rents among the leaves revealed horrible glimpses of dark-dripping rocks, and mysterious mouths of wolfish caves. Struck by this most unanticipated view, the tourist now quickened his impulsive steps to verify the change by coming into direct contact with so chamelon a height. As he would now speed on, the lower ground, which from the manor-house piazza seemed all a grassy level, suddenly merged into a very long and weary acclivity, slowly rising close up to the precipice's base ... (p. 343)

Taking up a landscape-as-seascape conceit, Melville laces his description with Oriental images of ruin; "efflorescent grasses" rippled against the cliff,

> as the efflorescent waves of some great swell or long rolling billow ripple against the water-line of a steep gigantic war-ship on the sea. And, as among the rolling sea-like sands of Egypt, disordered rows of broken Sphinxes lead to the Cheopian pyramid itself; so this long acclivity was thickly strewn with enormous rocky masses, grotesque in shape, and with wonderful features on them, which seemed to express that slumbering intelligence visible in some recumbent beasts — beasts whose intelligence seems struck dumb in them by some sorrowful and inexplicable spell. (p. 343)

Having pierced through a final fringe of vegetation, the narrator confronts an "impregnable redoubt" that had been "cunningly masked" by the "green tapestry of the interlacing leaves" (p. 244). All about rocks shoot up, "radiating with a hideous repellingness":

> Stark desolation; ruin, merciless and ceaseless; chills and gloom, — all here lived a hidden life, curtained by that cunning purpleness, which, from the piazza of the manor house, so beautifully invested the mountain once called Delectable, but now styled Titanic.

The immense "redoubt" of the mountain cliff, Melville's symbol of the Absolute, seems "not inaccessible" only when invested with the "cunning purpleness" of picturesque distance. The labyrinth of blasted boulders and trees and the ultimate redoubt that leaves the narrator "transfixed" (p. 344) must surely image the maze of epistemology and metaphysics in which Melville had struggled in that quest for the Absolute, *Moby-Dick*.

In "The Piazza" Melville turned from the exposure of the delusive effects of perspective to the disparity between aesthetic experience and the common exigencies of life. As Greylock's summit is a perpetual torment for the lost Marianna, so the upper reaches of the Mount of the Titans is a zone wherein "the multiple and most sterile inodorous immortalness of the small, white flower furnished no aliment for the mild cow's meditative cud" (p. 344). Descending in sadness from the dead, impenetrable wall of the summit the narrator encounters vestiges of human ruin that are apposite to the ruined cottage of Marianna. Melville again takes up flower symbolism in demonstrating that the sublime is inimical to humane values. "Here and there" near the summit

> you still might smell from far the sweet aromaticness of clumps of catnip, that dear farm-house herb. Soon you would see the modest verdure of the plant itself, and wheresoever you saw that sight, old foundation stones and rotting timbers of log-houses long extinct would also meet your eye; their desolation illy hid by the green solicitudes of the unemigrating herb. Most fitly named the catnip; since, like the unrunagat cat, though all that's human forsake the place, that plant will long abide, long bask and bloom on the abandoned hearth. Illy hid; for every spring the amaranthine and celestial flower gained on the mortal household herb; for every autumn the catnip died, but never an autumn made the amaranth to wane. The catnip and the amaranth! — man's earthly household peace, and the ever-encroaching appetite for God.[29] (pp. 344-345)

This strained passage may be unredeemable as art — it is as purple as the prospect from the Glendinning manor — but it is a valuable index of the aesthetic dilemma in which Melville found himself after *Moby-Dick*. That venture in the sublime had been driven by the "appetite for God," and, as is endlessly evinced in *Pierre*, Melville conceived of the personal price of

---

29. Cf. "The Piazza," in which the narrator laments that the "Hearth Stone Hills" cannot be framed in the same prospect as sublime Greylock (p. 3).

his venture to be the blight of nature. With *Pierre* he initially intended to try his hand at the popular, sentimental romance, but he found, perhaps before the early chapters of *Pierre* had been written, that the conclusions he had come to in *Moby-Dick* destroyed the creative possibilities in romance of nature. The frequent lapses of taste in *Pierre* as well the book's painful gropings toward psychological self-revelation suggest the real torments of Melville's situation; *Pierre* had necessarily to fail.

In the section on the Enceladus stone that concludes the mountain digression in *Pierre*, we find Melville striving to image personal tensions that he himself probably did not wholly understand. An important shift of perceptual vehicle occurs almost unnoticeably in the course of the mountain digression. The Saddle Meadows environs are first perceived through an omniscient eye that soon becomes that of a tourist. This perceiving identity is quickly supplanted by an inclusive "you," which draws the reader into a more intimate experience of the landscape evoked. But immediately after the strange, up-thrust rock at the base of the mountain cliff is described the passage is startlingly interrupted by an awakening Pierre:

> "Enceladus! it is Enceladus!" — Pierre cried out in his sleep. That moment the phantom faced him; and Pierre saw Enceladus no more; but on the Titan's armless trunk, his own duplicate face and features magnifiedly gleamed upon him with prophetic discomfiture and woe. With trembling frame he started from his chair, and woke from that ideal horror to all his actual grief. (p. 346)

The narrator's vision fuses with Pierre's dream vision, and Enceladus emerges as Melville's telling emblem of self.

The torso-shaped rock, which has been "stormed off" the summit of the Mount of the titans, is "deridingly left" at the cliff's base to "bay out his ineffectual howl" (p. 345) of defiance. "Fast frozen into the earth at the junction of the neck," Enceladus is armless and impotent. Like Pierre, who could not "leap the final barrier of gloom" (p. 346), Enceladus is the "son of incestuous Coelus and terra, the son of incestuous Heaven and Earth"; both are "heaven aspiring" and "sky-assaulting," but "not wholly earth-emancipated" (p. 347). Behind this murky, imperfectly controlled symbolism is the defeat of Melville's idealism.

Pierre may be heaven aspiring, but the primary direction of the book devoted to him is inward. The wrenching discordance between the Enceladus symbolism and the narrator's repeated insistence that he is writing an American Inferno may be recognized as the effect of a fundamental contradiction in the life of the mind in Melville's age. As Christopher Collins has put it, the transcendental cosmology "turned the rational Puritan cosmos inside-out: God was at the center of the undiscovered inner world, not at the rim of the outermost sphere."[30] Yet,

30. *The Uses of Observation*, p. 115.

abatted by the powerful strain of Lockean epistemology in America, the Puritan emphasis on experiential knowledge was as strong — in fact, stronger — than the transcendental emphasis on intuitive knowledge. Out of this tension of conflicting metaphysics and epistemologies Melville had managed to generate one masterpiece. Through the voyage motif of *Moby-Dick* he held Kant and Locke, Narcissus and sailor, in creative tension; in *Pierre*, which is imitative of a mode of fiction for which Melville had no talent, that tension becomes destructive conflict.

"The Piazza" concludes with the retreat from Greylock complete. The narrator attempts to settle back into a complacent aestheticism, "Launching [his] yawl no more for fairy-land." Yet his pleasure in nature's "amphitheatre" has been forever tainted by his mountain excursion, for

> every night, when the curtain falls, truth comes in with darkness. No light shows from the mountain. To and fro I walk the piazza deck, haunted by Marianna's face, and many as real a story.[31]

The concluding phrase suggests that as Melville selected the shorter fiction he would include in his modest collection he saw his best efforts after *Pierre* as rising from an impulse toward realism. But what he seems to have had in mind as "the real" while he composed the short fiction between 1853 and 1856 is difficult to define in any but a negative way. It would seem to be a world stripped of romance, something subtly but importantly different from the mere "actuality" that so troubled American Romantics as well as from the mechanistic world of Naturalism.

Pierre ends in an urban dungeon, and the circumscription of space of that romance lingers in the works that followed. One after another of the stories "presents an action of withdrawal, resignation, defeat," Warner Berthoff has remarked; "The whole frame of action has become less splendid and spacious."[32] The settings of the short fiction tend to be confining habitations like the law offices and prison courtyard in "Bartleby," the house with its tedious domestic tension in "I and My Chimney," the slave ship in "Benito Cereno," and the paper factory of the "Tartarus of Maids." As a student of the aesthetics of nature has observed, the garden or natural prospect is "the landing from which outer space is confronted," while buildings "turn the individual in on himself."[33] In nearly all of Melville's shorter work, drama is internalized.

"Bartleby," "Benito Cereno," and "The Encantadas" are the three great pieces among the *Piazza Tales*, and in the first two of these nature is

31. *Piazza Tales*, p. 15.
32. Introduction to *Great Short Works of Herman Melville* (New York: Harper & Row, 1966), p. 15.
33. Paul Shepard, *Man in the Landscape*, p. 116.

of little importance. In "Bartleby" the significance of nature is limited to
the pointedness of its exclusion. Describing the two windows of his law
offices that face a black and a white blank wall, the narrator remarks that
his view "might have been considered rather tame than otherwise,
deficient in what landscape painters call 'life'." In the Tombs he tells
Bartleby, "Look, there is the sky, and here is the grass." The prisoner's
enigmatic reply — "I know where I am"[34] — suggests that not only space
but meaning as well is circumscribed, entombed, in the shorter fiction.
The opening seascape of "Benito Cereno" is certainly memorable for its
evocation of a new variation of the "dumb blankness, full of meaning"[35]
that had so fascinated Melville in *Moby-Dick*:

> Everything was mute and calm; everything gray. The sea, though undulated into
> long roods of swells, seemed fixed, and was sleeked at the surface like waved lead
> that had cooled and set in the smelter's mould. The sky seemed a grey surtout.[36]

But the focus quickly becomes internal, psychological, and nature is not
broached significantly again until the close of the story. There Delano
attempts to revive the spirits of Don Benito through appeal to the
regenerative power of nature:

> "See, yon bright sun has forgotten it all, and the blue sea, and the blue sky; these
> have turned over new leaves"
> "Because they have no memory," he dejectedly replied; "because they are not
> human."
> "But these mild trades that now fan your cheek, do they not come with a human-
> like healing to you? Warm friends, steadfast friends are the trades."
> "With their steadfastness they but waft me to my tomb, Señor," was the
> foreboding response.

The American, whose perception remains limited by appearances, insists
on the possibility that any past, however horrid, might be blotted by life's
endless renewal. "You are saved," he cries to Don Benito, who, mired in
"shadow," goes to his death in a monastery on "Mount Agonia."[37] The
same darkness that blights the sensibility of the Spaniard is pervasive in
"The Encantadas," wherein nature's light is only a tormenting counterpoint to nature's gloom.

Masked by the suggestive pseudonym, "Salvator R. Tarnmoor,"
Melville creates in the series of casually connected sketches that comprise
"The Encantadas," a work that is sustainedly parodic of the conventional
picturesque tour-book. That this was Melville's intention is evinced by
the first sketch, "The Isles at Large," in which the death-ridden landscape
of the Galapagos is repeatedly connected with such American centers of

34. *Piazza Tales*, pp. 17, 51.
35. *Moby-Dick*, p.
36. *Piazza Tales*, p. 55.
37. Ibid., pp. 139, 140.

picturesque interest as the Erie Canal and Adirondack Mountains; "As for solitariness," the narrator writes,

> the greast forests of the north, the expanses of unnavigated waters, the Greenland ice-fields, are the profoundest of solitudes to a human observer; still the magic of their changeable tides and seasons mitigates their terror; because ... those forests are visited by the May; the remotest seas reflect familiar stars even as Lake Erie does.

But the "special curse" of the Encantadas is "that to them change never comes; neither change of seasons nor of sorrows."[38] They are, to be sure, as enchanting as their name suggests, but the trance-like state they effect is not the pleasing atmosphere of the conventional picturesque but the aura of despair and portentous evil. "In no world but a fallen one could such lands exist,"[39] remarks the narrator, and he suggests that since he has experienced the desert islands even his native New England landscape has somehow fallen from grace:

> Nor even at the risk of meeting the charge of absurdly believing in enchantments, can I restrain the admission that sometimes, even now, when leaving the crowded city to wander out July and August among the Adirondack Mountains, far from the influences of towns and proportionally nigh to the mysterious ones of nature; when at such times I sit me down in the mossy head of some deep-wooded gorge, surrounded by prostrate trunks of blasted pines and recall, as in a dream, my other and far-distant rovings in the baked heart of the charmed isles; ... I can hardly resist the feeling that in my time I have indeed slept upon evilly enchanted ground.[40]

Laced with allusions to Milton and tagged by epigraphs from romance, from *The Faerie Queene* and from *As You Like It* and *The Tempest*,[41] the sketches form an extraordinarily intense microcosm of a world that has lost romance as well as grace. "Take five-and-twenty heaps of cinders dumped here and there in an outside city lot," the narrator begins;

> imagine some of them magnified into mountains, and the vacant lot the sea; and you will have fit idea of the general aspect of the Encantadas .... A group rather of extinct volcanoes than of isles; looking much as the world at large might, after a penal conflagration.[42]

Beyond the "Ant-eaters, Man-haters, Lizards, Snakes, Spiders, Salamanders, Devils," and tortoises, the inhabitants of the islands are all "runaways, Castaways, Solitaries."[43] As Jones has pointed out, the sixth

38. Ibid., p. 150.
39. Ibid., p. 151.
40. Ibid., p. 153.
41. On Melville's careful choice and editing of these epigraphs see Russell Thomas, "Melville's Use of Some Sources in *The Encantadas*," *American Literature* 3 (January 1932): 432-456 and Buford Jones, "Spenser and Shakespeare in *The Encantadas, Sketch VI*," *Emerson Society Quarterly* 35 (Second Quarter): 68-73.
42. *Piazza Tales*, p. 149.
43. Ibid., pp. 166, 204.

sketch, "Barrinton Isle and the Buccaneers," is the least dark of the sketches:

> Barrington Isle, tentatively introduced as "the least unproductive isle of the group," is unobtrusively but distinctly developed as a tiny remnant of the unfallen world, a "harbour of safety, and bower of ease" for men who find civilization less conducive to regeneracy than stark isolation.[44]

The measure of harmony with the environment achieved by the buccaneers is suggested by the strange "seats" they have left in the landscape,

> Seats which might have served Brahmins and presidents of peace societies. Fine old ruins of what had once been symmetric lounges of stone and turf, they bore every mark of both artificialness and age, and were, undoubtedly, made by the Buccaneers. One had been a long sofa, with back and arms, just such a sofa as the poet Gray might have loved to throw himself upon, his Crebillon in hand.[45]

But, in spite of these marks of a small but precious measure of felicity, the Encantadas are both a spiritual and a physical desert. As Shepard has said of topographical symbolism, the sea, which Melville had left behind him, is "potential primitive, the beginning," while "the desert is the end, a place of purgation. ... and humility, and is crossed only with faith."[46] Melville does not cross the end, the desert, in faith, as is suggested by two other inhabitants of the islands.

The castaway Chola widow to whom the eighth sketch is devoted offers genuine potential for tragedy, yet her horrid witness of her husband's death is so unimaginably cruel that it seems beyond her, seems to be "some sham tragedy on the stage." The sense of a gulf between art and reality latent in this phrase is also present in the narrator, who says

> It is not artistic heartlessness, but I wish I would but draw in crayons; for this woman was a most touching sight; and crayons, tracing softly melancholy lines, would best depict the mournful image of the dark-damasked Chola widow.[47]

The widow's exposure to the sight of her husband's death is rendered through the telling use of a motif borrowed from American seascape:

> Before Hunilla's eyes they sank ... She was seated on a rude bower among the withered thickets, crowning a lofty cliff, a little back from the beach. The thickets were so disposed, that in looking upon the sea at large she peered out from among the branches as from the lattice of a high balcony. But upon the day we speak of here, the better to watch the adventure of those two hearts she loved, Hunilla had withdrawn the branches to one side, and held them so. They formed an oval frame, through which the bluely boundless sea rolled like a painted one. And there, the invisible painter painted to her view the wave-tossed and disjointed rafts; ... and then all subsided into smooth-flowing creamy waters, slowly drifting the splintered

44. "Spenser and Shakespeare in *The Encantadas*," p. 68.
45. *Piazza Tales*, p. 173.
46. *Man in the Landscape*, p. 154.
47. *Piazza Tales*, p. 181.

198

wreck; while first and last, no sound of any sort was heard. Death in a silent picture; a dream of the eye; such vanishing shapes as the mirage shows.[48]

In its conventional form, the painterly motif of the woman looking to the sea from a window or partially enclosed bower was meant to contrast garden and wilderness, pastoral and sublime. Here Hunilla's bower is itself a wilderness in which she is exiled, and the pathos of the conventional shipwreck scene is subordinated to the eerie emptiness of the silent calm.[49]

The position of "Hood's Isle and the Hermit Oberlus" as the ninth and penultimate sketch suggests that the image of man presented in it is more important than that offered by the earlier section on the Chola widow. The weird Oberlus stands as Melville's image of primordial, unregenerate man, and it is only fit that he should be at one with the fallen world of the Encantadas. He lives in a "den of lava and clinkers" and farms "among the rocks about two acres of soil capable of rude cultivation":

> It is ... reported to have been the strangest sight, this same Oberlus, of a sultry, cloudy morning, hidden under his shocking old black tarpaulin hat, hoeing potatoes among the lava. So warped and crooked was his strange nature, that the very handle of his hoe seemed gradually to have shrunk and twisted in his grasp ... When planting his whole aspect and all his gestures were so malevolently and uselessly sinister and secret, that he seemed rather in act of dropping poison into wells than potatoes into soil.[50]

Such a ghastly distortion of pastoral is appropriate in "The Encantadas," Melville's picturesque of a natural hell.

Whatever merit there may be to Melville's suggestion that the *Piazza Tales* are held together by a common strain of realism,[51] the collection is certainly unified by a consistently high quality. Among the lesser short fictions excluded from the volume, only four bear any relevance to the aesthetics of nature and these warrant only brief attention. In "The Two Temples" Melville seems to have returned to the epistemological issues that so concern him in *Moby-Dick*. The closed room in the tower of "Temple First" that is illumined by stained glass windows is, as Zoellner has pointed out,[52] symbolic of the dungeon of sensationally circum-

48. *Piazza Tales*, pp. 183-184; cf. the collapse of the vortex in *Moby-Dick* that "subsided to a creamy pool" (Epilogue).

49. On the motif and the shipwreck theme in American and British painting see Boase, "Shipwrecks in English Romantic Painting," pp. 337-344, and Stein, *Seascape and the American Imagination.*.

50. *Piazza Tales*, p. 195.

51. The slighter performances in the collection, "The Lightning-Rod Man" and "The Bell Tower," could hardly be termed realistic. Ilse Sofie Newbery has argued unconvincingly that the tales are unified thematically. ("The Unity of Melville's *Piazza Tales*," Ph.D. dissertation, University of British Columbia, 1964).

52. *Salt-Sea Mastodon*, p. 25.

scribed experience; not content in the luminously colored room, the narrator struggles with little success to see out. But the epistemological symbolism is only half realized, and it would seem to bear no clear relation to the satire of the fashionable Grace Church in New York that is the primary intention of the sketch.[53] In "The Two Temples" ambiguity subverts rather than expands meaning, a problem also found in "Cock-a-Doodle-Doo!" While it is a more interesting piece than "The Two Temples," the latter seems a hash of possible meanings, no one of which is sufficiently developed to warrant priority. It has been cogently read as a satire of transcendental faith in the imagination,[54] as a "paean of Christian faith,"[55] and as a thinly disguised sexual allegory.[56] The opening passages of the tale are clearly parodic of "Resolution and Independence," and affinities between Merrymusk, the owner of the magical cock, and Wordsworth's Leech Gatherer prepare the reader for an affirmation of the power of imagination. But the glibness of the narrative voice and the flippancy of the title hint of an abiding irony throughout.

"The Apple-Tree Table" is the only tale of the 'fifties that celebrates the redemptive power of nature without a subversive undercurrent of irony. The resurrection of the beautiful insect that had been entombed for more than a century suggests to the narrator and his family the possibility of spiritual resurrection. But the extraordinarily circumscribed range of vision in the story, coupled with the familial tensions so typical of Melville's domestic fiction, limits its affirmative note; it is as though Melville could find grace in natural processes only by focusing on nature's minutia. In any case, the more powerful "The Tartarus of Maids," published in April, 1855, thirteen months before "The Apple-Tree Table," presents a more compelling picture of how Melville had come to regard biological nature. It is amazing that "The Tartarus of Maids" ever saw print in Melville's lifetime, so raw and hideous is its allegory of sexual reproduction. Of the Pittsfield mountain locale he fashions an elaborate landscape-as-body conceit in which the female

53. Charles Briggs of *Putnam's Magazine* rejected the tale in consideration of "the religious sensibilities of the public" (letter to Melville, May 12, 1854; reprinted in Leyda, *The Melville Log*, I, 487).

54. See Egbert S. Oliver, "'Cock-a-Doodle-Doo!' and Transcendental Hocus-Pocus," *New England Quarterly* 21 (Summer 1948): 204-215 and William B. Stein, "Melville Roasts Thoreau's Cock," *Modern Language Notes 74 (March 1959): 218-219.*

55. Fogle, *Melville's Shorter Tales*, p. 33. Fogle goes on to say that "One inclines to think finally that the story means what it says but betrays something else. Intended as a trumpet call of affirmation, it reveals in its dissonances the note of underlying despair" (p. 35).

56. Berthoff sees in the tale a "bitter sub-theme of men's enslavement to the force of sex" (*Great Short Works*, p. 75).

genitals figure as a nightmarish paper factory. The man who had esteemed the Kantian whale-head in *Moby-Dick* and disparaged the Lockean again expresses his aversion to mechanistic epitemology; the narrator flees in disgust as the pallid factory girls mechanically turn out reams of blank white paper.

Melville returned to an expansive stage of fiction in *Israel Potter*, which is by no means a work of the first order. An enthusiastic nationalism is undeniably at play in it, but so, too, is a deep anxiety concerning America's future. The finest qualities of the Republic, Melville suggests, will perhaps be the agency of its doom. He proudly deems America the John Paul Jones among nations, but observes that the savage exuberance of that war hero's kind may be inimical to social and political stability. The enterprising spirit of utilitarianism is exemplified in the figure of Franklin, whose remarkable energies are described as at once exploitative and life-denying. It is a most significant irony that Potter himself, another Ishmael and a son of the wilderness, should disappear amid the squalor and industrial filth of London. If the final circumscription of space signals Melville's shift of impulse from the outward quest to the quest within, then *Israel Potter* may be seen as a kind of preliminary to the exclusively interior landscape of *The Confidence-man*.

It is difficult to accede to Newton Arvin's view that an "obsessive sense of the lurking treacheries in both nature and man is at the heart of this uncomfortable book,"[57] since in *The Confidence-Man* all vestiges of a natural landscape are obliterated. The work might be said to have no setting whatsoever, save perhaps the dream setting of the collective American unconscious. Having found profoundly unsettling ambiguity in the sublime view from the mast-head, Melville descended in *The Confidence-Man* to the darkest reaches of the nation's forecastle and presented a world in which doubt, deception, and uncertainty infect every word, face, and distinction.

The very fact that Melville's philosophical voyage down the Mississippi entirely lacks a sense of place must surely be an important source of what Arvin rightly calls the *"infidel"*[58] quality of the book. For Melville's refusal to admit any sensuous or pictorial detail in a voyage down America's greatest river and her greatest topographical symbol fosters a powerful nihilistic statement, a final, damning rejection of nature. That such a statement through negation was intended is suggested by his apparent excision of a pictorially evocative passage from his manuscript that would have been the only sequence of natural description in the

57. *Herman Melville*, p. 249.
58. Ibid., p. 251.

book.[59] But the absence of a sense of place in *The Confidence-Man* is justified on other grounds than the implicit rejection of nature it effects. A sense of place can only be achieved through a discrete vision or point of view, and Melville's dark moral argument,[60] rising from the endlessly ambiguous shiftings of identity aboard the riverboat, precludes fixed perspective. As the *Fidèle* sails down the river toward a moral midnight of the soul, it is appropriate that the book should end with the closing motif of "The Piazza": the waning light is finally extinguished.

59. The fragment, referred to as "The River," is reprinted by Elizabeth S. Foster in her edition of *The Confidence-Man* (New York: Hendricks House, 1954), pp. 379-380. The fact that it was found among portions of the manuscripts of the finished work and that it was written on the same paper suggests that it was written for possible inclusion.

60. It is notable that Melville builds this moral argument largely by subverting the ideas of eighteenth-century moral philosophers (see Fred E. Brouwer, "Melville's *The Confidence-Man* as Ship of Philosophers," *Southern Humanities Review* 3 [Autumn 1969]: 158-165. Similarly, he was inclined to define his aesthetic position through negation of eighteenth-century aesthetic ideas.

CHAPTER IV

CONCLUSIONS

"The Piazza" is a telling paradigm of the quest in nature set forth in Melville's prose fiction in the great decade of 1846 through 1856. Like the South Sea romances and like *Mardi* and *Moby-Dick*, the sketch records a quest for light in the natural world. Its concluding statement — "No light shows from the mountain" — signalizes the retreat from nature that begins after *Moby-Dick*. To borrow the theatrical trope established at the end of "The Piazza," the great stage of wild nature, the stage of most of Melville's major fictions, was closed in darkness after 1851. We are thus left with the paradox that through the composition of *Moby-Dick*, the greatest fictive rendering of America's pre-eminent theme of man in nature, Melville felt compelled to reject the aesthetic ideas with which his culture structured and defined its relation to the world.

The fact that, as Morse Peckham has put it, the history of the United States is the history of "the progressive westward movement of European culture into alien physical environments"[1] must be recalled if we are to come to terms with the aesthetic problems confronted by Melville and his contemporaries. Man's vision of himself and of his social, economic, and political life is no doubt antecedent to his vision of nature, and the grafting of eighteenth-century European aesthetics to the American environment was inevitably attended by conflict. As Paul Shepard has written,

> The wilderness sentiment was born where there was no wilderness ... The Americans, moving in this tradition, were presented with the dubious opportunity of trying out the nature aesthetic at the edge of a real wilderness — an aesthetic which had been known to Western civilization for two hundred years at the most.[2]

Through the early decades of the nineteenth century, the sublime of nature was for Americans not an aesthetic experience that might be sought or avoided at will so much as a fact of life that was a threat and a challenge. Melville, to be sure, lived and wrote after the wilderness of the West had been largely subdued, but the *Pequod*'s errand on a watery wilderness is necessary business and not diversion or pleasure. The alien

1. "Hawthorne and Melville as European Authors," in Howard, ed., *Melville and Hawthorne in the Berkshires*, p. 43.
2. *Man in the Landscape*, p. 151.

quality of European aesthetics in America is more evident in regard to the picturesque. As is abundantly evinced in Irving and Hawthorne, American writers were hard pressed to accommodate the picturesque in a landscape with no past and in a nation as contemptuous of tradition as it was intent on generating a future. The calculated disjunctions of "the Piazza," the clash between the imagery and idiom of European aesthetics and the harsh realities of the mountain world, and the conflict between the aesthetically pleasing decay of Marianna's hut and the sordid reality of her isolation and poverty, stand as testimony to Melville's subtle awareness of his and his fellow artists' predicament.

The peculiar urgency with which American writers of the age grappled with the aesthetics of nature stems in large measure from the evolution of wild nature as a national symbol. However, it was not simply the hopes of "Young America" that drove Melville to nature's center and to despair in *Moby-Dick* any more than it was the imported legacy of British Romanticism. Not the sublime of Shelley or Byron or, for that matter, of Cornelius Mathews, the sublime in Melville is a subtle confluence of European aesthetic tradition and the thought of New England Puritanism. The millennialist and typological currents of Puritan thought had fostered in America a conception of sublimity as dramatic and immediate revelation of Spirit a century before the importation of European Idealism and the rise of the Transcendentalism. Melville, who was as if by instinct drawn to those passages of the Old Testament richest in natural revelation, seems to have absorbed this tradition in its original form. The residue of Puritan typology is of course everywhere evident in the popular culture of his age, but there it takes a thoroughly tempered form. As Perry Miller has argued, the culture of nineteenth-century liberal Protestantism "dallied with the sublime and failed to comprehend the sinister dynamic of Nature."[3] They wrote and painted the sublime melting into the beautiful. Melville did not share their error.

It is probably true that the ideas a writer embraces or rejects are less the basis of his identity than the superfices by which he lends structure and communicable form to his basic desires and aversions. The factors behind what Leon Howard has called the "unusual energy of intellectual strife"[4] in Melville's works no doubt lie deeper than aesthetic theory and deeper still than Puritan tradition. After all, virtually all of the major writers of his age successfully attuned a selection of European traditions to their own experience and needs; in fact, that very task of adjustment might be said to be at the center of the achievements of Irving, Cooper, Hawthorne, Emerson, Thoreau, and others. What sets Melville apart is the

3. "The Romantic Dilemma in American Nationalism and the Concept of Nature," *Nature's Nation*, p. 207.

persistence of "intellectual strife," the fact that negation becomes first a favored method and finally, in *The Confidence-Man*, an exclusive end.

The strife in Melville's work must surely rise from that pair of personal qualities so often remarked by his biographers: the will to believe and the obsessive inclination to doubt, or, as William Ellery Sedgwick has put it, the opposition of heart and mind.[5] Hawthorne's famous portrait of Melville in 1856 reveals this conflict: "He stayed with us from Tuesday till Thursday," wrote Hawthorne,

> and, on the intervening day, we took a pretty long walk together, and sat down in a hollow among the sandhills, ... and smoked a cigar. Melville, as he always does, began to reason of Providence and futurity, and everything that lies beyond human ken, and informed me that he had "pretty much made up his mind to be annihilated;" but still he does not seem to rest in that anticipation and, I think, will never rest until he gets hold of a definite belief. It is strange how he persists — and has persisted ever since I knew him, and probably long before — in wandering to and fro over these deserts, as dismal and monotonous as the sandhills amid which we were sitting. He can neither believe, nor be comfortable in his unbelief; and he is too honest and courageous not to try one or the other.[6]

An artist of such psychic conflicts would be unusually susceptible to the aesthetic strife endemic to early nineteenth-century America. Caught between Mechanism and Idealism, between Locke and Kant, he would vacillate between the reduction of aesthetic experience to a mere function of mood and the expectation that it might yield up something like religious revelation.

The dismal deserts through which Melville wanders in the Hawthorne portrait are, like the desert islands in "The Encantadas," a fallen world, a world without grace. If, as Ernest Tuveson has argued, the imagination was for the romantic artist a means of grace and of reconciling the heart and mind in nature,[7] then the fall from grace that is chronicled in "The Piazza" and verified in Hawthorne's portrait of Melville finally relates to the loss of faith in the imagination. In a passage in *Biographia Literaria* that Melville surely knew, Coleridge offers a topographical image of the imagination that contrasts revealingly with "The Piazza." "It is time to tell the truth," wrote Coleridge;

> There is a *philosophic ... consciousness*, which lies beneath or (as it were) *behind* the spontaneous consciousness natural to all reflecting beings. As the elder Romans distinguished their northern provinces into Cis-Alpine and Trans-Alpine, so we

4. "Americanization of the European Heritage," in *The American Writer and the European Heritage*, ed. Margaret Denny and William H. Gilman (Minneapolis: Minnesota University Press, 1950), p. 83.

5. *Herman Melville: The Tragedy of Mind* (New York: Russell & Russell, 1962).

6. Hawthorne's journal entry for November 12, 1856; reprinted in *The Melville Log*, II, 529.

7. *The Imagination as a Means of Grace*, especially pp. 132-220.

may divide all the objects of human knowledge into those on this side, and those on the other side of the spontaneous consciousness ... The latter is exclusively the domain of PURE philosophy, which is therefore properly entitled *transcendental*, in order to discriminate it at once, both from mere reflection and *re*-presentation on the one hand, and on the other from those flights of lawless speculation which, abandoned by *all* distinct consciousness, ... are justly condemned, as *transcendent*. The first range of hills, that encircles the scanty vale of human life, is the horizon for the majority of its inhabitants. On *its* ridges the common sun is born and departs ... by the many, even this range ... is but imperfectly known. Its higher ascents are too often hidden by mists and clouds from uncultivated swamps, which few have courage or curiousity to penetrate. To the multitude below these vapors appear, now as the dark haunts of terrific agents, on which none may intrude with impunity; and now all *a-glow*, with colors not their own, they are gazed at as the splendid palaces of happiness and power. But in all ages there have been a few, who measuring and sounding the rivers of the vale at the feet of their furthest inaccessible falls have learned, that the sources must be far higher and far inward; a few, who even in the level streams have detected elements, which neither the vale itself or the surrounding mountains contained or could supply.[8]

At the foot of ultimately inaccessible reaches, Melville found that what he sought was far higher. For him the sublime was, like the mountain crest in "The Piazza," a pass between two worlds but participant of neither. Retreating from nature, he sought truth far inward, but the enigmatic shadow of Greylock was always with him.

8. *Biographia Literaria*, I, 163-166.

SELECTED BIBLIOGRAPHY

General Works

Adams, Richard P. "American Renaissance: An Epistemological Problem." *Emerson Society Quarterly* 35 (second quarter 1964); 2-7.
——. "Romanticism and the American Renaissance." *American Literature* 23 (January 1952): 419-432.
Adams, Robert Martin. *Nil: Episodes in the Literary Conquest of Void During the Nineteenth Century*. New York: Oxford University Press, 1966.
Addison, Joseph. *The Spectator*. Edited by Donald F. Bond. Vol. III. Oxford: Clarendon Press, 1965.
Alison, Archibald. *Essays on the Nature and Principles of Taste*. Hartford, Conn.: George Goodwin & Sons, 1821.
Allen, Gay Wilson. "The Influence of Space on the American Imagination." In *Essays on American Literature in Honor of Jay b. Hubbell*, pp. 329-342. Edited by Clarence Ghodes. Durham, N. C.: Duke University Press, 1967.
Allen, Walter. *The Urgent West: The American Dream and Modern Man*. New York: E. P. Dutton & Company, 1969.
Allston, Washington. *"Lectures on Art" and "Poems" and "Monaldi."* Edited by Nathalia Wright. Gainesville, Fla.: Scholars' Facsimiles & Reprints, 1967.
Arnheim, Rudolf. *Art and Visual Perception*. Berkeley: University of California Press, 1954.
Auden, W. H. *The Enchafed Flood; or, The romantic Iconography of the Sea*. New York: Random House, 1950.
Baillie, John. *An Essay on the Sublime*. London, 1747; reprinted Los Angeles: Augustun Reprint Society, 1953.
Bate, Walter Jackson. *From Classic To Romantic: Premises of Taste in Eighteenth-Century England*. New York: Harper & Row, 1946.
Bayle, Pierre. *Historical and Critical Dictionary*. 5 vols. London: J. J. and P. Knapton, 1734-38.
Baym, Max ZI. *A History of Literary Aesthetics in America*. New York: Frederick Ungar Publishing Company, 1973.

Bell, Millicent. *Hawthorne's View of the Artist.* New York: State University of New York, 1962.

Bier, Jesse. "Hawthorne on Romance: His Prefaces Related and Examined." *Modern Philology* 53 (August 1955): 17-24.

Blair, Hugh. *Lectures on Rhetoric and Belles Lettres.* New York: George Long, 1817.

Boas, George. "Romantic Philosphy in America." in *Romanticism in America*, pp. 191-202. New York: Russell & Russell, 1961.

Boase, T. S. R. "Shipwrecks in English Romantic Painting." *Journal of the Warburg and Courtauld Institute* 22 (1959): 337-344.

Born, Wolfgang. *American Landscape Painting; an Interpretation.* New Haven: Yale University Press, 1948.

Boudreau, Gordon V. "H. D. Thoreau, William Gilpin, and the Metaphysical Ground of the Picturesque." *American Literature* 45 (November 1973): 357-369.

Brooks, Van Wyck. *From a Writer's Notebook.* New York: E. P. Dutton & Company, 1958.

Burd, Van Aiken. "Background to *Modern Painters*." *PMLA* 74 (June 1959): 254-267.

Burke, Edmund. *A Philosophical Enquiry into the Origins of Our Ideas of Sublime and Beautiful.* Edited by J. T. Boulton. London: Routledge and Paul, 1958.

Burroughs, Bryson. *A Catalogue of Paintings in the Metropolitan Museum Art.* 7th ed. New York: Metropolitan Museum of Art, 1924.

Callow, James t. *Kindred Spirits: Knickerbocker Writers and Artists, 1807-1855.* Chapel Hill: University of North Carolina Press, 1967.

Carritt, E. F. "The Sources and Effects in England of Kant's Philosophy of Beauty." *Monist* 35 (1925): 315-328.

——. *The Theory of Beauty.* 6th ed. London: Methuen, 1962.

Chambers, Ephraim. *Cyclopaedia: or, An Universal Dictionary of Arts and Sciences.* 2 vols. London: Knapton, etc., 1728.

Charvat, William. *The Origins of American Critical Thought, 1810-1835.* Philadelphia: University of Pennsylvania Press, 1936.

Chase, Richard. *The American Novel and Its Tradition.* New York: Doubleday & Company, 1957.

Collingwood, R. G. *Principles of art.* Oxford: Oxford University Press, 1963.

Collins, Christopher. *The Uses of Observation: A Study of Correspondential Vision in the Writings of Emerson, Thoreau, and Whitman.* Paris and The Hague: Mouton, 1971.

Conron, John. *The American Landscape: A Critical Anthology of Prose and Poetry.* New York: Oxford University Press, 1973.

Cornish, Vaughn. *Scenery and the Sense of Sight.* Cambridge: Cambridge University Press, 1935.

Coursen, Herbert R. "Nature's Center." *College English* 24 (March 1963): 467-469.

Cowdrey, Mary Bartlett, ed. *The American Academy of Fine Arts and American Art Union, 1816-1852.* 2 vols. New York: New York Historical Society, 1953.

Curti, Merle. *The Growth of American Thought.* New York: Harper & Row, 1943.

Curtis, George William. *Lotus Eating: A Summer Book.* New York: Harper & Brothers, 1852.

Dahl, Curtis. "The American School of Catastrophe." *American Quarterly* 11 (Fall 1959): 380-390.

——. "Bulwer-Lytton and the School of Catastrophe." *Philological Quarterly* 32 (October 1953): 428-442.

Dennis, John. *Critical Works.* Edited by Edward Niles Hooker. Baltimore: Johns Hopkins University Press, 1939.

Duffy, John J. *Coleridge's American Disciples: The Selected Correspondence of James Marsh.* Amherst: University of Massachusetts Press, 1974.

Eastlake, Charles Lock. *Eastlake's Contributions to the Fine Arts.* London: John Murray, 1848.

Eliade, Mircea. *The Myth of the Eternal Return.* Translated by Willard R. Trask. New York: Pantheon Books, 1954.

Feidelson, Charles N., Jr. *Symbolism and American Literature.* Chicago University of Chicago Press, 1953.

Fisher, Marvin. "The Iconology of Industrialism; 1830-1860." *American Quarterly* (Fall 1961): 347-364.

Fletcher, Angus. *Allegory: The Theory of a Symbolic Mode.* Ithaca, N.Y.: Cornell University Press, 1964.

Flexner, James Thomas. *The Light of Distant Skies.* New York: Harcourt, Brace, & Company, 1954.

Frye, Northrop. *Anatomy of Criticism: Four Essays.* Princeton: Princeton University Press, 1957.

——. "The Four Forms of Prose Fiction." *Hudson Review* 2 (Winter 1950): 582-595.

Fussell, Edwin. *Frontier: American Literature and the American West.* Princeton: Princeton University Press, 1965.

Gibson, J. J. *The Perception of the Visual World.* Boston: Houghton Mifflin, 1950.

Gilpin, William. *An Essay upon Prints, containing Remarks on the Principles of Picturesque Beauty.* London: J. Robson, 1768.

——. *Three Essays: On Picturesque Beauty; On Picturesque Travel; and On Sketching Landscape: to Which is Added a Poem, on Landscape Painting.* London: R. Blamire, 1792.

Goethe, Johann Wolfgang von. *Goethe's Theory of Colours.* Translated by Charles Lock Eastlake. London: Frank Cass & Company, 1967.

Gombrich, E.H. *Art and Illusion: A Study in the Psychology of Pictorial Representation.* New York: Pantheon, 1960.

Guetti, James. *The Limits of Metaphor: A Study of Melville, Conrad, and Faulkner.* Ithaca, N.Y.: Cornell University Press, 1967.

Gussow, Alan. *A Sense of Place: The Artist and the American Land.* New York: Saturday Review Press, 1972.

Hagstrum, Jean H. *The Sister Arts: The tradition of Literary Pictorialism and English Poetry from Dryden to Gray.* Chicago: University of Chicago Press, 1958.

Harris, Neil. *The Artist in American Society.* New York: George Braziller, 1966.

Hazard, Lucy Lockwood. *The Frontier in American Literature.* New York: Thomas Y. Crowell Company, 1927.

Heiser, M.F. "The Decline of Neo-Classicism, 1801-1848." In *Transitions in American Literary Culture*, pp. 93-159. Edited by Harry Hayden Clark. Durham, N.C.: Duke University Press, 1953.

Hipple, Walter John. *The Beautiful, the Sublime, and the Picturesque in Eighteenth-Century British Aesthetic Theory.* Carbondale, Ill.: Southern Illinois University Press, 1957.

[Holmes, Oliver Wendell] "Exhibition of Pictures Painted by Washington Allston at Harding's Gallery, School Street." *North American Review* 50 (1840): 358-381.

Howard, Leon. "Americanization of the European Heritage." In *The Writer and the European Tradition*, pp. 78-89. Edited by Margaret Denny and William H. Gilman. Minneapolis: Minnesota University Press, 1950.

Hussey, Christopher. *The Picturesque: Studies in a Point of View.* New York: G.P. Putnam's Sons, 1927.

Huth, Hans. *Nature and the American: Three Centuries of Changing Attitudes.* Berkeley: University of California Press, 1967.

Jackson, Wallace. *Immediacy: The Development of a Critical Concept from Addison to Coleridge.* Amsterdam: Rodopi, 1973.

——. "Wordsworth and His Predecessors: Private Sensations and Public Tones." *Criticism* 17 (Winter 1975): 41-58.

Jeffrey, Francis. 'Alison's *Essay on Taste."* *Edinburgh Review* 18 (May 1811): 1-45.

Jones, Buford. "The 'Fairy Land' of Hawthorne's Romances." *Emerson Society Quarterly* 48 (Third Quarter 1967): 106-124.

——. "'The Man of Adamant' and the Moral Picturesque." *American Transcendental Quarterly* 10 (1972): 33-41.

Jones, Howard Mumford. "Landscape as Religion." In *Belief and Dis-*

belief in American Literature, pp. 25-47. Chicago: University of Chicago Press, 1969.

———. "Prose and Pictures: James Fenimore Cooper." *Tulane Studies in English* 3 (1952): 133-154.

Jones, William Alfred. *Characters and Criticism*. 2 vols. New York: I.Y. Westervelt, 1857.

———. *Literary Studies: A Collection of Miscellaneous Essays*. New York: Edward Walker, 1847.

Kallich, Martin. *The Association of Ideas and Critical Theory in Eighteenth-Century England*. Paris and The hague: Mouton, 1970.

Kant, Immanuel. *Kant's Critique of Aesthetic Judgment*. Translated by James Creed Meredith. Oxford: Oxford University Press, 1911.

Kiely, Robert. *The Romantic Novel in England*. Cambridge: Harvard University Press, 1972.

Knight, Richard Payne. *An Analytical Inquiry into the Principles of Taste*. London: T. Payne and J. White, 1805.

Landow, George P. *The Aesthetic and Critical Theories of John Ruskin*. Princeton: Princeton University Press, 1971.

Larkin, Oliver W. *Art and Life in America*. New York: Rinehart & Company, 1949.

Leonard, William Ellery. *Byron and Byronism in America*. Boston: n.p., 1905.

Levin, Harry. *The Power of Blackness: Hawthorne, Poe, Melville*. New York: Alfred Knopf, 1958.

Levy, Leo B. "Hawthorne and the Sublime." *American Literature* 37 (January 1966): 391-402.

———. "The Landscape Modes of *The Scarlet Letter*." *Nineteenth-Century Fiction* 23 (March 1969): 377-389.

———. "Picturesque Style in *The House of the Seven Gables*." *New England Quarterly* 39 (June 1966): 147-160.

Lewis, R.W.B. *The American Adam: Innocence, Tragedy, and Tradition in the Nineteenth Century*. Chicago and London: University of Chicago Press, 1955.

Ljungquist, Kent P. "Poe and the Sublime: His Two Short Sea Tales in Context of an Aesthetic Tradition." *Criticism* 17 (Spring 1975): 131-151.

Lowenthal, David. "Geography, Experience, and Imagination: Towards a Geographical Epistemology." *Annals of the Association of American Geographers* 51 (1961): 241-267.

McCoubrey, John w., ed. *American Art, 1760-1960: Sources and Documents*. Englewood Cliffs, N.J.: Prentice-Hall, 1965.

———. *American Tradition in Painting*. New York: George Braziller, 1963.

McKenzie, Gorden. *Critical Responsiveness: A Study of the Psychological*

Current in Later Eighteenth-Century Criticism. Berkeley: University of California Press, 1949.

McLuhan, Marshall. *The Interior Landscape: The Literary Criticism of Marshall McLuhan, 1943-1962.* Edited by Eugene McNamara. New York and Toronto: McGraw-Hill Book Company, 1969.

Magoon, E.L., ed. *The Home Book of the Picturesque.* New York: Wiley and Putnam, 1852.

Malins, Edward. *English Landscaping and Literature.* London: Oxford University Press, 1966.

Manwaring, Elizabeth W. *Italian Landscape in Eighteenth-Century England.* New York: Oxford University Press, 1925.

Martin, Terrence. *The Instructed Vision: Scottish Common Sense Philosophy and the Origins of American Fiction.* Bloomington: Indiana University Press, 1961.

———. *Nathaniel Hawthorne.* New York: Twayne Publishers, 1965.

———, "Rip, Ichabod, and the American Imagination." *American Literature* 31 (May 1959): 137-149.

Marx, Leo. *The Machine in the Garden: Technology and the Pastoral Ideal in America.* New York: Oxford University Press, 1964.

Matthiessen, F.O. *American Renaissance: Art and Expression in the Age of Emerson and Whitman.* New York: Oxford University Press, 1941.

Miller, Perry. *Errand into the Wilderness.* Cambridge: Belknap Press of Harvard University Press, 1956.

———. *Nature's Nation.* Cambridge: Harvard University Press, 1967.

———. *The New England Mind: The Seventeenth Century.* New York: Beacon Press, 1961.

———. *The Raven and the Whale: The War of Words and Wits in the Era of Poe and Melville.* New York: Harcourt, Brace and Company, 1956.

Monk, Samuel Holt. *The Sublime: A Study of Critical Theories in Eighteenth-Century England.* New York: Modern Language Association, 1935; reprinted ed. Ann Arbor: University of Michigan Press, 1960.

Murphy, Morriss. "Wordsworthian Concepts in 'The Great Stone Face.'" *College English* 23 (February 1962): 364-365.

Nash, Roderick. *Wilderness and the American Mind.* New Haven: Yale University Press, 1967.

Nechas, James W. "Ambiguity of Word and Whale: The Negative Affix in *Moby-Dick*." *College Literature* 2 (Fall 1975): 198-225.

Nicolson, Marjorie Hope. *Mountain Gloom and Mountain Glory: The Development of the Aesthetics of the Infinite.* Ithaca, N.Y.: Cornell University Press, 1959.

Nicolson, Marjorie Hope. *Newton Demands the Muse: Newton's "Optics" and the Eighteenth-Century Poets.* Princeton: Princeton University Press, 1946.

Noble, David W. *The Eternal Adam and the New World Garden: The Central Myth in the American Novel Since 1830.* New York: George Braziller, 1968.

Noble, Louis Legrand. *The Life and Works of Thomas Cole.* Edited by Elliot S. Vesell. Cambridge: Belknap Press of Harvard Univesity Press, 1964.

Pauly, Thomas H. "The Literary Sketch in Nineteenth-Century America." *Texas Studies in Literature and Language* 17 (Summer 1975): 489-503.

Pochmann, Henry A. *German Culture in America: Philosophical and Literary Influences, 1600-1900.* Madison: University of Wisconsin Press, 1957.

Prall, D.W. *Aesthetic Judgment.* New York: Thomas Y. Crowell and Company, 1967.

Price, Martin. "The Picturesque Moment." In *From Sensibility to Romanticism: Essays Presented to Frederick A. Pottle,* pp. 259-292. Edited by Frederick W. Hilles and Harold Bloom. New York: Oxford University Press, 1965.

Price, Uvedale. *An Essay on the Picturesque, as Compared with the Sublime and the Beautiful; and on the Use of Studying Pictures for the Purpose of Improving Real Landscape.* London: J. Robson, 1794.

Pritchard, John. *Literary Wise Men of Gotham: Criticism in New York, 1815-1860.* Baton Rouge, La.: Louisiana State University Press, 1963.

Ringe, Donald. "Kindred Spirits: Bryant and Cole." *American Quarterly* 6 (Fall 1954): 233-244.

——. *The Pictorial Mode: Space and Time in the Art of Bryant, Irving, Cooper.* Lexington: University of Kentucky Press, 1971.

Roche, Arthur John. "A Literary Gentleman in New York: Evert A. Duyckinck's Relationship with Nathaniel Hawthorne, Herman Melville, Edgar Allen Poe, and William Gilmore Simms." Ph.D. dissertation: Duke University, 1973.

Rosenberg, John D. *The Darkening Glass: A Portrait of Ruskin's Genius.* New York: Columbia University Press, 1961.

Ruskin, John. *Modern Painters.* New York: Wiley and Putnam, 1847.

Sanford, Charles L. *The Quest for Paradise: Europe and the American Moral Imagination.* Urbana: University of Illinois Press, 1961.

Schneider, Richard J. "Reflections in Walden Pond: Thoreau's Optics." *ESQ* 21 (Second quarter 1975): 65-75.

Shepard, Paul. *Man in the Landscape: A Historical View of the Esthetics of Nature.* New York: Alfred Knopf, 1967.

Slotkin, Richard. *Regeneration through Violence: The Mythology of the American Frontier, 1600-1860.* Middletown, Conn.: Wesleyan University Press, 1973.

Smallwood, William Martin. *Natural History and the American Mind.* New York: Columbia University Press, 1941.

Smith, Henry Nash. *Virgin Land: The American West as Symbol and Myth.* Cambridge: Harvard University Press, 1950.

Spencer, Benjamin. *The Quest for Nationality: An American Literary Campaign.* Syracus, N.Y.: Syracuse University Press, 1957.

Spiller, Robert E. "Critical Standards in the American Romantic Movement." *College English* 8 (April 1947): 344-352.

Soby, James Thrall, and Miller, Dorothy C. *Romantic Painting in America.* New York: Museum of Modern art, 1943.

Sparshott, F.R. *The Structure of Aesthetics.* Toronto: University of Toronto Press, 1963.

Stafford, John. *The Literary criticism of "Young America": A Study in the Relationship of Politics and Literature, 1837-1850.* New York: Russell and Russell, 1967.

Stein, Roger B. *John Ruskin and Aesthetic Thought in America, 1840-1900.* Cambridge: Harvard University Press, 1967.

———. *Seascape and the American Imagination.* New York: The Metropolitan Museum of Art and Clarkson N. Potter, Inc., 1975.

Stewart, Dugald. *Elements of the Philosophy of the Human Mind.* 2 vols. Cambridge, England: James Munroe and Company, 1833.

Stone, Edward. *Voices of Despair: Four Motifs in American Literature.* Athens: Ohio University Press, 1966.

Stovall, Floyd, ed. *The Development of American Literary Criticism.* Chapel Hill: University of North Carolina Press, 1955.

Sweet, Frederick A. *The Hudson River School and the Early American Landscape Tradition.* New York: Whitney Museum of American Art, 1945.

Templeman, William D. "Thoreau, Moralist of the Picturesque." *PMLA* 47 (September 1932): 864-889.

Tinker, Chauncey Brewster. *Painter and Poet: Studies in the Literary Relations of Painting and Poetry.* Cambridge: Harvard University Press, 1938.

Townscend, Francis G. "The American Estimate of Ruskin, 1847-1860." *Philological Quarterly* 22 (January 1953): 69-82.

Turner, Frederick Jackson. *The Frontier in American History.* New York: Holt and Company, 1921.

Tuveson, Ernest lee. *The Imagination as a Means of Grace: Locke and the Aesthetics of Romanticism.* Berkely and Los Angeles: University of California Press, 1960.

———. *Redeemer Nation: The Idea of America's Millennial Role.* Chicago: University of Chicago Press, 1968.

———. "Space, Deity, and the 'Natural Sublime.'" *Modern Language*

Quarterly 12 (Spring 1951): 20-38.

Van Nostrand, A.D. *Everyman His Own Poet: Romantic Gospels in American Literature.* New York: McGraw-Hill Book Company, 1968.

Wasserman, Earl. "Nature Moralized: The Divine Analogy in the Eighteenth Century." *ELH* 20 (1953): 39-78.

Williams, George H. *Wilderness and Paradise in Christian Thought: The Biblical Experience of the Desert in the History of Christianity and the Paradise Theme in the Theological Idea of the University.* New York: Harper & Brothers, 1962.

Winters, Ivor. *Maule's Curse: Seven Studies in the History of American Obscurantism.* Norfolk, Va.: New Directions, 1938.

Woodson, Thomas. "Thoreau's Excursion to the Bekshires and Catskills." *ESQ* 21 (Second quarter 1975): 82-92.

Wooley, Mary E. "The Development of the Love of Romantic Scenery in America." *American Historical Review* 3 (1897): 56-67.

Works on and by Melville

Anderson, Charles Robert. *Melville in the South Seas.* New York: Dover Publications, 1966.

Arvin, Newton. *Herman Melville.* New York: William Sloane Associates, 1950.

——. "Melville and the Gothic Novel." *New England Quarterly* 22 (March 1949): 33-48.

Baird, James R. *Ishmael: The Art of Melville in the Contexts of International Primitivism.* Baltimore, Md.: Johns Hopkins Press, 1956; reprint ed., New York: Harper & Brothers, 1960.

Beatty, Lillian. "Typee and Blithedale: Rejected Ideal Communities." *Personalist* 37 (1956): 367-378.

Bell, Michael D. "The Glendinning Heritage: Melville's Literary Borrowings in *Pierre.*" *Studies in Romanticism* 12: 741-758.

Blansett, Barbara. "'From Dark to Dark': *Mardi* as a Foreshadowing of *Pierre.*" *Southern Quarterly* 1 (April 1963): 213-227.

——. "Melville and Emersonian Transcendentalism." Ph.D. dissertation, University of Texas, 1964.

Boudreau, Gorden V. "Herman Melville: Master Mason of the Gothic." Ph.D. dissertation, Indiana University, 1967.

Bickley, Robert B., Jr. "Literary Influences and Techniques in Melville's Short Fiction, 1853-1856." Ph.D. dissertation, Duke University, 1970.

Braswell, William. "The Early Loves Scenes of Melville's *Pierre.*" *American Literature* 22 (January 1951): 382-389.

——. "Melville as a Critic of Emerson." *American Literature* 9 (November 1937): 317-334.

——. *Melville's Religious Thought: An Essay in Interpretation.* Durham.

N.C.: Duke University Press, 1943; reprinted New York: Pageant book Company, 1959.

Bredahl, Axel Carl. *Melville's Angles of Vision*. Gainesville: University of Florida Press, 1972.

Breinig, Helmbrecht. "The Destruction of Fairyland: Melville's 'Piazza' in the Tradition of the American Imagination." *ELH* 35 (1968): 254-283.

Brodtkorb, Paul, Jr. *Ishmael's White World: A Phenomenological Reading of "Moby-Dick."* New Haven: Yale University Press, 1965.

Brooks, Van Wyck. "Melville in the Berkshires." In *The Times of Melville and Whitman*, pp. 165-179. New York: E.P. Dutton, 1953.

Brouwer, Fred E. "Melville's *The Confidence-Man* as Ship of Philosophers." *Southern Humanities Review* 3 (Autumn 1969): 158-165.

Cecchi, Emilio. "Two Notes on Melville." *Sewanee Review* 68 (July 1960): 398-406.

Cowen, Wilson Walker. "Melville's Marginalia," Ph.D. dissertation, Harvard, 1965.

Creeger, George R. "Color Symbolism in the Works of Herman Melville, 1846-1852." Ph.D. dissertation, Yale University, 1952.

——. "The Symbolism of Whiteness in Melville's Prose Fiction." *Jahrbuch fur Amerikastudien* 5 (1960): 147-163.

Dahl, Curtis. "Moby Dick's Cousin Behemoth." *American Literature* 31 (March 1959): 21-29

Davis, Merrell R. *Melville's "Mardi": A Chartless Voyage*. New Haven: Yale University Press, 1952.

Donaldson, Scott. "The Dark Truth of the *Piazza Tales*." *PMLA* 85 (October 1970): 1082-1087.

Drummond, C.Q.: "Nature: Meek Ass or White Whale?" *Sage* 1 (Spring 1966): 71-84.

Dryden, Edgar A. *Melville's Thematics of Form: the Great Art of Telling the Truth*. Baltimore: Johns Hopkins University Press, 1968.

Eby, E.H. "Herman Melville's 'Tartarus of Maids.'" *Modern Language Quarterly* 1 (March 1940): 95-100.

Finkelstein, Dorothy. *Melville's Orienda*. New Haven and London: Yale University Press, 1961.

Fisher, Marvin. *Going Under: Melville's Short Fiction and the American 1850's*. Baton Rouge: Louisiana State University Press, 1977.

Fogle, Richard Harter. *Melville's Shorter Tales*. Norman, Ok.: Oklahoma University Press, 1960.

Foster, Charles H. "Something in Emblems: A Reinterpretation of Moby Dick." *New England Quarterly* 34 (March 1961): 3-35.

Foster Elizabeth. "Another Note on Melville and Geology." *American Literature* 22 (January 1951): 479-487.

——. "Melville and Geology." *American Literature* 17 (March 1945): 50-65.

Frank, Max. *Die Farb- und Lichtsymbolik im Prosawerk Herman Melvilles.* Heidelberg: Carl Winter, 1967.

Franklin, H. Bruce. *The Wake of the Gods: Melville's Mythology.* Stanford: Stanford University Press, 1963.

Frederick, John T. "Melville's Early Acquaintance with Bayle." *American Literature* 39 (January 1968): 545-547.

Furrow, sharon. "The Terrible Made Visible: Melville, Salvator Rosa, and Piranesi." *ESQ* 19 (Fourth Quarter 1973): 237-253.

Gardner, John "Bartleby: Art and Social Commitment." *Philological Quarterly* 43 (January 1964): 87-98.

Gary, Lorena M. "Rich Colors and Ominous Shadows." *South Atlantic Quarterly* 37 (1938): 41-45.

Gilman, William H. *Melville's Early Life and "Redburn."* New York: New York University Press, 1951.

Gilmore, Michael T. "Melville's Apocalypse: American Millennialism and *Moby-Dick.*" *ESQ* 21 (Third Quarter 1975): 154-161.

Glenn, Barbara. "Melville and tne Sublime in *Moby Dick.*" *American Literature* 48 (May 1976): 165-182.

Granger, Bruce Ingham. "The Gams in *Moby-Dick.*" *Western Humanities Review* 8 (Winter 1953): 41-47.

Hayman, Allan. "The Real and the Original: Herman Melville's Theory of Prose Fiction." *Modern Fiction Studies* 8 (Autumn 1962): 211-232.

Heimert, Alan. "*Moby-Dick* and American Political Symbolism." *American Quarterly* 15 (Winter 1963): 498-534.

Hetherington, Hugh W. *Melville's Reviewers, British and American, 1846-1891.* Chapel Hill: University of North Carolina Press, 1961.

Hillway, Tyrus. "Melville and the Spirit of Science." *South Atlantic Quarterly* 48 (January 1949): 77-88.

Hoeltje, Hubert H. "Hawthorne, Melville, and 'Blackness.'" *American Literature* 37 (November 1965): 41-51.

Horsford, Howard C. "The Design of the Argument in *Moby-Dick.*" *Modern Fiction Studies* 8 (autumn 1962): 223-251.

Hoyle, Norman Eugene. "Melville as a Magazinist." Ph.D. dissertation, Duke University, 1960.

Jones, Buford. "Spenser and Shakespeare in *The Encantadas, Sketch VI.*" *Emerson Society Quarterly* 35 (Second quarter 1964): 68-73.

Lebowitz, Alan. *Progress into Silence: A Study of Melville's Heroes.* Bloomington and London: Indiana University Press, 1970.

Levy, Leo B. "Hawthorne and the Idea of 'Bartleby.'" *Emerson Society Quarterly* 47 (Second quarter 1967): 66-69.

Leyda, Jay. *The Melville Log: A Documentary Life of Herman Melville,*

1819-1891. 2 vols. New York: Harcourt, Brace and World, 1951; reprinted with additional materials New York: Gorden Press, 1969.

McCarthy, Paul. "Elements of Anatomy in Melville's Fiction." *Studies in the Novel* 6 (Spring 1974): 38-61.

———. "Melville's Use of Painting in *Pierre.*" *Discourse* 2 (Autumn 1968): 490-505.

MacDonald, Allan. "A Sailor Among the transcendentalists." *New England Quarterly* 8 (September 1935): 307-319.

Mansfield, Luther Stearns. "Glimpses of Herman Melville's Life in Pittsfield, 1850-1851." *American Literature* 9 (March 1937): 26-48.

Mason, Ronald. *The Spirit above the Dust: A Study of Herman Melville.* London: John Lehmann, 1951.

Melville, Herman. *The Complete Stories of Herman Melville.* Edited by Jay Leyda. New York: Random House, 1949.

———. *The Confidence-Man: His Masquerade.* Edited by Elizabeth S. Foster. New York: Hendricks House, 1954.

———. *The Encantadas: or, Enchanted Isles.* Edited by Victor Wolfgang von Hagen. Burlingame, Cal.: William P. Wreden, 1940.

———. "Hawthorne and His Mosses." *Literary World* 17 (August 17, 1850; August 24, 1850): 125-127, 145-147.

———. *Journal of a Visit to London and the Continent by Herman Melville, 1849-1850.* Edited by Eleonor Melville Metcalf. Cambridge: Harvard University Press, 1948.

———. *The Letters of Herman Melville.* Edited by Merrell R. Davis and William H. Gilman. New Haven: Yale University Press, 1960.

———. *Moby-Dick.* Edited by Luther S. Mansfield and Howard P. Vincent. Chicago and New York: Hendricks House, 1952.

———. *Piazza Tales.* Edited by Egbert S. Oliver. New York: Hendricks House, 1962.

———. *The Writings of Herman Melville.* Edited by Harrison Hayford, Hershel Parker, and G. Thomas Tanselle. Vols. 1-6. Evanston and Chicago: Northwestern University Press and The Newberry Library, 1969-1972.

Miller, James E. "Hawthorne and Melville: No! in Thunder." In *Quests Surd and Absurd*, pp. 186-208. Chicago: University of Chicago Press, 1967.

Moore, Richard S. "Piranesi, 'The Blanket,' and the 'Mathematical Sublime' in *Moby Dick.*" *Melville Society Extracts* 47 (September 1981): 1-4.

Newbery, Ilse Sofie. "*The Encantadas:* Melville's *Inferno.*" *American Literature* 38 (March 1966): 49-68.

———. "The Unity of Melville's *Piazza Tales.*" Ph.D. dissertation, University of British Columbia, 1964.

218

Oliver, Egbert S. "'Cock-a-Doodle-Doo!' and Transcendental Hocus-Pocus." *New England Quarterly* 21 (1948): 204-215.

Olson, Charles. *Call Me Ishmael.* San Francisco: City Lights Books, 1947.

Osbourn, R.V. "The White Whale and the Absolute." *Essays in Criticism* 6 (April 1956): 160-170.

Parker, Hershel. "Melville's Satire of Emerson and Thoreau: An Evaluation of the Evidence." *American Transcendental Quarterly* 7 (Summer 1970): 61-67.

Parker, Hershel, and Hayford, Harrison, eds. *"Moby-Dick" as Doubloon: Essays and Extracts.* New York: W.W. Norton & Company, 1970.

Parker, Hershel, ed. *The Recognition of Herman Melville: Selected Criticism Since 1846.* Ann Arbor: Michigan University Press, 1967.

Penicke, Klaus. "A View from the Piazza: Herman Melville and the Legacy of the European Sublime." *Comparative Literature Studies* 4 (1967): 267-281.

Polk, James. "Melville and the Idea of the City." *University of Texas Quarterly* 41 (summer 1972): 277-292.

Pommer, Henry F. *Milton and Melville.* Pittsburgh: University of Pittsburgh Press, 1950.

Pops, Martin Leonard. *The Melville Archetype.* Kent, Ohio: Kent State University Press, 1970.

Ross, Morton L. *"Moby-Dick* as an Education." *Studies in the Novel* 6 (Spring 1974): 62-75.

Rosenberry, Edward H. *Melville and the Comic Spirit.* Cambridge: Harvard University Press, 1955.

——. "The Problem of *Billy Budd.*" *PMLA* 80 (December 1965): 489-498.

Rust, R. Dilworth. "Vision in *Moby-Dick.*" *Emerson Society Quarterly* 33 (Fourth quarter 1963): 73-75.

Schiffman, Joseph. "Melville's Final Stage, Irony: A Re-examination of *Billy Budd* Criticism." *American Literature* 22 (November 1950): 128-136.

Scott, Sumner W.D. "The Whale in *Moby-Dick.*" Ph.D. dissertation, University of Chicago, 1950.

Sealts, Merton M., Jr. "Approaching Melville through 'Hawthorne and Mosses.'" *Emerson Society Quarterly* 28 (Third Quarter 1962): 12-15.

——. "Melville's 'Neoplatonical Originals.'" *Modern Language Notes* 67 (February 1952): 80-86.

——. *Melville's Reading: A Checklist of Books Owned and Borrowed.* Madison: University of Wisconsin Press, 1966.

Seelye, John D. "The Golden Navel: The Cabalism of Ahab's Doubloon." *Nineteenth-Century Fiction* 14 (March 1960): 350-355.

——. *Melville: The Ironic Diagram*. Evanston: Northwestern University Press, 1970.

Schlers, H.H. "Flaxman, Dante, and Melville's *Pierre*." *Bulletin of the New York Public Library* 64 (February 1960): 65-82.

Slater, Judith. "The Domestic Adventurer in Melville's Tales." *American Literature* 37 (November 1965): 267-279.

Stanton, Robert. "*Typee* and Milton: Paradise Well Lost." *Modern Language Notes* 74 (May 1959): 407-411.

Star, Morris. "Melville and the Fine Arts." Ph.D. dissertation, Northwestern University Press, 1964.

——. "Melville's Markings in Walpole's *Anecdotes of Painting in England*." *Papers of the Bibliographical Society of America* 66 (July-September 1966): 321-327.

Stein, William Bysshe. "Melville's Comedy of Faith." *ELH* 27 (Decmeber 1960): 315-333.

——. "Melville Roasts Thoreau's Cock." *Modern Language Notes* 74 (March 1959): 218-219.

Stern, Milton R. *The Fine Hammered Steel of Herman Melville*. Urbana: University of Illinois Press, 1960.

Thompson, Lawrence. *Melville's Quarrel with God*. Princeton: Princeton University Press, 1952.

Turner, Darwin T. "A View of Melville's Piazza." *CLA Journal* 7 (1963): 56-62.

Vargish, Thomas. "The Gnostic Mythos in *Moby-Dick*." *PMLA* 81 (January 1966): 272-277.

Vincent, Howard P. "Ishmael, Writer and Art Critic." In *Themes and Directions in American Literature*, pp. 69-79. Edited by Ray B. Browne and Donald Pizer. Lafayette, Ind.: Purdue University Press, 1969.

——. *The Trying-Out of "Moby-Dick."* Carbondale: Southern Illinois University Press, 1949.

Vincent, Howard P., ed. *Melville and Hawthorne in the Berkshires*. Kent, Ohio: Kent State University Press, 1968.

Ward, J.A. "The Function of the Cetological Chapters in *Moby-Dick*." *American Literature* 28 (January 1967): 164-183.

Watts, Robert Alan. "'The Seaward Peep' Ahab's Transgression." *University Review* (Kansas) 31 (December 1934): 133-138.

Widmer, Kingsley. *The Ways of Nihilism: A Study of Melville's Short Novels*. N.P.: The California State Colleges, 1970.

Wright Nathalia. *Melville's Use of the Bible*. Durham, N.C.: Duke University Press, 1949.

——. "*Moby-Dick*: Jonah's or Job's Whale?" *American Literature* 37 (May 1965): 190-195.

——. "*Mosses from an Old Manse* and *Moby-Dick*: The Shock of Discovery." *Modern Language Notes* 67 (1952): 387-392.

Yu, Beongcheon. "Ishmael's Equal Eye: The Source of Balance in *Moby-Dick*." *ELH* 32 (March 1965): 110-125.

Zoellner, Robert. *Salt-Sea Mastodon: A Reading of "Moby-Dick."* Berkeley: University of California Press, 1973.

INDEX